REASON AND THE QUESTION OF GOD

REASON AND THE QUESTION OF GOD

An Introduction
to the Philosophy of Religion

RICHARD SCHAEFFLER

Translated from the German
by
Robert R. Barr and Marlies Parent

A Herder & Herder Book
The Crossroad Publishing Company
New York

The Crossroad Publishing Company
370 Lexington Avenue, New York, NY 10017

Originally published in German under the title *Religionsphilosophie*
© 1983, 1997 by Verlag Karl Alber, Freiburg and Munich

English translation Copyright © 1999 by The Crossroad Publishing Company

Printed in the United States of America

Library of Congress Cataloging-in-Publication Data

Schaeffler, Richard.
   [Religionsphilosophie. English]
   Reason and the question of God : an introduction to the philosophy of religion / Richard Schaeffler ; translated by Robert Barr.
      p. cm.
   Includes bibliographical references and indexes.
   ISBN 0-8245-1804-7 (pbk.)
   1. Religion—Philosophy. I. Title.
   BL51.S418313   1999
   210—dc21   99-38950
                                                     CIP

1   2   3   4   5   6   7   8   9   10   04   03   02   01   00   99

Contents

—————

FOREWORD   ix

FOREWORD TO THE SECOND EDITION, 1997   xiii

INTRODUCTION   xv

Chapter
1. The Oldest Type: Philosophy of Religion
   as Critique of a "Prerational Consciousness"   1

2. A Widely Diffused Type: Philosophy of Religion
   as Conversion of Religion into Philosophy   5
   A First Program: Philosophical Allegorization
   *   of Religious Tradition*   5
   The Platonic Source of a Second Program:
   *   Philosophy as Religion Become Conscious of Itself*   6
   Modifications of This Program in the History of Philosophy   8
   Philosophy of Religion as Transformation of Religion
   *   into Philosophy: Backward Glance on a Journey*   16

3. The Prevailing Type in Several Eras: Philosophy of Religion
   on the Basis of Philosophical Theology   17
   Theme and Argumentation of Philosophical Theology   18
   From the Critical Hermeneutics of Religion to Onto-Theology   21
   Kant's "Copernican Revolution" and the Crisis of
   *   Onto-Theology*   25
   On the History and Typology of Discourse upon God
   *   in Transcendental Philosophy*   30
   Discourse upon God in Transcendental Philosophy,
   *   and Theology of Hope*   38

Philosophy of Religion on the Basis of Philosophical Theology:
   Review of a Journey and Critical Evaluation   45

4. A More Recent Type of Philosophy of Religion:
   The Phenomenology of Religion   50
   Phenomenology of Religions: Outcome of an Encounter
      between Philosophical Phenomenology and
      Empirical Religious Science   51
   Phenomenology of Religion as Doctrine of the Apparition
      of the Holy: Positions, Programs, and Developments   57
   The Question of Possibilities and Boundaries of the
      Phenomenological Method in Religious Science   61
   Outlook: The Program of the Phenomenology of Religion
      and Its Maintenance by Way of a Transcendental
      Analytics of Religious Language   71

5. The "Linguistic Turn," and the Philosophy of Religion
   as Analysis of Religious Language   73
   Positivism and the Analysis of Religious Language   74
   The "Linguistic Turn" and Transcendental Philosophy: Analysis
      of Religious Language beyond the Struggle with Positivism 84
   Philosophy of Language and Theology of the Word: The
      Linguistic Turn in the Encounter of Philosophy of
      Religion and Christian Theology   96

6. Philosophical Theology, Phenomenology of Religion,
   Analytics of Religious Language: A Review of Three
   Methodological Approaches to the Philosophy of Religion,
   and a Systematic Outlook   106
   Comparative Review and Critical Evaluation   106
   A Systematic View   119

SUPPLEMENTARY MATERIAL FOR THE SECOND EDITION   139
An Altered Orientation Requirement   139
   The Secularization Process as a Question to Be
      Addressed to the Philosophy of Religion   139
   Secularization of Politics and Environmental Ethics,
      and the Need for a New Orientation of the
      Philosophy of Religion   142
   Intercultural Encounter and Dialogue of the Religions   146

"New Religions" and the Question of Criteria for the
Distinction of the "Genuinely Religious" from
"Pseudomorphoses of Religion"   149
Questions for the Philosophy of Religion on the
Part of Theology   153

Problems of Method   155
The Method-Combination Suggested in This Book   156
Methodological Objections   157
Attempts at an Application   159
Religion's Rationality and Capacity for Critique   159
Differentiation of the Religious from Its
Distortions as Task of Argumentation in Theology
and the Philosophy of Religion   164
Religion, Culture, and Society   169
On the Question of Method: Primacy of Intentionality?   175

WORKS CITED   178

INDEX   192

Foreword

———•◦•———

$\mathbf{M}$AY I BE PERMITTED to preface the following presentation with a personal observation. When the editors and the publisher of *Handbuch der Philosophie* did me the honor of inviting me to take responsibility for the volume *Religionsphilosophie*, I had the boldness to consent. Having published a number of works in the area of the philosophy of religion (for example, *Religion und kritisches Bewußtsein* (Religion and critical consciousness); "Die Religionskritik sucht ihren Partner" (Critique of religion seeks its partner); or "Der Kultus als Weltauslegung" (Worship as interpretation of the world), I felt prepared for this task. And long-cherished plans to merge drafts on the phenomenology of worship or on the analysis of religious language in a systematic overall presentation seemed somewhat closer to realization. As I gathered and surveyed the materials, however, the question occurred to me: What can the reader rightly expect from a "handbook"? And my response was: Not the individual contribution of a given author to discussion (or this only peripherally), who may more or less deviate from the "prevailing opinion," but above all, solid information on what is available in the area of the philosophy of religion in terms of secure conclusions, tested methods, and the current state of discussion. However, it soon appeared that in philosophy across the board—but especially in the field of the philosophy of religion—secure results are a problematic affair. And even on the characteristics of the questions that must be broached in the philosophy of religion, no consensus obtains among the specialists. Attempts to assign the philosophy of religion a solid place in the comprehensive field of philosophy—even, for instance, after Hegel's example, a place in the "system of philosophy"—are more and more the object of skepticism. And even the new basis of the philosophy of religion in philosophical phenomenology, which was undertaken in the first half of our century and which found wide acceptance, today seems, to a large extent, a purely

ix

academic undertaking, still worth reflection but by no means generating uncontested preliminary decisions. There is no such thing as the philosophy of religion as a discrete field of themes and questions, methods, and conclusions. There may have been such earlier; it may be that there will be such later. But what we have today is a multiplicity of questions, premises for solutions, and methods, which seems confusing.

For a long time it seemed to me that the assignment I had undertaken placed me before the following alternatives: Either I must decide to write one philosophy of religion, in full awareness that, in this field, there are not only other opinions than mine (which is self-evident), but, especially, other convictions as to what a philosophy of religion ought to accomplish, what questions it ought to pose, what themes it ought to handle. Or else I must rest content with playing the role of a neutral reporter and transmitting, in compendious synopsis, an overview of the history and present stage of development of the philosophy of religion. The first way seemed to me not to correspond to the character of a manual or handbook. The necessary one-sidedness with which a certain understanding of the philosophy of religion—namely, my own—would stand in the limelight would, it is true, be as necessary as it would be permissible, if it were a matter of submitting a contribution for discussion among specialists (and I should like to reserve such a contribution for another occasion); but the balance of information rightly expected from a handbook would have to suffer. The second way, the way of neutral reporting, seemed to me inadequate to the philosophical theme. One cannot report on philosophical undertakings of thought from the distance of the indifferent observer. Nor can a reader put together a picture of philosophical argumentations and discussions without digesting the questions coming up for discussion one after another. Aristotle's indication that one becomes a zither-player not by way of reports on zither-playing, but by playing the zither (*Eth. Nik.* 1103 a 34) holds for the philosophy of religion as well. Information about questions, premises, and methods of the philosophy of religion remains unintelligible unless it stimulates one to join personally in the questioning, the argumentation, the philosophizing.

Thus, I sought a third way for the presentation given here: Instead of giving *one* philosophy of religion, or reporting compendiously on the *many* philosophies of religion, I have attempted to expound, by way of example, certain questions that, in various periods of history, have led this discipline to undertake the philosophical interpretation and evaluation of religious phenomena; to expound premises on whose basis attempts have been made, and can be made even today, to clarify these questions; and finally, to determine methods whereby one can walk the way from premise to possible conclusions.

Readers will therefore feel the lack, in this book, of a great deal that they might rightly expect from a comprehensive and minute treatment of the philosophy of religion. The abundance of religious phenomena described in the empirical religious sciences, which become the objects of interpretation, sifting, and appraisal by philosophers of religion, can be named in only a few indications. There is also much that readers will not find that they could expect from a comprehensive presentation of classical and scholastic directions in the philosophy of religion. Certain individual persons and positions that have played a role in the history of the philosophy of religion will be presented only very sketchily. The present volume *is* neither a philosophy of religion, nor does it *describe* the many philosophies of religion produced in the course of history. In strict concentration on the problems, it attempts to describe questions, premises, and methods, and thus to transmit an overview of the variety of ways in which the philosophy of religion has been understood and practiced, yesterday and today.

The tones generated by philosophers of religion, in various directions, on their very differently built instruments, produce no concert: and so a harmonized presentation is impossible. And yet today one cannot begin to play in one's own style without listening to all these tones: this forbids one to start right out playing one's own zither, like a soloist, in one's own way, in neglect of the multiplicity of philosophies of religion. Our critical sorting-out of questions, premises, and methods posed and used by the philosophy of religion is intended to assist readers to become practiced in the different manners of thought in the philosophy of religion, in order that they may be able to judge, from the experience of their own reflection, what it is that they are doing when at last they decide to play their zither in their own way: that is, to practice the philosophy of religion in the way that seems to them to be adequate for their theme.

I am happy at the opportunity to discharge a manifold debt of gratitude. I thank the editors, Professor Dr. Elisabeth Ströker and Professor Dr. Wolfgang Wieland, for their confidence, their patience, and much instructive counsel. I have the publisher, Dr. Meinolf Wewel, to thank for his precious collaboration during the time of the development of this book. I thank my colleagues Julie Kirchberg and Johannes Müther for the care with which they have assisted with the final draft of the manuscript and with corrections, as well as with the creation of the bibliography. I thank Anneliese Kaufhold for her careful work of producing the typescript.

Bochum, June 1983
Richard Schaeffler

Foreword to the

Second Edition, 1997

———⊰•⊱———

SINCE THE APPEARANCE of the first edition of this book (1983), the state of discussion prevailing in the field of the philosophy of religion has changed in a number of respects. These changes have not so much occasioned new types of philosophy of religion, else chapters 1–5 of this book would have to be expanded with an additional chapter. But the tasks that the philosophy of religion is expected to perform today have certainly been altered.

The appended "Supplementary Material for the Second Edition" is therefore of a different literary genre from that of the text of the first edition, adopted here without change. Here it will be necessary for the author, who until now has worked predominantly as a reporter and therefore has taken care to preserve a certain neutrality in order to do justice to the different types of philosophy of religion, to set forth his own position in the philosophy of religion more emphatically. Such a procedure does, it is true, deviate from the task that is specific for a handbook. But such a deviation may well seem justified in this particular case: the altered state of the discussion, which transcends the circle of specialists to reach a broader public, has occasioned the appearance of a need for orientation, which the philosopher of religion can only satisfy by undertaking the attempt, through the combination he recommends of the methods of phenomenology, linguistic philosophy, and transcendental philosophy, to reach answers to the questions posed to the philosophy of religion through social developments calling for an even more precise description.

Munich, June 1997
Richard Schaeffler

Introduction

—————»·o·«—————

A S LONG AS PHILOSOPHY has existed, it has taken religion as one of
its themes. After all, most questions philosophers sought to answer
had already been the themes of mythological recitals, ritual celebrations,
and religious aphorisms. For example, there were the questions of the origin of the world, the position of the human being in the cosmos, the moral
norms of behavior, the possibilities and limits of cognition. Thus, in its origins as again and again in the course of its history, philosophy has gained
its distinguishing self-concept through the fact that it has taken its critical
distance from religion, whether authentic or self-styled. This is the case
with Heraclitus's criticism of the Homeric tales of the gods no less than
with Hans Albert's effort to define his "critical rationalism" by way of a distinction from the "revelational model of cognition."

But religion is not only older than philosophy; it has also remained its
contemporary. At least until today, religion has not allowed itself to be con-
verted into philosophy. Nor has it in the least submitted to being side-
tracked into those theoretical questions and practical tasks for which
philosophy and science have declared their incompetence. Rather, it has
critically and competitively intervened, if in varying degrees of courage and
intensity, wherever it has judged the questioning and attempts at answers
on the part of philosophers and scholars to be an invasion of its own
province. Thus, to our own day, philosophy has confronted the task of finding and explaining its self-concept, not only by way of distinguishing itself
from religion (especially in the manner and way of posing and answering
questions) but also in orientation to it (especially by reason of its partially
overlapping thematic fields).

And so, over and over, religion is *the other vis-à-vis philosophy,* even when
one and the same person attempts to confront the same questions now as a
philosopher, now as a religious individual and a member of a religious com-

munity. But religion, for philosophy, is *the other belonging to it in a particularly characteristic fashion*—the "other from itself," inasmuch as, with its continually strange formation, for philosophy, of human thinking, speaking, and acting, philosophical thinking comes to a clearer understanding of its uniqueness and its task.

But the perseverance with which philosophy has struck a relationship with this "other from itself" has never precluded religion's being discussed philosophically, and in the most varied ways. The one philosophy of religion has unfolded into a multiplicity of philosophies of religion. These philosophies of religion are distinguished from one another not only in the response they give to the question, What is religion? Their basic multiplicity lies also in the manner of asking the question. The content of that complex of phenomena, unified under the heading of "religion," which registers as needing presentation or explanation—like the presentations or explanations deemed "adequate"—varies from age to age, as well as from school of philosophers to school of philosophers within the same age.

However, the history of the philosophy of religion does not develop rectilinearly, any more than does the history of philosophy across the board. Questions of philosophy, and so of the philosophy of religion, are never "exhausted"—they are dealt with until they are either adequately answered or recognized as ill-posed. Frequently they are simply "dropped." After passionate and lengthy discussion, they will be regarded by a coming generation as unimportant, or at least as less urgent. Then, often after the lapse of centuries, they may be "rediscovered."

What holds for the questions, holds as well for the premises, or "points of departure"—those observations and reflections that afford the philosopher the prospect that, once the investigation of the questions has been initiated in their terms, the questions can be formulated in a way that will do justice to the matter, and finally be answered in a way that will do justice to the problems. Such points of departure are often simply "given up," because other, newly discovered phenomena or considerations have opened broader prospects for a quicker, or more certain, increase in cognition. And in this respect as well, there are rediscoveries and renaissances.

Accordingly, for a presentation of the starting points, questions, and methods of the philosophy of religion, it will be in order to combine a historical, chronological approach with that of the classification of types. This means that, with each manner of philosophical inquiry into religion, we shall begin by seeking out where it first enters the historical scene; then we shall devote to it, even over the course of a rather long span of historical time, considerations akin to it in starting point and methodology.

In the interest of due brevity, our presentation will be limited to the fol-

lowing types: philosophy of religion as critique of a "pre-rational consciousness"; philosophy of religion as transformation of religion into philosophy; philosophy of religion on the basis of philosophical theology; the
phenomenology of religion; philosophy of religion according to the "linguistic turn," that is, the analytics of religious discourse.

A concluding review of these questions, starting points for solutions, and
methods is intended to facilitate a systematic outlook on future tasks of the
philosophy of religion.

CHAPTER 1

The Oldest Type

Philosophy of Religion as Critique of a "Prerational Consciousness"

THE FACT THAT PHILOSOPHY and science deal so extensively with problems that have begun as themes of religious proclamation and wisdom enables us to understand a datum of the history of philosophy: When the history of philosophy began, philosophy's concern with religion was governed by the intent to show the necessity of philosophy and science on the basis of the inadequacies of religious interpretations and explanations of the phenomena of nature and society. Aristophanes' ridicule of mythological explanations of events in the star-studded heavens, or in the atmosphere, attests a consciousness and conviction on the part of persons who had learned to investigate, interpret, and render intelligible these occurrences in scientific fashion (Aristophanes, *Clouds*, 367–411).

In this wise, antiquity itself developed a type of philosophy of religion, which experienced multiple rebirths in later ages of the history of philosophy. All of these forms of the philosophy of religion owned a common principle: religion as a system describes phenomena of nature and society in prescientific interpretations and explanations.

A question akin: How is it to be explained that the scientific approach to these problems arose so late, while prescientific approaches held on tooth and nail? The towering achievements in technology, and even in practical politics, at the hands of these long-ago generations preclude an ascription of this to some lack of intelligence on their part. Thus it is likely that the responsible factor for the tardy appearance of science and the tenaciousness of religious notions was the hegemony of the affect. Among these manifestations of affect, *fear* seems the most likely element to which we may look to explain the fact that human beings dared not make free use of their altogether ready rationality. The excessive fear inspired by, for example, lightning, or the sun's scorching heat, created a concept of superhuman powers: "Fear first created the gods on earth" (Statius of Thebes 3.661). But reci-

1

procally, the concept of such powers evoked a new sort of fear: fear of becoming a "sinner," and thus of arousing the wrath of the gods, were one to seek a rational explanation of these shattering occurrences (Lucretius, *De rerum natura* 1.62–67, 80–81). But if religion is an indication of a thinking under ban, then "free thinkers," who in their questioning and investigating take no notice of the reproach of sinfulness, will understand themselves as the representatives of authentic human dignity, and will call to their fellow human beings, "Dare to be one who knows" (Horace, *Epist.* 1.2.40; cf. Collins).

Like fear, its complement, *hope,* can create these hesitations. Here religion appears as a kind of substitute satisfaction for unfulfilled intramundane hopes. Persons more or less hope that their seemingly so feeble life will survive the demise of this seemingly so mighty cosmos, and will win participation in a "next world." Or they may hope that the social and political helplessness they feel will be counterbalanced in a coming judgment that will "exalt the lowly and topple the mighty" (cf. Luke 1:51–53). In such a view, religion can easily seem the expression of resentment on the part of persons "cheated in life": Thus Friedrich Nietzsche sees, especially in the Judeo-Christian tradition, the clear stamp of a priestly revenge on the powerful, disguising itself in the vesture of a love for the lowly (see Nietzsche, *GdM,* 281–82).

Such substitute satisfactions afford the suffering a subjective solace, it is true; objectively, however, they have the effect of assuaging these persons' anger and shame in the face of prevailing relationships, thereby sidetracking these energies of theirs from an effort to alter such relationships. And so, in Karl Marx's mind, it is precisely the powerful in a society that are interested in seeing religious concepts command the consciousness of the population, shifting their hope to a "next world," and thereby contributing to a stabilization of relations prevailing in the present one. Religion is not only a substitute satisfaction for unfulfilled hopes ("opiate *of* the people"); it is also a means of satisfying a protest against misery in a way that will be innocuous for the prevailing order ("opiate *for* the people"). Thus, anyone seeking to mount an effective critique of religion has the task of altering those relationships that ever and again generate religion, since these relationships continually stimulate the emergence of the disappointed hopes that occasion the need for substitute satisfaction and therefore for religion (see Marx, KHegRPh, 378–79).

Finally, along with physical or societal misery, one can impute those fears and hopes to which religion owes its origin and stability to the traumas of the soul occurring in various crises of individual development. We suffer these traumas of the soul especially in the transition from childhood to maturity. We have to pay for the new freedom of adulthood with a loss of security, which can generate the yearning to be able to "be a child again": only this time the child not of an earthly parent but of a heavenly one. According to Sigmund Freud, fears and guilt feelings unleashed by our loss of security and the hope of a new kind of childhood stimulate the imagination to generate fantasies calculated to vanquish fear and attain the imaginary satisfaction of a hope unfulfillable in reality. These ideals are illusory but hardy, because the fear and hope from which they spring are hardy. Religion is an illusion, therefore, but an illusion with a future (cf. the title of Freud's *chef d'oeuvre* in the critique of religion, "The Future of an Illusion").

In the minds of all of these critics, now that philosophy and science have provided such questions with a solution based on a real foundation—questions to which in earlier times religion had to furnish the sole available answers, inadequate as they were—religion has lost its justification for existence. The tenacity of religion since the appearance of philosophy and science is to be explained only as an outgrowth of the affect, which hinders the free activity of the powers of understanding. The demise of religion, then, is to be expected when the occasions of these affective movements are removed, be it through revolutionary changes in social relationships or through therapeutic changes in the individual consciousness. This pair of programs—revolution and psychotherapy—has long been regarded as irreconcilable. Especially, Marxists rejected psychotherapy as a bourgeois theory that sought to describe psychic phenomena apart from their economic conditions—the development of the individual without insertion into the social framework. However, the two programs were also susceptible of merger. Here, the class-society theory reveals the societal conditions that generate neuroses in the individual, while psychoanalysis shows the psychopathological results of these societal conditions. Thus, the ancient theory of the emergence of religion from fear has found its most recent expression in the "Freudian left."

Marx and Freud represent limit cases within the type of philosophy of religion under consideration. On the one hand, they are convinced that religion is the expression of a prerational consciousness that is bereft of all right in our age of science and philosophy. At the same time, religion is a revealing symptom to be studied if one is to come to know the true status of the human being: "religious distress" is a reflection of "real distress" (Marx, KHegRPh, 378) and at the same time it is an expression of hope for victory over real distress. The truth contained in religious concepts (namely, the reflection of the human being's social, or psychopathological, situation) must be recognized, and the will at work in religion (victory over this distress) must be fulfilled, if the religious "illusion" is to be vanquished.

With this program, Marx and Freud stand in the tradition of another type of philosophy of religion, which likewise harks back to antiquity. Religion is understood when its implicit truth is divested of its specifically religious form, and it is transformed into philosophy or science. The origin of philosophy and science from religion is now to be complemented by the transformation of religion into philosophy and science.

CHAPTER 2

A Widely Diffused Type

Philosophy of Religion as Conversion of Religion into Philosophy

A FIRST PROGRAM: PHILOSOPHICAL ALLEGORIZATION OF RELIGIOUS TRADITION

THE ALLEGORIZATION OF MYTH prevailing in the age of Hellenism sought to extract the authentic meaning of religious discourse from its mythic language and to translate it into the language of philosophy and science. As myth has understood the entire gamut of phenomena of nature and society as "manifestations" of gods, so the allegorization of myth interpreted these gods as "personifications" of the forces of nature, society, or the human soul. In this view, the truth of myth lies in its anticipation in religious form (that is, both prephilosophical and prescientific form) of the later insights of the sciences of nature, politics, or psychology. One in control of these scientific insights today can retrospectively explain, and at the same time criticize, myth. "To set myth aright" is the slogan of this procedure. (For the concept of this endeavor, see Plato, *Phaedr.* 229C–230B).

Herewith, once more in antiquity, a type of religion was created to which interpretations of religion from various periods in the history of philosophy can be referred—especially modern attempts to seek the fund of truth contained in religious traditions in the form of data on the powers of the human soul (especially in the various schools of the psychology of the unconscious) disguised as tales of the gods.

As science understands itself in terms of an explication of the core of truth that had been more concealed than revealed in religious discourse, so science can be critically interrogated as to whether it has succeeded in translating all truths of religion into that discourse of rationality that will do justice to its object and allow for its scientific treatment. Now the investigation of myth will take as its method the discovery of themes that have not as yet been translated into scientifically developed questions. Thus, to cite

5

only one example, F. W. J. Schelling expects, from mythology, information as to the nature of those "potencies" through which the divorce and mutual orientation of subject and object assume ever new configurations over the course of history. For Schelling, myth becomes a source of an insight that transcendental philosophy before Schelling was not yet in a position to acquire: the insight into the historicity of subject and object (see Schelling, *Einl. Mythol.*, 209). In this wise, the philosophy of religion becomes the heuristics (method of discovery) of heretofore neglected themes of philosophy and science.

THE PLATONIC SOURCE OF A SECOND PROGRAM:
PHILOSOPHY AS RELIGION BECOME CONSCIOUS OF ITSELF

As Plato portrays him, Socrates understands his philosophy as "service to the Muse" (Plato, *Phaedo* 60E–61A). He even characterizes his critique of the oracle as "reverence for the god" (*Apol.* 23C). He is conscious of his calling "to produce not arguments, but mythic narratives" (*Phaedo* 61B): however, he answers this call by reworking the mythic texts of tradition (ibid.). This program is the key to a revision of the myths of tradition in the Platonic dialogues, which relate especially to myths of the judgment of the dead.

In all of these self-expressions and procedural routes, the will is at work to fulfill the authentic concern of religion through the transformation of religion into philosophy. At the same time, however, philosophy itself is to be understood in religious terms. The challenge "Know yourself," which became the program of the Socratic philosophy, is expressly ascribed by the Platonic Socrates to an inscription on the temple at Delphi, which, Socrates insists, is to be understood not as "wise counsel" (*symboulē*), but as a "greeting of the divinity to those who enter there" (Plato, *Charm.* 165A). And the Socrates of the *Symposium* emphatically credits "a seer woman," Diotima, with his interpretation of philosophy as an "erotic passion" (*Symp.* 201D).

The religious character of Socratic-Platonic philosophy is especially evinced in the manner in which it seeks to overcome the twin danger of an overappreciation of the human logos and its disdaining—in modern terms, the twofold threat of dogmatism and skepticism (Plato, *Phaedo* 89D–90C). This is achieved through a "knowing ignorance," with its two elements: the capacity to render one's own ignorance expressly conscious in reflection, and thereby to distinguish what is to be sought as the unknown (capacity for questioning); and the capacity to adduce criteria on which one is able to judge whether and when the object sought has been found. But precisely these capacities—to recognize oneself as the ignorant one, to identify the unknown in a spirit of questioning, and to grasp the truth of the proffered answer—are common to the philosopher and the visitor to the Oracle. And like the visitor to the Oracle, Socrates ascribes this capacity to the fact that he has been greeted by the god. On the basis of this greeting on the part of the deity, philosophers too keep on the inquiring track of a truth they do not know but seek—and yet, like a misty reminiscence of forgotten knowledge, a truth that serves them as a rod by which to measure all of their own opinions as well as those of others. And because this capability has sprung from the deity's greeting, the way of reminiscence is a homeward-bound journey of the soul to the gods, who stand near human beings in earthly realities, which are their images, and thus "inspire" the soul and render it capable of the ascent (cf. *Phaedr.* 249C–D).

A philosophy that thus understands itself—in a religious manner—can precisely understand religion conversely: philosophically. Now the true sense of initiation into mysteries consists in grasping corporeal, sensory eros as an image of passion for divine truth, and at the same time as the triggering power of this celestial eros. The authentic sense of the myths of the judgment of the dead consists in their purification of the soul whose goal is to behold in sensory phenomena the "images" that "remind" it of the world of ideas. Thus, philosophy becomes the interpreter of religious tradition, and at the same time legislator for those "mythmakers" who can enjoin upon the philosopher the task of producing new religious discourse in the light of the textbook of philosophical insight (Plato *Pol.* 377B–C).

Here (together with the project of "setting the myths aright" in the sense of scientific insights) another type of philosophy of religion makes its appearance; and to this type, as well, philosophical endeavors of the most varied epochs can be referred. All of the philosophies of religion of this type have a common point of departure: the observation of a paradoxical peculiarity of human reason consisting in that reason's power to submit to its critique any manifestation of the world of objects, and any appraisal of the subjective meaning summoned forth by that manifestation (*doxa,* then, in the double sense of the word), without having to lay claim to and presuppose a content-knowledge of the manifestation. Thanks to this capacity, human reason vanquishes the double threat of dogmatism and skepticism, since it owes its debt not to a certitude of its critical judgment but to the truth it seeks. Reliance on this truth, which is always greater than its human comprehension, founds the religious self-understanding of the philosophies under consideration, here and in the following section, as examples of a common type. The same confidence in a *veritas semper major,* according to the conceptualization of these philosophers, is the kernel of all of those manifestations that we group together under the name of "religion." Here, therefore, a philosophy in terms of religion, and a religion in terms of philosophy, merge to the point of indifferentiation. Augustine's programmatic declaration is characteristic: "Where I found truth, there I found my God" (*Conf.* 10.24).

MODIFICATIONS OF THIS PROGRAM
IN THE HISTORY OF PHILOSOPHY

Plotinus and Neoplatonism

The doctrine of the cognitive ascent as the homecoming of the soul to the gods, which in Plato himself is expressed only in certain loci (significant though they are) becomes the constructive principle of an entire philosophical system. In Plotinus's view, the soul, as a cosmic power, mediates the emergence of the sensible world from the divine One, and its return thither. From the encounter of the soul with the divine Nous, the logos of the world springs forth (Plotinus, *Enn.* III,2, chap. 16). Its kinship with the oneness of the divine Idea founds the temporal ordering in the movements of the corporeal world. Its descent into matter is the ground of existence of all bodily things; its return to the divine One is the ground for the teleology of the world process (*Enn.* IV,2, chap. 2). Philosophy is understood as the guide of the human soul to integration into this cosmic event. The cognitive activity of the soul is a part of its labor of reconciliation between the visible and invisible worlds (*Enn.* VI,2, chap. 2; IV,7, chaps. 6–8).

Philosophy, then, is service to the world and to its return to its divine source; but at the same time it is service to this divine source itself, which utilizes the human soul and its cognitive powers to subordinate the corporeal world to the logos generated in the encounter between Nous and Psyche.

This religious understanding of philosophy passes over to a philosophical understanding of religion in Plotinus as well. Plotinus's doctrine of the emanation of multiplicity from the divine One permits him to reconcile the worship of the many gods of tradition with a philosophical monotheism. He sets forth the mythologic accounts of the generation of the gods and of the world, from the sacred marriage of divine powers of the primordial moment, as imagery, whose true sense is that, in order to realize itself as Spirit (Nous), the One must posit the Other (Heteron) as its contrary, thus to span the gamut of all world-founding productions in a confrontation of

Spirit and object (Plotinus, *Enn.* V,4, chap. 2). Later Neoplatonists returned from such considerations to a philosophical interpretation of the whole of mythological tradition, which at first they had sharply criticized in the name of a philosophical monotheism. (Cf. Porphyry, *Philosophy from the Oracular Pronouncements, Images of the Gods, The Divine Names, The Philosophy of Homer.* Correspondingly, Proclus sought in his *Plato's Theology* to derive the gods and heroes of myth from the One as the "First God.")

Augustine's Special Position

Like the Neoplatonists, Augustine understands the philosophical ascent of cognition as a return of the soul to its divine source. With Augustine, the human being's position between God and the world is to be understood in the sense that reason, through its subordination to the divine truth, wins a critical superiority over the totality of all objects: it does not judge of the truth but judges all objects in the light of this truth (Augustine, *VR* no. 158). However, Augustine departs from the usual Neoplatonic understanding of philosophy in three important ways. First, he eschews the relative justification of polytheism in favor of a worship of one God, and this, he holds, is "religion" in the full sense of the word (ibid., nos. 25, 29). Second, he understands the relationship of the soul to truth not merely religiously, in a generic sense, but specifically in a Christian sense: as the consequence of the grace of divine forgiveness. The *veritas* that empowers us to cognition is identical in reality with the *caritas* that forgives us our sins: and both together are an expression of that divine "constancy" that offers us the opportunity of conversion in the vagaries of our ways (Augustine, *Conf.* 11.8). But third, Augustine seeks to avoid the transformation of religion into philosophy. And so, in the religious proclamation, he seeks, along with such elements as he "has found also in the books of the Platonics," elements that neither are nor can be found there. Here especially is the message of the incarnation of the Word, that not only, as the Platonists too say, is the source of all worldly reality and leads the cosmic process to its goal, but is become identifiable at a specific locus in time and space within the world (see *Conf.* 7.9). By way of these deviations from the general type of Neoplatonic philosophy of religion, Augustine lays the groundwork for another type of philosophy of religion: the philosophical grounding of the decision for religion *simpliciter* (against atheism), and the decision for a specific "true" religion (against idolatry), as well as the distinction between religious truths that are available to philosophical argumentation and religious truths that can be made known only through divine revelation (in later terminology: the distinction between natural and revealed religion). We shall speak in a later section of this type of philosophy of religion, in whose center a philosophical doctrine of God stands.

From Neoplatonism to Idealism

The older Neoplatonic program had attempted, first, to reduce to its philosophical concept all manifestations of the religious, wherever these might be found, including, therefore, the polytheistic manifestations; and, second, to exclude no religion, and therefore not even the Christian faith, from transformation into philosophy. Now these aims found their resumption in the philosophy of religion of German Idealism. Here a particularly important element was Plotinus's basic thought, now taken up anew: the emergence of the multiplicity of the world from the original divine oneness is mediated by the motion of the divine Spirit—which, in order to be spirit, posits as its opposite a different-from-itself as its object. Its purpose in doing so is to assimilate this necessary, essentially belonging to it, "other," the other-from-itself. "Spirit is essentially this: from its being-other, and from the overcoming of this being-other, by the negation of negation, to come to itself" (Hegel, *Phil. Rel.* I, 435; see also *Gesch. Phil.*, 52). In German Idealism, this dialectic of spirit becomes the general basis for explaining the world process, the phenomenon of cognition, and the relation of the finite spirit to the infinite, that is, religion.

To be sure, with the Idealists this dialectic of spirit is marked by a specific element of Christian theology: the doctrine of the Spirit as one of the three divine persons. Idealistic philosophy of religion, in key respects of its foundation, and in broad areas of its application, is a trinitarian theology transformed into a philosophical dialectic. According to the Idealist philosophy of religion, a philosophical exegesis of the proposition "God is Spirit" evidences the superiority of Christianity over the other religions, and philosophical means are utilized to establish this. Let us sketch the journey from ancient Neoplatonism to the Idealism of the nineteenth century, at least in its most important stages.

Plotinus himself had posed the question of human freedom in connection with his doctrine of spirit. On the one side, according to his conceptualization, the divine Spirit (Nous) as foreseeing, and predetermining Spirit (Pronoia) as seeing all things in advance and determining them, determines the course of the world. But on the other side, the moral responsibility of the human being can only be preserved when that being is not a mere link in the chain of cause and effect but a "source of its own," so that it "co-weaves at the weft of the whole" (Plotinus, *Enn.* III,1, chap. 8). Thus the question arose how divine foreknowledge and human freedom can be conceptually reconciled. Plotinus devoted two of his writings to this problem (*Enn.* III,2 and III,3).

In Augustine, and under his influence in the Christian theologians, the problem of human freedom acquired a further urgency in the combining of the Plotinian doctrine of *pronoia* (translated as "foreseeing") with the Pauline concept of *prohorismos* (translated as "predetermination")—cf. Romans 8:29–30. Human beings are found to be sinners—in a condition of being deprived of their freedom through their own fault, from which condition they can be delivered only through God's grace of forgiveness. But this grace of forgiveness is imparted by God in a free, unmerited bestowal on those predetermined by God to participation in the glory of the Resurrected One. This doctrine of predestination, however, seemed to exclude the sovereignty of the human will over its own decisions. In his early writing *On Free Choice* (*De libero arbitrio*), Augustine still held: "Nothing is so much in our power as our will" (*Lib. arb.* 3.27). In his late writing *On Grace and Free Will* (*De gratia et libero arbitrio*), to the contrary, he says that the decisions of the will "are so much in God's power that he allows them to burgeon forth whence and when he will" (*GLA* 20). Now the philosophy of religion became, to a great extent, the attempt to find a way between the horns of this dilemma.

Philosophers found the right slogan for these attempts in another Pauline text: the expression "indwelling of the divine Spirit" (cf. Romans 8:11; 1 Corinthians 2:12). Paul's concept of the Spirit binds two moments together that could have seemed irreconcilable: the moment of interiority, removed from any theoretical or practical intervention from without, and the moment of mediation. Spirit, as Paul describes it, is the unique self-consciousness of God or of the human being: "Who knows what is truly human other than the human spirit within? So neither does anyone comprehend what is genuinely God's but the Spirit of God" (1 Corinthians 2:11). And yet, God can select persons upon whom to bestow this divine Spirit. In this way, and only in this way, the human being knows "what is in God": the secret counsel of the divine election of grace (cf. 1 Corinthians 2:12–13). In this Pauline doctrine of the Spirit, the philosophers of German Idealism found the basis for a solution to two questions: How can the consciousness of the finite human being be at the same time the consciousness of the infinite God? And how can the will of the finite human being relate to the will of the universal cause, the infinite God, in free decision? The answer was in both cases the same: Through a participation in the self-awareness, or free self-determination, of God.

The response to the question of the relationship between the finite human being and the infinite God had first been given by Spinoza: Our knowledge of God is a "mode" of the divine self-knowledge; our love for God is a mode of the divine love. Our un-freedom consists in the vain attempt to win, with regard to God and at the same time apart from God, an independence in being and an independent legislation in behavior. But our freedom consists in the insight into and acquiescence in the fact that all of our cognizing and willing is but a manner in which God's infinite knowledge and infinite love "express" themselves in a finite manner: in the mode of our finitude (Spinoza, *E* II, Theorem 11, Appendix; V, Theorem 36).

But Spinoza's mistake, concluded the Idealists, was not to have grasped our human cognizing and willing as a moment in the inner life of the divinity and as a finite manner of the divine "self-expression." And yet only thus could the human being's subjectivity and freedom be rescued (see Schelling *WmF,* 231; see also pp. 239, 303). Instead, Spinoza's mistake consisted in the fact that, from his concept of God (the concept of infinite substance) there is no basis for God's infinite essence to be able to express itself in a finite manner. Only if God is Spirit *in se,* in the divine essence, and therefore relates in trinitarian wise to that divine essence in Another from God, in the divine Son, can God now be shared "without," in the finite human being, as Spirit. The proposition from the Gospel of John "God is Spirit" (John 4:24) thus becomes, on the one side, the key to an understanding of religion in general, since all forms of relationship of the finite to the infinite are but manners in which the infinite transmits itself to itself in the Other from itself. On the other side, the same statement becomes the slogan for the difference of the Christian faith from other religions, since only the Christian dogma of the Trinity adequately names the condition under which this religion as such is possible. Hence Christianity is the "absolute religion." And thus Hegel can formulate:

> The Absolute is Spirit: this is the supreme definition of the Absolute. To find this definition, and to grasp its sense and content—this, one can say, was the absolute tendency of all formation and philosophy. To this point have all religion and science bent their efforts, and out of this endeavor alone is it possible to grasp world history. The word and conceptualization of Spirit was an early discovery, and the content of the Christian religion is to know God as Spirit. To grasp this content in its proper elements is the task of philosophy. (Hegel, *Syst. Phil.* III, 35–36)

> The nature of God, to be pure Spirit, is revealed to the human being in the Christian religion. (Hegel, *Phil. Gesch.,* 415)

From an Explication of Religion to Its Abolition

A backward glance at Hegel's explication of religion in general and the Christian message in particular shows us that in Hegel's conviction, without a philosophical dialectic, the proposition "God is Spirit," while it is the central content of the Christian message, is impossible to understand. On the other hand, it must be asked whether the proposition "The Absolute is Spirit," or its converse, "Spirit is the Absolute," can be formulated, understood, and based apart from a relationship to the Christian message. According to this explanation, indeed, not only can Christianity not be understood apart from philosophy, but philosophy ultimately cannot entertain an adequate self-understanding apart from Christianity. Thus, an Idealist understanding of religion now contains the germ of the abolition of religion in itself.

To this corresponds Hegel's understanding of the position of Christianity in the history of religions. Christianity represents the consummation of that history; at the same time, in many respects, it marks its end. In Christ, after all, the "abstract" relationship to God maintained by the religions became "concrete": the unity of the Absolute Divine was now no longer generic and abstract—no longer a generic concept under which "the gods" could be subsumed, but also no longer abstract in the sense of the unmediated encounter of God with the human being and the world. The unity of the Absolute Divine becomes the mediated oneness of God-and-the-human-being: "immediate unicity" (see Hegel, *Phil. Rel.* II, 283, 285).

Precisely for this reason, Jesus' death becomes the death of God. God has definitively ceased to be present at any special point in space and time. And this is the condition under which God can be revealed as Spirit. Not coincidentally, holds Hegel, the Gospels present the death of Jesus as the prerequisite for the outpouring of the Spirit (*Phil. Gesch.*, 417). Henceforward, God's presence in the world is to consist exclusively in God's being the Spirit of a community, a Spirit-in-common (ibid., 420–21). "This is the Spirit of God, or God as present, real Spirit: God dwelling in his community" (*Phil. Rel.* II, 315). True, God is now the spirit of a community that is designated, in its particular form of today, in which it exists in separation from pagans and Jews, to anticipate the single community of tomorrow. The community will be "fulfilled, through the negation of its directness, to generality—a fulfillment that is not, as yet, and that is thus to be grasped as future (*Phil. Rel.* II, 221).

But if religion in general is an externalization of this dialectic of spirit, and if Christianity in particular, as "absolute religion," seizes this Spirit as the Spirit of the community, which in turn is the anticipation of a coming humanity, then the question arises: Is the word "God" anything but a metaphor for the dialectic of this Spirit, which is finally to prove the common Spirit of the human race? L. Feuerbach says that this is all that the word means. In order to come to self-knowledge, the human being must make an object of its own being and essence; and this "objectified being" appears before it as its God (Feuerbach, *WdChr*, 41; see also pp. 5, 15). All service of God, all consciousness of any obligation to be obedient to God and obliged to God's service, is an unconscious service of the individual to human beings and thereby to the human species, to humanity—an indirect consciousness of belonging to it and being under obligation to serve it.

But then, granted, religion is a precious testimonial to the human being's consciousness of self and of an inner wealth that is at the same time, in terms of a concept of God, turned outward (Feuerbach, *WdChr*, 10, 15). But religious consciousness misunderstands itself (ibid., 16). And as soon as the religious person is brought to true self-consciousness through philosophical criticism, the metaphors "God" and "Spirit" can be dispensed with. They are replaced with the expressions, "essence of human beings," and "human race." At last the philosophical interpretation of religion has led to the dissolution of religion.

The one remaining question: How comes it that the religious person so long, so fiercely, and so successfully resists enlightenment as to the true content of these misunderstood religious conceptualizations? Marx responds: Human beings will resist the philosophical explanation so long as, on the basis of the real anguish of their life conditions, they have need of the fictitious consolation of religion. In this sense, for Marx, "the requirement of surrendering the illusions concerning their condition" is tied up with the more primordial requirement of "surrendering a condition that has need of illusions" (Marx, KHegRPh, 379).

Bloch's Religion without God

Taking his point of departure from Marx's thesis that it is the needs of human beings that give rise to religion, and that will continue to do so as long as these needs go unfulfilled, E. Bloch asks whether these needs of the human being are exclusively directed to victory over socioeconomic misery. He judges this conception as the expression of an underestimation of the longings and requirements of the human being (Bloch, *GdU*, 407, 409–10; *AiChr*, 98). After all, this longing and these requirements aim not only at the improvement of the situation of the human being within a tenacious structure of that being's life conditions, but at a new world *simpliciter*. The requirement that this world pass and a new world replace it constitutes the core of all religious conceptualizations, as Bloch understands them (*AiChr*, 59ff.; cf. also pp. 291, 302–3). But now the religious requirement of the demise of this world, as Bloch understands that requirement, cannot co-exist indefinitely with the worship of God. God remains compromised by having created the world and "still finding it very good" (*AiChr*, 144). "The Principle that is supposed to have created the world cannot be the same as the one that leads out of this world," for the aim of hope for a new world is "as superior to Yahweh's entire product as the meaning of Canaan was superior to what was experienced as 'Egypt'" (*AiChr*, 290–91). The exodus of the hopeful ones from the entire system of "this world," symbolically anticipated and handed down as Israel's exodus from Egypt, must therefore be consummated in an exodus from any relation to any God at all—in the exodus from Yahweh himself into the unknown [land of] Canaan, of which he was the unkept promise" (Bloch, *PH*, 1456).

The true core of religion, the absolute hope in a "kingdom," drops its disguise only when it is recognized that the word "God" is an unconsidered metaphor for that "kingdom" that can only come when it is no longer expected of a God: "The truth of the God ideal is merely the utopia of the kingdom; for this, the prerequisite is precisely that no God remain on high, inasmuch as there is none there and never was" (Bloch, *PH*, 1524; identical with *AiChr*, 218).

Thus, religion understood aright lays the groundwork for its own demise. And as for Hegel, so for Bloch, Christianity is the fulfillment and perfection of the history of religion because it has made this true core of all religion the express content of its proclamation. "Atheism in Christianity," in Bloch's conviction, is the core of the Christian message and at the same time the goal to which the entire history of religions is directed.

The Christian ideal [that of the eschatological reign] has wandered with the three wise men of the entire East. These have forgotten their own stars for the one over the manger, but have brought gifts from all earlier religions—frank-incense, myrrh, and gold. They have surrendered tradition, together with . . . their myths of alienation, at the birthplace of the Present Moment, [where their star] finally comes to rest. The star has moved over the manger, where God ceases. (Bloch, *PH*, 1533–34)

There and nowhere else has the whole of the history of religion moved. (Bloch, *PH*, 1533)

PHILOSOPHY OF RELIGION AS TRANSFORMATION OF RELIGION
INTO PHILOSOPHY: BACKWARD GLANCE ON A JOURNEY

In our introductory considerations on the concept of the philosophy of religion, we stated that this philosophy is necessary in order for philosophy as a whole to understand itself. After all, to the latter purpose philosophy must grasp that its emergence is part of the history of religions, that this emergence presupposes a crisis within the history of religions, and why this is the case. The type of philosophies of religion here described produces a certain conclusion, if by no means the only possible one: the emergence of philosophy from religion will culminate in the transformation of religion into philosophy.

Plato, the Neoplatonists, and the Idealists sought to reach this goal by understanding religion philosophically, on the one hand, and, on the other, by understanding their own philosophizing in a religious manner. This symmetry was abolished by Feuerbach and Marx. Here, the philosophical understanding of religion was drawn from a profane self-understanding on the part of philosophy, which also sought to interpret the "true core" of religious conceptualizations in a fully profane manner. Bloch's philosophy of hope reestablished the symmetry, inasmuch as, to his atheistic understanding of religion, a religious understanding of his own atheism corresponded.

In order to justify the program of a transformation of religion into philosophy, it is necessary to uncover in religion itself the germ of its future self-abolition. Hegel and Bloch, each in his own way, have undertaken such a presentation of religion and its history. The presentation of Christianity as the religion of Spirit with Hegel and the presentation of Christianity as an "atheistic" religion with Bloch are attempts to demonstrate that each one's own philosophy is the legitimate heir of the complete history of religion. In both cases, it is Christianity that is appointed to prepare for this self-abolition of religion. And in this hermeneutic claim lies the challenge presented to theology by a religious philosophy of this kind, inasmuch as theology seeks to offer resistance to a transformation of religion into philosophy (see Schaeffler 1979, esp. 289–308).

CHAPTER 3

The Prevailing Type in Several Eras

Philosophy of Religion on the Basis of Philosophical Theology

I N OUR DISCUSSION of the type of philosophies of religion just addressed, we had occasion to mention Augustine. In a historical respect, Augustine is to be ranged in the tradition that has led from Platonism to Idealism (and from there to Feuerbach, Marx, and Bloch). In a systematic respect, however, Augustine departs from this type of philosophy of religion. He sought not to convert religion into philosophy but to present, on philosophical grounds, that religion, not atheism, is correct, and that, to boot, not all religions correspond to the philosophical definition of religion—that is, that not all are "true religions," but that this designation can be ascribed only to one of them, the biblical religion.

With this program, Augustine has an important position within another type of philosophy of religion: religion as service to God or the gods. That religion *simpliciter* is correct rather than atheism is to be evidenced by philosophical proofs for the existence of God. But the question of which religion among the many is the "true religion" is to be decided through philosophical arguments that describe God's being. Only service to the "true God" (therefore, to a God who corresponds to the concept of God) can be "true religion." Thus, from a systematic viewpoint, Augustine represents the type of philosophy of religion whose basis is a philosophic doctrine of God. The main questions of such a philosophical theology are the questions of God's existence and essence. (These can alternate their order, with pregnant consequences. Anselm of Canterbury, in his *Proslogion*, first posits a definition of God's essence and then proceeds to the question of whether God exists. Thomas Aquinas asks first whether God exists and then addresses the question of the divine essence (*S. Th.* I, q. 2, intro.).

17

THEME AND ARGUMENTATION OF PHILOSOPHICAL THEOLOGY

The Difference between Religious Questions and Those of Philosophical Theology

In order to evince the peculiarity of the main questions of philosophical theology—the questions of God's existence and essence—it will be helpful to consider what these questions are not. The religious person generally does not ask whether there is a God, but can altogether easily wonder whether "this" is God—that which appears here. In such cases it is not existence that is in question, nor is it essence—not whether there is a God and what a God is—but *who* is a God, and how God can be recognized. (A characteristic example of such a question is found in Virgil's *Aeneid* 1.326–29.) Both questions must be decided apart from religious philosophy. A contest over a will does not ask whether there is such a thing as a will, or what a will is, but *who* the legitimate heir is, and how that heir can be identified. Aeneas, too, in the locus just cited, asks not whether there are gods, or in what their essence consists, but whether in the concrete situation he is encountering a being worthy of divine worship.

Another kind of question is not to be confused with the question of God's existence or essence: the question of the divine names (cf. Exodus 3:13). While the question of God's essence presupposes that that being is at all times the same being as its essential concept represents, for religions it is altogether possible that the same God be addressed under different names in different situations. The name need not designate the "eternal essence" of the object named. The name indicates that the God who has once upon a time appeared and revealed the divine name, can be called upon in coming situations, so that the divine apparition is no ephemeral, single event, but rather leaves a memorial, and in this memorial renews the divine presence. Exactly this we find in the God who speaks from the burning bush, revealing the divine name and then adding: "This is my name for everlasting, and this my title from generation to generation" (Exodus 3:15). At issue here is not the divine essence but the fidelity of the divine attention to the chosen people and the possibility of human memory of the event.

Philosophical theology inquires as to God's existence and essence. Religion inquires into theophanies and into the "name" revealed in such theophanies as make it possible to call upon God and establish the divine presence ever and again.

The difference in these questions corresponds to a distinction in the manners in which religion, on the one hand, and philosophical theology, on the other, speak of God. The philosophical concept of the divine essence, which answers the question What is (a) God? is the object of a definition; the name of God, by contrast, into which religious persons inquire, is used in narrative. The existence or nonexistence of God, which is debated in philosophical theology, is to be established by arguments; theophanies, on the other hand, are not conclusions to be drawn from series of arguments, but are the content of experiences. But if religion and philosophical theology speak of God in such different ways, then it appears doubtful whether they are speaking of the same God at all when they use the word "God." Thus, the "God of the philosophers" seems a different God from the one prayed to in religions and whose mighty deeds are proclaimed in those religions.

The Word "God" in the Transition
from the Religious to the Philosophical Context

Of course, we must not forget the link between religious and philosophical language about God. The first element in this bond is that, in both discourses, "beginnings" are spoken of. Rightly has Plato called the tales of the gods "archaeologies," language about the beginnings (see *Hipp. M.* 285D). But "beginnings" here has a special meaning. A first distinction obtains in the fact that these beginnings do not recede into the past with the passage of time, do not lose their importance for the present, but are ever present and effective. In particular, acts of worship, and narrative, transmit an ever new and renewing presence of these sources. This suggests to the philosophical observer that the "archai" of which tales of the god speak are not temporal "beginnings" but abidingly effective "principles," which themselves do not fall under designations of time. Thus, religions are subject to a critical yardstick: To what extent have they at least approached this concept of the "eternity of the divine"?

A second criterion of distinction of the divine "beginnings" consists in the fact that myths frequently emphasize that "at that time," that is, "in the beginning," the situation was altogether different from "today." On the one hand, decisions were then open that today are irrevocable, and these have stamped the course of things with a permanent law—for example, the decision on the place and path of the stars, on the mortality or immortality of the human being, on the victory or defeat of the powers of chaos. Again, persons "of that time" were immediate witnesses, if not indeed co-agents, of the divine activity, whereas "today" the gods and their deeds continue to be present among human beings only in the graphic representation of worship, the place of worship, and in some cases the images to be worshiped. This suggests to the philosophical observer that the "divine sources" are qualitatively distinct from all "causes" observed within the world of our experience. The fact that myth, finally, speaks of a "span" of time that must be expressly bridged by the memorial of narrative and the activity of worship, indicates that the qualitative difference between these sources and the world of our experience is grounded in a "difference in essence." Religions are thus open to a value judgment on the basis of the extent to which they have at least approached this concept of the "essential difference of the divine."

Eternity and transcendence, we can conclude, are at least semiconsciously present in the religious discourse on the divine beginnings. But they are not brought to adequate expression in mythological discourse. Thus, the philosophical attempt to designate the subject of religious discourse crosses over into the critique of religion. After all, if God must be conceptualized as the eternal and transcendent principle of the world of experience, then one can precisely not speak of God in the manner in which religious discourse speaks of God: in narratives that report a temporal series of events and thus seem to disregard God's eternity, and, in the description of sensibly graspable encounters, to prescind from God's transcendence and invisibility.

Philosophical theology, which first seeks to grasp what it is that is reported in religious narratives concerning the gods (concerning the "divine sources") now passes over into a critique of the way in which religions speak of these divine sources (in the form of narratives of sensible theophanies). Philosophical theology specifies criteria for the assessment of such discourse. (The sources sought must be conceptualized as eternal and transcendent.)

Only when this transition from the hermeneutics of religious discourse to its philosophical critique has been accomplished do the two key questions of philosophical theology arise: Has this temporal world an eternal, transcendent principle at all? And of what kind or essence will such a principle be, in case it exists, in order to explain this temporary, experientially accessible, world?

Surely one can, with a philosophical theology thus effected, once again attempt to rehabilitate myth. In that locus in the dialogue *Phaedo,* where the Platonic Socrates speaks of having seen a dream image challenging him to produce myths rather than philosophical arguments, the specific strength of myth (in contrast to logos) is defined: Myth is able to show how opposites are inseparably "joined at the heads" (*Phaid.* 60B). What appears paradoxical, and therefore impossible for logos, is expressible by myth because it divides the paradox into the time sequences of a story. There the relevant grounding factor of the described unity-of-opposites is presented as prior in time, the relevant grounded factor as the one following in time.

This suggests to any philosophical spectator the judgment that the God of whom religion speaks is in such a way the eternal and transcendent principle of the experienced world, that from this principle even that connection of opposites can be comprehended which (despite all of the rules of the logicians against contradictions) is the basic law of our experienced world. This God is the unity out of which the opposites of the world of appearances unfold and in which, as inseparably attached opposites, they abide (see Heraclitus B 51, 67).

To be sure, this philosophical hermeneutic of myth occasions a critique of religion of a new kind. Certain directions in philosophical theology emphasize the oneness of God so strongly that every distinction and connection of subject and predicate in an affirmative proposition is *eo ipso* judged an offense against that oneness. The divine One, which precedes all opposites, is without predicate and in this sense is unnamable. Every naming bears upon the divine principle not in its undifferentiated, all-opposites-preceding unity but in its subsequent explication of the diversity arising from it. Every naming bears, in this way, upon a mere secondary, and, furthermore, variable aspect of the divine oneness, not (the godly unity) itself: "The One, which alone grants understanding, does and does not wish to be named with the name of Zeus," but rather "earns its name as fire takes on the scent of what burns within it" (Heraclitus B 32, B 67).

FROM THE CRITICAL HERMENEUTICS OF RELIGION
TO ONTO-THEOLOGY

Preparatory Steps

Heraclitus and Plato serve as examples of how, from reflections on religious narratives that are transmitted, concepts emerge that could be used as a critique of these very same narratives. Religious discourse, it appears, is rightly understood only when one comprehends the "divine origin" as the eternal and unchanging, essentially different from the world of experience and therefore invisible, simple and yet diversity-originating principle.

But once criteria for a proper discourse upon the divine has been established, the opposite proposition suggests itself: Wherever there is talk of a principle of such kind, there is simultaneously talk of God. Then every philosophical teaching-of-principles could be called "theology," without the necessity of a reference to traditional religious imagery. And indeed Aristotle has used the word "theology," namely, "discourse about God," in the sense of such a philosophical teaching-of-principles (see Aristotle, *Metaphys.* K7.1064B 1–3).

Plato, on the other hand, had not used the word "God" for designating the highest principle, but had spoken of a divine "artisan" (*demiourgos*) who creates temporal images of the eternal ideas and thereby makes it possible for himself to produce time as the "eternal numerically progressing image of eternity abiding in oneness" (Plato, *Tim.* 37D). Later tradition, however, has merged the concept of the founder of this numerical/temporal world order with the concept of the eternal, transcendent principle and has therefore produced the God-concept which so long ruled philosophical theology.

Aristotle took an important step in this direction by attributing the numerical order of time to the rotational movements of the sky, but ascribed these to the activity of the "first unmoved mover," which is "always in action" because its specific kind of action, the "self-thinking thought," needs no foreign object but is self-sufficient (Aristotle, *Metaphys.* AΛ 8 1074 A–B). The concept of such a self-sufficient thought, simultaneously the first cause of the moved, temporal world, becomes afterwards the leading concept of philosophical theology.

"God" and "Being"

The question of the *archai*, first discussed in mythological archaeologies, then in the search for highest principles on the part of the pre-Socratics, finds its answer with Aristotle in the concept of "being." Philosophy in the strict sense is ontology. So the question arises: How does the self-thinking thought, that first cause of all movement and its numerical/temporal order, relate itself to "being" as the one, eternal, and transcendent principle of all diverse experiential reality?

Philosophical theology, as practiced in the following centuries, rested on this thesis: The two just-mentioned concepts apply to an essential identical reality. God is "being" and the "self-thinking thought" simultaneously. On the one hand, "being itself" has to include every "degree of being," but on the other hand must demonstrate a higher degree of being than all that does not "think itself." According to the first argument, the "spirit nature" of the highest principle flows from its "fullness of being." In the second argument, the "fullness of being" is developed from the "first-cause-ness" of the self-thinking thought. (For these two kinds of arguments, see Augustine, *On the True Religion* (*De vera religione*), and Thomas Aquinas, *Summa Theologiae*.

The philosophers who in one way or another sought to prove that the "first unmoved mover" is identical with the "absolute being," stood under the influence of biblical tradition as well, when it came to these attempted arguments. The God of whom the Bible speaks has brought forth, through the work of creation, the succession of "evening" and "morning," and therefore has founded that which the philosophers have called the "numerically progressing order of time." Thus far, the Aristotelian concept of the "first unmoved mover" is applicable to this God, and even more so than in Aristotle, inasmuch as God's work of creation springs from a "taking counsel with himself" ("Let us make the human being . . .")—an expression of self-knowledge. But precisely this God is self-naming, if one follows the Greek translation of the Old Testament for the scene of the burning bush, with the expression, "I am the 'being' one," the one who *is* (Exodus 3:14). This suggests the interpretation that God is the one who, in an unlimited sense, is the "'being' one" and thus "'being' itself."

God's self-naming in the burning bush, read in the wording of the Greek Bible, now counts as the classic reference for the identity of essence (*Realidentität*) of the world-creating Spirit (the "first mover") with "'Being' Itself" (the highest, transcendent principle—see Thomas Aquinas, *S. Th.* I, q. 13, a. 11, c). Precisely this identity permits one to consider discourse upon God, namely, theology, and discourse upon being, namely, ontology, as materially identical. Philosophical theology and ontology thus merge into onto-theology. (An example of this merger appears in the iconography of the Eastern Church: To signify the divinity of the one who appeared in human form, written into Christ's halos is *ho on*, "the One who is.")

Such an onto-theology could now, on the one hand, serve the philosophical foundation of religion in its debate with atheism, in that it sought to prove that the denial of God denounces the last rationale that alone explains beings as such and "being" as a whole. Simultaneously, onto-theology served to support the status of the biblical religions as the only true ones. In no other religion—it is said in ontologically oriented philosophies of religion—is God expressly honored as the "'being' one." No other divinities manifest the marks of eternity, transcendence, and unity of absolute being. The first step in onto-theology, therefore, always consists in reducing all being to "being itself," and in explaining that "being itself" is identical in essence with God (proofs of God). The second step consists in the differentiation between being-itself and all finite beings, and therewith in the denunciation of service to "false gods." Attempts to practice onto-theology with this double assignment have been produced in many variations, up to modern times. Above all, Catholic theology has always been interested in an ontological understanding of discourse upon God (see Schaeffler 1980, esp. 22ff., 319ff., 357ff.). A more recent variation of this ontological understanding of God has been developed (without regard for Kant's protest!) where the ontological question of "being" has been intertwined with the transcendental question of the terms of possibility (*Möglichkeitsbedingungen*) for experience and its objects (see the section below "On the History and Typology of Discourse upon God in Transcendental Philosophy").

Onto-Theology and the Relation of Faith and Knowledge

Philosophical theology in the particular form of onto-theology seemed to have given a definitive answer to the question of God's existence and essence: God is "being itself" (*ipsum esse*), and this being is the pure, self-sufficient being-by-itself of a "self-thinking thought." But being itself is at the same time the necessarily existing being. Thereby the question of the true religion is finally answered as well: the true religion is service to that God who has made a self-revelation as "the Being."

This type of philosophy of religion, however, is distinguished from the previous type in not seeking to transform religion into philosophy. And so the question arises: What is the specifically religious moment of the true religion that is not available to a transformation into philosophy? Or more specifically: What is left to the Christian proclamation to say, once the philosopher has cognized God's essence and existence from arguments from reason? To put the same question in respect of the acts of the cognizing subject: What is the difference between the act of faith (listening to the word of revelation) and the act of knowledge (the result of the "natural" concern with cognition)?

If we inquire into the specific content of the religious proclamation, the content not available to transformation into philosophy, then the following response suggests itself: What cannot be cognized through philosophical arguments are God's free salvific counsels, those not prejudiced by way of any necessity of being. It is for these that, in the New Testament, the word "mystery" is used (1 Corinthians 2:7; Romans 11:25). The "unfathomability" of the free decisions of the divine will is also spoken of earlier, in texts of Greek religion (Pindar, frag. 50; Heraclitus B 18). If religion's special matter is the unfathomable mysteries of the divine salvific will, then its specific form will be faithful listening to God's self-communication: faith.

In those eras of the history of philosophy in which onto-theology served as the basis of all philosophy and religion, this opposition of faith and its mysteries, on the one hand, and knowledge and its "fathomable" objects, on the other, became the leitmotif of the question of the essence of religion. This opposition between faith and knowledge acquired a specific stamp at the hands of Anselm of Canterbury, who through his (later so-called) "Ontological Proof for God" became the classic representative of an onto-theology. At the end of his proof for God he thanks God "that I . . . now,

. . . even if I were not to wish to believe in your existence, could still not escape an insight into it" (Anselm of Canterbury, *Prosl.* 4). Faith (and with it, religion) is a matter of the will, and therefore ever threatened: it could happen that I might not "wish to believe." Knowledge, by contrast, as a result of reasoning argumentation, is a matter of necessity. The will is free; the intellect is not. Therefore it appears as a reasonable task to wish to advance from faith to knowledge. (Anselm designates the content of his *Proslogion* as *"fides quaerens intellectum"*: "faith seeking understanding"— *Prosl.*, praef.; cf. Barth 1931).

Understood from a religious viewpoint, the will to proceed from faith to knowledge is an anticipation of that "beatific vision" that the believer hopes for in the life after death (cf. Anselm, *CDH,* dedic.). This is the sense in which Thomas Aquinas appraises faith as a provisional form of the human relationship to the divine truth (cf. *S. Th.* I-II, q. 67, a. 3, c; II-II, q. 1, a. 7, c). But the program, "From faith to knowledge" was also understood in the sense of a critique of religion: an expression of the wish to leave the "unsure ground" of religious convictions and to shift to the "sure ground" of knowledge gained by argumentation. Therefore that consent of the will that, in the conception of Anselm and Thomas, belongs to the act of faith, is only accorded that truth susceptible of compelling argument. Thus this truth is withdrawn from the domain of the will and its capacity for resistance and objection. This is the step taken by Descartes, in clear dependence on Anselm of Canterbury and at the same time in differentiation from him. We must see how this produced a new form of philosophical theology and a new understanding of religion. But the meaning of this shift is especially clear when we grasp it as a prelude to Immanuel Kant's "Copernican revolution."

KANT'S "COPERNICAN REVOLUTION" AND THE
CRISIS OF ONTO-THEOLOGY

From Ontology to the Analytics of the Understanding

Two sources, as we have seen, have given rise to onto-theology by their confluence: the Aristotelian thesis that the supreme principle of all that we perceive is "being as such" and the Greek translation of the Old Testament, according to which God announced the divine name in the burning bush as "the One who is." Philosophers who thus discover that the true sense of all discourse upon God, all theology, consists in the discourse of Being, become interpreters of religion. They remind religion that, in all of their mythological "archaeologies," they are following the traces of the one and true *Archē*, Being. And they serve notice to the devotees of the biblical religion that, among the many biblical names of God, the only adequate one is the one claimed by God: "Being"; and this gives the biblical religion its preeminence among all religions.

The effectiveness of this conceptualization is also due to the fact that a particular, philologically altogether questionable translation of the locus cited in the book of Exodus prevailed for so many centuries among theologians as well. Only in an environment in which it had become an evidence that philosophy must understand itself as ontology, and an environment in which this understanding of philosophy had become the prevailing one for the interpretation of religious traditions as well, could, among the many translations of the narrative of the burning bush that would have been possible, the one prevail in which God's self-designation is "I am the one who is."

But this understanding of philosophy of itself is the one that ruled as the sole adequate one on the European continent for several centuries. Only Kant, finally, sought to show that philosophy, if it would be a science, must divest itself of "the proud name of ontology" and rest content with being a "simple analytics of pure understanding" (Kant, *KrV,* A, 247). But if philosophy as a whole no longer aims at an ontology, then the philosophy of religion can no longer be grounded in an onto-theology. With all consistency, Kant's critique of ontology climaxes in the rejection of the "Ontological Proof" for the existence of God. If, on the other hand, philosophy across the board becomes an "analytics of pure understanding"—or more generally, a theory of subjectivity, inasmuch as the latter renders itself suitable for the encounter with potential objects— then the philosophy of religion, too, will have to be based on such a transcendental theory of subjectivity.

Religion, as Kant understands it, emerges from that dialectic in which the understanding is inevitably caught in its theoretical, and especially practical, usage, once it seeks to acquire a concept of that concatenation of phenomena within which we encounter the objects of our experience. But this dialectic cannot be solved apart from the "postulates" of the existence of God, the survival of the human being in a coming world, and the justification of the sinner through a juridical "sentence of grace." After all, without out a hope in such a "sentence of grace," the law of morals would suffice, it is true, for human beings to experience themselves as convicted, but not for showing them how they can become human beings pleasing to God. For this, Kant expressly says, a "bad tree" would have to "bring forth good fruit," which obviously is inconceivable without contradiction (Kant, *Religion,* A, 46). Only the postulates of hope (of which hope in God's grace of justification is the most important) remove the contradiction of the moral goal (see Schaeffler 1981b).

Such considerations accomplish the transition from ontology to a transcendental theory of subjectivity as a manner of founding religion and the understanding of religion. Religion is intrinsically the totality of those postulates (that is, assumptions not demonstrable theoretically but necessary practically) that are necessary for a resolution of the logical contradiction of the moral idea and thereby for the liberation of reason for its self-legislation.

The End of a Rational Foundation of Religion?

Kant's critique of all ontology and his resulting consistent rejection of ontotheology necessarily awakened the impression that a philosophical grounding of religion across the board and a philosophical acquisition of criteria for the decision among the religions were now no longer possible. The decision between religion and atheism, as well as the second decision (in case the first came down on the side of religion) for or against a particular religion (for instance, "between God and the gods") would now become a blind decision made on the basis of emotions, and beyond the purview of rational criticism.

More than a century after Kant, then, Pope Pius X thought that the influence of this Kantian philosophy on an understanding of religion ought to be described in this way: In "that doctrine, . . . according to which the human understanding is entirely restricted to phenomena" (*Pasc.*, 596), "any approach to God from the side of the intellect is closed off" from the human being (ibid., 633). And so, instead of being grounded on reason, religion is based on "that religious sense [*sensus*] that fosters the interiority of life from the hidden caverns of the unconscious [*e latebris subconscientiae erumpit*]" (ibid., 600).

It was surely not Kant's intent to reduce religion to a matter of feelings at work in the subconscious and exempt from rational control. But this interpretation coincides with an observation from the history of science: Post-Kantian philosophy of religion—with regular appeal to Kant's critique of ontology—has understood traditional religion, including the Christian faith (to the extent that it cannot be transformed into philosophy) to be an expression of human emotionality. (Thus, especially, the religious philosophies of the late nineteenth century.)

Now, this effect of the Kantian critique on the history of philosophy not only contradicts Kant's subjective intentions but also the objective content of his positions and arguments. On the contrary, Kant's whole argumentation was geared to producing for religion a legitimizing foundation "within the limits of pure reason," and to bestow on its revelation content a rational basis of understanding.

The opinion, so effective in the history of science yet supported neither by the wording nor the intended meaning of the Kantian message, that Kant's critique meant the end of all rational arguments for religion and the loss of all criteria that would make a decision possible among religions, is thus based on a misunderstanding. The occasion of the misunderstanding is the fact that Kant did dismiss such arguments: only he dismissed them not simply but with respect to their hitherto practiced usage. In the history of philosophy in general, and in the history of the philosophy of religion in particular, this critique signifies a turning point that Kant himself called "Copernican." The pre-Copernican astronomy took it for granted that we deal with the sky and the stars in it as immediately given realities. Copernicus, however, reflected on the fact that the position of the subject in the universe defines the mode of presentation of these objects. In like manner, pre-Kantian philosophy assumed that we deal with the world and the beings in it in their immediately given reality. Kant reflected that the peculiarity of the subject defines the mode of presentation of these objects, their way of "appearance for us." Whence he concluded that, when inquiring into the conditions that make possible the "oppositeness" of objects, their "standing athwart" the subject, we are dealing not with special hyperempirical objects but with subjective conditions determining the structure of our experiential connections. Thus, what previous metaphysics sought as a "transcendent" reality (that is, lying beyond the totality of possible experience) is to be found only as the "transcendental" (that is, as the form of our own acts that makes possible the object relation of our regard and thought).

It followed from this, for the sort of metaphysics that Kant at first wanted to elevate to the rank of science, that either this metaphysics is the vehicle of the proof that this subjectivity of ours is the last unconditioned condition of the entire world of appearances—then any talk of God is objectless—or else it undertakes the attempt to reduce once again human subjectivity itself, and its transcendental (object-relation enabling) power, for its part, to a condition independent of human beings. In the latter case a philosophical theology would emerge that is no longer ontological but is founded on a theory of subjectivity. Kant's teaching on postulates is a first suggestion as to what such a philosophical theology could look like.

A Comprehensive Context for the History of Philosophy

The thought of a philosophical theology founded on a theory of subjectivity surrenders some of its outlandishness when one realizes that Kant's philosophy, despite all of the radicalism it comports in terms of a "Copernican turning point of thought," still remains embedded, to a higher degree than Kant himself knew, in the comprehensive tradition of European metaphysics.

First one needs to recall that the kind of ontology Kant was fighting was Aristotelian in character. Further, there had existed, since Plato, a metaphysics of reflection upon the source that gave "cognition its power and objects of cognition their cognizability" (Plato, *Pol.* 508D–E). Because this source is neither spirit nor object, it cannot be identified with any kind of being (ibid., 509B). In the various forms of Christian Platonism, a philosophical doctrine of God was attempted, over and again, which made no effort to describe God as an object "above" worldly objects, but in which God is this condition of subjectivity (the power of cognition) and its connection to objects (the "cognizability of objects"). Even when this source above all objects was called "being," it was in sharp contraposition to all that existed that this was done. The transcendental condition of cognizability relates to all objects, as light—which as such remains invisible—relates to color, which becomes visible through that light:

> As the eye, when it turns toward the manifold variations of color, cannot see light, . . . so the eye of our mind, when it turns toward beings in particular and as a whole, notices not being itself, . . . even though . . . only through being does it encounter all else. . . . The eye of our mind . . . has the impression of seeing nothing, . . . even as the eye, if it sees pure light, believes it sees nothing. (Bonaventure, *ImD* 5.4)

The theme of a philosophical theology of this type is: God is the non-objective light for the eye of the mind and its objects, not the unmoved mover of the starry sky and all of the moving things that this sky envelops. There is a tradition of transcendental theology, then, that is older than Kant. And this theology returns today, having taken up Kantian elements, in the attempts at a transcendental theology—now, granted, tied up with the attempt to reconcile the critical arguments of Kant with an Aristotelian and Thomistically oriented ontology.

Joseph Maréchal, founder of the more recent transcendental-philosophical doctrine of God, has given one of the drafts of his later work "The Starting Point of Metaphysics," the title "Transposition of Kantianism" (*Mél.*, 289ff.). And he has added to the title this comment:

> This reconciliation in principle with the past [of classic metaphysics] certainly cannot be required of Kant at the cost of a wholesale sacrifice of his *Critique of Pure Reason*, but can indeed through the transposition of a certain number of his agnostic theses. We use the term "transposition" advisedly, preferring it

to other expressions that would indicate a more radical correction. (*Mél.*, 290)

Kant's doctrine of the postulates therefore remains inscribed in a tradition stretching from Plato and Christian Platonism to Maréchal's and Rahner's transcendental theology, and is determined by the one, tenacious thought that the human power of perception itself, and its connection to possible objects, is the place where God's reality "enlightens." Religion, according to this understanding, is the relationship of the human being as a subject to that supraobjective ground that alone empowers the human regard of and thinking about the transcendental—that is, enables one to open up the horizon of possible experience.

ON THE HISTORY AND TYPOLOGY OF DISCOURSE UPON GOD IN TRANSCENDENTAL PHILOSOPHY

Descartes and the Proof for God in a Theory of Subjectivity

At this point we must speak of Descartes. Not only did he discover (through his radical doubts) the basis for a new certitude (in the self-consciousness of the thinking "I"); he also was able to establish (through further inquiry into the conditions of this self-consciousness) a new form of philosophical theology. This type of philosophical theology ruled early modern times, was the immediate object of Kant's critique, but has been taken up once more—passing by way of the Kantian critique—in another form by modern transcendental theology.

The Cartesian doctrine of God, as primarily expressed in the proofs for God of the *Meditations,* can be comprehended only if one recalls how Descartes understands the *"cogitare"* that is the nature-specific act of the human "ego." Decartes' *"cogito"* is not about the secure possession of a knowledge but about a movement of seeking and testing possible answers, which movement continues to be activated by doubt as by a sting (see Descartes, *Medit.* 2.9). At the beginning of this path is not just simple ignorance (*ignorantia* as *negatio*) but the experience of error (error as *privatio*)—not only the missing of knowledge but the discovery of misleading appearance: "Even some years ago I experienced how much falsehood I have let pass for truth in my youth, and how doubtful, therefore, is all that I have built upon it since" (*Medit.* 1.2). Whoever begins with this experience cannot—on this seemingly natural, organic, although as yet uncultivated ground—build a cognition system, but must first remove what is built faultily: indeed, topple it from its foundations (*"funditus . . . esse evertenda,"* ibid.).

The fundamental question of method here is therefore not Socratic-Platonic—How we can know ourselves as the unknowing one?—but the more radical question of how we can judge ourselves as the erroneous ones. What we need for this—to use a word from Augustine—is not merely the *veritas lucens,* the light that the followers of Plato themselves knew, which renders the eyes able to see and objects visible. It is the *veritas redarguens,* the normative standard, before which we learn to judge ourselves as the failing ones (see Augustine, *Conf.* 10.23).

Following the example of Augustine, Descartes too thinks of human self-consciousness under the condemning standard of truth as the self-awareness of a sinner. Error, for Descartes, means the consequence of a false use of free will, and therefore the consequence of sin (*Medit.* 4.9, 12). And this sin can only be discovered as such inasmuch as we know that we stand before God. Thus, the very first experience (*animadversio*) of which the *Meditations* speak—namely, the personal experience of the human being as settled in error—confirms the concept of that God before whom alone human beings can discover themselves as sinners. In this sense the knowledge of God precedes the human self-consciousness, enabling it. "So I obtain, in a certain sense, the concept of the infinite earlier than that of the finite—that is, the concept of God before the concept of myself" (*Medit.* 3.24).

The proofs of God established by Descartes in his *Meditations* do not bring in from the outside the knowledge of something hitherto unknown, but merely render explicit that knowledge of God which—in the self-consciousness of human beings, in the experience of their error and in the movement of their doubt—has always been implicitly present. Because error is understood as sin, this God, before whom alone human beings know themselves as sinful, must be known directly as the morally perfect one. Therefore, the morally grounded truth of this God guarantees the truth of human understanding wherever human beings limit the assent of their judgment to that which challenges (from necessity of thought) the attempt to doubt it. It would not be consistent with the perfection of God to keep the human being the prisoner of insurmountable error.

Trust in reason, which limits itself to accepting only that which is proved from necessity of thought, is therefore the result of one's trust in the absolute goodness of God. A reason-renouncing skepticism amounts to a mistrust in the Creator (cf. *Medit.* 4.17; 6.11). "And so I clearly see that the certainty and truth of all knowledge is solely dependent on the perception of the true God, and this to such a degree that, before I knew him, I was unable to know anything in a perfect way" (*Medit.* 5.16).

Development of a Religious Rationalism
and the Deification of Reason

Cognition of God is the human being's cognition of self plumbed to its remotest depths; hence, as countermove, trust in reason is trust in God, applied; finally, strictness of method is the guideline to express God's truthfulness through the truth in human perception. These key phrases can be used to describe the peculiarity of a thinking that can be designated "religious rationalism." Such an understanding of trust in reason made it possible for the theologians of the immediate post-Cartesian era to combine enlightenment and religious tradition all but seamlessly. The opinion that enlightenment and its rationalism must be in principle the enemy of religion became dominant only in the romantic age. Even the above-cited papal condemnation of "modernism" by Pius X, indeed even certain formulations of Vatican Council II, were based on the conviction that an attack on reason would simultaneously be an attack on the fundamentals of religion, because of human beings' relationship to God being grounded in their dignity as subjects of reason. "Man judges rightly that by his intellect he surpasses the material universe, for he shares in the light of the divine mind. . . . For his intelligence is not confined to observable data alone. It can with genuine certitude attain to reality itself as knowable" (Vatican II, *GS* §15).

To be sure, a rationalism that understood itself as religious could also posit altered criteria, in order to discern the one "true religion" among the many empirically existing ones. And it became possible that the determination thus founded would not fall in favor of Christianity. At the end of the Enlightenment period—quite in keeping with "religious rationalism"— stood the attempt, in revolutionary France, to replace the Christian worship service with a "cult of the supreme being," or even through paying homage to the "Goddess of Reason" (cf. Decree of the National Assembly of Floreal 18 of the year 2—May 7, 1794), which Robespierre established in his address "Concerning the Relationships of Religious and Moral Ideas to the Principles of the Republic, and concerning the National Feasts" (Robespierre, *Werke* 10:442–65).

It would be precipitous, here and in comparable cases, to speak of "religious substitution," let alone "imitation of religion." Repeatedly, we observe the attempt to combine in the mind the absolute demand for the validity of reason-generated insights with the self-perception of human beings as not only in error but also guilty. Human beings have lost the freedom of their judgment in a "self-inflicted immaturity"—indeed, they have "alienated" their inalienable human dignity, that is, surrendered to their rulers the right of the firstborn in exchange for the "mess of pottage" of easy living and security. Reason, therefore, appears to human beings ever less as a merely human "inheritance," and ever more as the way that a superhuman power, before which human beings know themselves guilty, still works actively for their freedom.

A religious foundation for trust in reason, a hope to be delivered from sin and error through this reason, could therefore lead to a deification of reason, which was understood no longer as a power of the human being but as a divine power working in the human being. To boot, the battle for the public rule of reason (i.e., for the construction of societal and political conditions corresponding to the rules of reason, and therefore making a rational manner of life possible for the individual), joined forces with the religious pathos of a battle for the divine light against the armies of darkness.

Even the terror of the French Revolution can be explained on the basis of the conviction that it is not only ignorance but sinful denial that stands against the light of divine and liberating reason. And the "Committees of Public Safety"—in the original French *Comités du Salut Publique*—which exercised the new rule of force and terror, derive their name from the fact that they sought not only human beings' "welfare" but their "salvation" as well.

The French Revolution ranked for its contemporaries as unforgettable in two ways. On the one hand, reason had proved itself capable of becoming a politically effective force, which all of the power of the rulers could not withstand. On the other hand, the danger became apparent that a deification of reason might create a new turnabout, from liberation to oppression, from a struggle for human ideals to a new inhumanity. Kant has expressly commented on this twofold experience:

> The revolution of a spirited people, which we have seen to occur in our days, may succeed or fail. It may be so filled up with misery and cruel deeds that a well-thinking person, undertaking it a second time and hoping to carry it out successfully, still would not decide to make the experiment at such costs—this revolution, I say, finds in the hearts of all observers (who are not themselves caught up in the game) a longing for participation verging on enthusiasm— and the expression of which longing was connected with danger—which therefore can have, as a cause, nothing else but a moral disposition in the

human race. . . . For such a phenomenon in the history of human kind can never be forgotten. (Kant, *SF,* A, 143–44, 149)

If we place Kant's critique of reason in this context, then that critique becomes an attempt to uphold the religious understanding of reason and at the same time avoid the deification of reason.

Defeat of Reason's Deification through a Demonstration of Its Dialectic

Not only with Descartes but also with Spinoza, Leibniz, and other writers of the Enlightenment era, the argument for the existence of God became the indispensable means for the foundation of knowledge. Only if there is a God can human beings be sure of truth, be it that—in the *amor Dei intellectualis*—they gain access to God's self-consciousness and self-love, or be it that they trust in the "preestablished harmony" through which God ordained the contingent order of thought in the human being as part of the objective world order. In no earlier or later era of the history of philosophy did proofs for God play such a central role in the comprehensive act of philosophizing, as in the age of rationalism (see Schulz 1957). Whoever, in this position, not only criticized one or other attempt at a proof of God, but sought to extend the argument and hold that proofs for God were impossible on principle, would seem to have deprived not only religion of its rationale, but also rationality of its religious foundation—and thereby once more to have dissolved that certitude which Descartes had won in his passage through his radical doubts.

And yet Kant returned to the two discoveries from which Descartes' thinking as well had taken its point of departure: to the experiences of error and sin. Granted, he treated these experiences with a new radicality. And from this radical reflection on the subjectivity of the erroneous and guilty human being came a new way of understanding trust in reason—religiously—and at the same time, religion rationally.

As to error, Kant speaks not merely of careless transgressions of the rules of the acquisition of cognition, mistakes that persons occasionally make, but of an "appearance" that inescapably enters the picture. Kant calls it the "transcendental appearance" (*KrV,* A, 293–98, esp. 297–98). Error results from the "demand" that reason must impose on itself if it is to lead the mind to the cognition of objects. Reason "demands," then, that every content of our perception and cognition take an unequivocal place in the world of appearances or the world of purposes. Only in that way does an object differentiate itself from the mere subjective play of representations. And yet, with the attempt to represent objectively the totality of conditions, and therefore the unconditional—namely, the "world" (the totality of objects of cognition) or "the highest good" (the goal-perspective of all objects of volition)—reason falls both times into a self-contradiction, into an "antinomy." By this it proves itself "dialectical," that is, generative of contradictions and entangling itself in contradictions. This dialectic is "transcendental," in that it results from a demand to integrate every entity into the all-embracing totality, which demand must elevate reason if it would pass from subjective representations to the cognition of objects.

The transcendental and therefore inevitable dialectic of reason is now the *mark of finitude*, through which human reason is distinguished from the archetype of the divine intellect. Simultaneously, however, only this dialectic opens the door to an understanding of the true nature of the autonomy of reason. Because the antinomies are resolved only through the insight that the world in its totality of all objects is not "given" to us but "assigned," therefore, the world is not an object lying ahead of cognition but a regulative idea leading the process of cognition. However, the perceiving and thinking "I" is not a member of this cohesive totality. Rather it lies as pure act ("I think") before this world assemblage, making the condition of the latter possible. The "transcendental error" that was based on confusing that totality "assigned" to us with an object that could be "given" to us, thus proves itself to be the "most benevolent error" (Kant, *KpV*, A, 193). This error, namely, has made necessary a reflection through which philosophers found more than they asked for. They looked for the source of a correctible error, to overcome the antinomies of their worldview. Instead, they found a new self-understanding of the "I" and its relation to the world of objects.

Not only the experience of error, but the experience of sinfulness becomes radicalized by Kant in a decisive way. Like "error," sin too is more than an occasional, unavoidable failing. It is a condition in which human beings find themselves from the outset, and for their whole lifetime. After all, moral wrong must spring from a free act; yet the free act of self-determination cannot be an event in time, otherwise it would fall under the law of causality. Rather, human beings endow themselves through this act with their "intelligible character," that is, their constant—and characteristic for each individual—way of reacting to the surrounding world by deeds of their own. As with every free act, so can the human being's sinful self-determination become effective only by the formation of that human being's intelligible character, which stamps—by means of the empirical character—all modes of behavior in time. This character is presupposed "from the outset"—whenever human beings strike a relationship. The deed that defines them has therefore occurred "from the outset." The human being "began . . . from evil" (Kant, *Religion*, 88). And even if an unending

life span were at our command, so that we might embark on an endless path
of self-improvment (Kant's "postulate"), then this ethical "progress," precisely because it is necessary, would only be the clearest demonstration that
the human character is wholly defined by sinfulness. The state of goodness
is for the human being never reality, but at best "always only in the mere
state of becoming" (ibid., 94).

But just as with error, sinfulness does not exhaust itself in particular
wrongdoing. It defines the quality of human life as a whole. And suddenly
the law of ethics becomes self-contradictory. The law of ethics addresses the
human being as a free creature, and thus, according to Kant's interpretations, presupposes that persons, in their very being, do not fall under the
order of time; and yet it demands of those persons simultaneously a change,
an "ethical progress." From this develops the first contradiction: between
timeless freedom and time-bound progress. The law of ethics prescribes a
goal for this progress; but this goal is unreachable through any progress.
Thus arises the second contradiction: between endless becoming and the
being that is demanded. The law of ethics, finally, demands that we make
the transition from the merely interior disposition to effective deed; and yet
the possibility of the law of ethics rests precisely on the principle that the
moral order of goals and the causal order are essentially distinct (Kant,
KpV, 204–5). Now arises the third contradiction: between the presupposed
independence, from the causal order, of the free will, and the physical operation that this independence demands.

Also in the area of the practical exercise of reason, as previously in the
field of theory, there therefore arises a variance of reason with itself, a
"dialectic." And once more, this dialectic is a *signpost of finitude,* through
which finitude human reason is distinguished from the divine. As previously with the dialectic of the theoretical use of reason, so now with that of
the practical, a reflection is constrained through which more is found than
was sought (KpV, A, 193). What was looked for was a way to defeat the
unfreedom that we have brought upon ourselves—a way to the subjugation
of reason to those foreign grounds of determination on which the fulfillment of our needs and inclinations is dependent. Instead, we have found,
as the sole means for a solution of the contradictions, the right to "postulates," that is, to theoretical suppositions that are necessary if the practically
obligatory is not to be logically impossible (see KpV, A, 219–20, 238).

The *Critique of Practical Reason* contains the postulates of the existence
of God, who, as common author of the law of nature and of the moral law,
is supposed to guarantee the physical effectiveness of moral dealings and of
the eternal continuation of the soul, which grants us an endless progress of
amelioration. Kant's *Religion within the Limits of Reason Alone* presents the

postulate of the "gracious verdict"—Kant's unorthodox appropriation of the Christian doctrine of the justification of the sinner (*Religion*, 95). It must not be forgotten, however, that all of these postulates are seen as establishing the practical possibility of a service to a coming "moral world order"—a goal, then, that, owing to the divergence between natural causality and "causality through freedom" (between the condition in which human beings find themselves and the condition to which they are to pass) cannot be effected by the human being alone, but must be hoped for, if moral praxis is not to remain "oriented to empty goals."

Thus, the postulates indicate the content of a hope that reconciles the theoretical use of reason with the practical. "All of the interest of my reason (the speculative as well as the practical) is joined in the following three questions: What can I know? What am I to do? What may I hope? The first question is purely speculative. . . . The second question is purely practical. . . . The third question is practical and theoretical at once" (Kant, *KrV,* A, 804–5). "The first question corresponds to metaphysics, the second to ethics, the third to religion" (Kant, *Logik*, A, 25). Now the postulates of hope, through which the dialectic of the practical use of reason is solved, at the same time designate the content of religion as Kant understands it.

A New Understanding of Religion

In the way that we have just described, Kant creates a new manner of philosophical discourse upon God. Granted, the word "God" no longer designates, in its first and immediate application, as it does in onto-theology, the ultimate ground of the world of being beheld by human persons, of which these latter are a part. God is now that reality to which human beings must address themselves in hope if the autonomy of their reason, which seemed to be dissolved in dialectic, is to be restored. The dialectic of the theoretical use of reason prevents human beings from forgetting the self-legislative character of their reason, prevents them from holding the world of objects as "given" instead of "assigned." The dialectic of the practical use of reason reminds them that the duties reason must set itself become internally contradictory unless human beings relate, in hope, to a ground of their autonomy that is distinct from themselves, and not at their disposition.

Hence, however, the basic question of the philosophy of religion—what religion essentially is—is answered in a new way. *Religion is that basic relationship of human beings to an object of their hope that frees reason from its internal contradiction, preserving it from self-destruction and rendering it capable of legislation over the world of phenomena and goals.* This understanding of religion performs, now in an altered way, the same tasks as had been perceived by onto-theology as well. Such discourse upon God justifies, as against the arguments of atheism, the decision in favor of religion generally. After all, a reason that would make its decision against the postulates, and thereby against faith, would abide in its self-contradiction, and thereby would ultimately destroy itself. The same philosophical discourse upon God justifies, in the competition of the religions with one another, a decision for the Christian faith. After all, only this faith contains an acceptance of the justification of the sinner by God's grace, through which the dialectic of the practical use of reason is defeated at its sharpest point.

But the certitude with which human beings know that they stand on this ground of the possibility of the autonomy of their reason has the character of hope.

DISCOURSE UPON GOD IN TRANSCENDENTAL PHILOSOPHY, AND THEOLOGY OF HOPE

Kant's Critique and the "Secularization of Philosophy"

In the post-Kantian age of the history of philosophy, philosophical theology could not regain that rank of a philosophical basic discipline that it had enjoyed in the age of religious rationalism. Reason's self-assurance, it now appeared, no longer needed a founding through evidence that the truth of rational cognition was guaranteed by the truth of a God.

But neither did the attempt of the Idealists, portrayed above, to understand philosophy as the path by which religion attains to a consciousness of itself, find any appreciable discipleship in the further course of the history of philosophy. Now it was thought appropriate not only to convert religion into philosophy but to remove the "religious remnants" that continued to work within philosophical thought. Otherwise, so the thinking went, philosophy, despite emphatic criticism of religious consciousness, remained a simple attempt to disguise the continuing theological character of its own thought. It became, as Nietzsche put it, "insidious theology" (*Antichrist*, 174).

Attempts to preserve religion by way of a "transformation into philosophy" now were regarded as indications that the devotees of such religious thinking, without admitting it, were convinced that religion's time is over. Thus, not even they themselves believe, basically, what they so assiduously defend with seemingly rational arguments. They no longer speak *bona fide*, in good faith. Their religious understanding of philosophy is an expression of "bad faith." This charge has been made especially by Sartre (Sartre

1946, 56–57). The unmasking of the interests that lurk in this "bad faith" therefore becomes the central task of the philosophy of religion. The latter now takes the form of a criticism of ideology.

Under the influence of this development in the history of philosophy in the nineteenth century, many theologians of the twentieth century as well came to the conviction that the secularization of thought was not only irreversible but also normative. According to this conceptualization, the task of theology consists, first, in the acknowledgment of contemporary thought as the legitimate heir of the Christian faith proclamation, and, second, in its application as a key to the presentation of the Christian proclamation. Thus, Friedrich Gogarten calls secularization "a legitimate and necessary consequence of the Christian faith" (Gogarten 1953, 214), and indeed for this reason: that the Christian faith leaves human beings' justification and salvation to the exclusive activity of grace, thereby delivering human activity from the burden of being salvific. The renunciation of human merit leaves "all activity, including the aspect of moral quality, a purely worldly affair" (Gogarten 1926, 141). The Christian faith proclamation has the task of effecting a "secularization," as opposed to an un-Christian "secularism," since the latter insidiously leads to an ever new sacralization and deification of the realm of human life (Gogarten 1926, 127; 1953, 224).

In this conception, Christianity not only stands factually at the end of the history of religion, as Feuerbach and Bloch had taught; but the announcement of the event in which religion comes to its end becomes the central content of the proclamation of the Christian faith. "Religion is unbelief; religion is an affair, we must come right out and say it, of the godless person" (Barth, *KD* I/2, 327). The task of the Christian is "to break free of his religious needs, . . . to surrender his heretofore, known to others, identity, and to win in faith the identity of Christ" (Moltmann 1972, 43).

Hegel teaches that, with Jesus' death on the cross, God has ceased to be experienced as the human being's "opposite number" anywhere, and now becomes active only as the Spirit of a community. This doctrine now finds its expression in a theology that interprets the cross as the "death of God," proclaiming the community led by the Spirit to be the only locus of the divine presence (Hegel, *Phil. Rel.* II, 301–16; cf. Vahanian 1961).

A glance at this position in the history of philosophy and theology reveals the courage it took in the twentieth century to swim against the tide of a solid contemporary consensus and to undertake once more an attempt at a philosophical theology, as well as a philosophy of religion based thereon. Apart from returns to pre-Kantian metaphysics, this attempt was undertaken in two ways: in the form of a doctrine of God in terms of a transcen-

dental philosophy, and in that of a theology of hope. Each of these paths —
consciously, in part, and in part without express consciousness of the history of philosophy—continues along the lines of Kantian argumentations.

Philosophy of Religion on the Basis
of Transcendental Theology

Joseph Maréchal has undertaken the attempt so to develop transcendental
reflection that it not replace the earlier ontology with an analytics of the
understanding, as it does with Kant, but can become the "point of departure" of an ontology and metaphysics understood in a new way. The title of
his *chef d'oeuvre*, then, is *The Point of Departure of Metaphysics* (Maréchal,
AdM).

The attempt at such a reconciliation between ontology and transcendental philosophy seemed promising, in view of the observation in the history of philosophy that Kant's central thought of a constitution of the object
through the acts of reason and the understanding was by no means foreign
to such determinedly ontologically oriented thinkers as Aristotle and
Thomas Aquinas. The immediate object of cognition, as these two writers
understand it, is neither the ideal and general as such (as in Platonism) nor
the sensory and individual as such (as in empiricism), but the individual as
exemplar of the general, and the general as the essential form of the individual, as the *quidditas rei sensibilis*. This object is given in immediate observation neither to the senses nor to the understanding. It is not given as such,
apart from the activity of our understanding (*"non existit in rerum natura"*),
but only emerges from the processing of residues of the memory of sensory
observations (*phantasmata*) through the active understanding or agent
intellect (*intellectus agens*) (Thomas Aquinas, *De an.* a 4, c; *Comm. de an.* III,
10. Vorl. no. 730).

Not only Kant, but Aristotle and Thomas Aquinas as well, have therefore
spoken of a function of the intellect consisting in the constitution of objects.
They have, however, linked this transcendental reflection with ontological
thinking. Thomas managed this especially by attending to where and how
the individual, as exemplar of the general, encounters the general as an
essential form of the individual. The answer: In the judgment ("This is a
rose"; "this rose is red."). But such judgments arise from an activity of the
understanding, which links the individual ("This . . .") with the general (". . .
rose," or ". . . red") and at the same time vouches for the validity of the "linkage" ("So it is"). Both functions of the judgment, however—Maréchal calls
them predication and affirmation—find their expression in the copula "is."
And so it is the concept of being of which we make use in every judgment;

and only the judgment produces the object of cognition, the "general in the individual" as such. Thus understood, the concept of being has transcendental meaning: it alone renders the encounter with the objects of cognition possible. Consequently, ontology alone shows us the doctrine of being— how those acts of the understanding are structured that render us capable of the encounter with objects. Transcendental philosophy does not replace ontology, as it does with Kant, but forms its "point of departure."

From this starting point, in terms of a transcendental transformation, Maréchal also manages an onto-theology and the philosophy of religion based on it. Every determinate judgment upon any determinate object ascribes to the latter "being," as indicated by the copula "is," in a determinate and therefore limited way. ("This is, in a determinate and limited way, to be a rose." "This rose is, in a determinate and limited way, to be red.") We can bring such a specification and circumscription to expression in the judgment only if we have at our disposition a concept that, for its part, is by no means indeterminate and yet is uncircumscribed: the concept of being in the unrestricted sense, measured by which every finite specification can at last be thematized as finite. In every predication and affirmation, therefore, this infinite being is copredicated and coaffirmed. In all knowledge that we gain through a judgment thus structured, the infinite being is co-known. Thus the transcendental analysis of the judgment leads back to Thomas Aquinas's thesis: "All cognizing beings implicitly cognize God in every judgment that they know" (*De verit.* 22 a 2, ad 1).

Granted, we do not know of God as we know of other objects, which stand before our eyes. We know God only in the infinite perspective of an approach" (Maréchal, *AdM*, 5:542). We "know" God as one "knows" the point of arrival that gives to all of the steps of the movement of cognition their direction in advance—or, with Karl Rahner, "without thematization, in the infinity of our transcendency" (Rahner, An. Chr, 549), that is, in a movement of cognition through which we have already overreached every individual and finite being and left it behind us.

From this point of departure it is clear in what way religion must be understood. Religion renders that act of going-beyond that we implicitly execute in every act of cognition expressly a theme of its proclamation. This is the common mark of all religions. The latter distinguish themselves from one another, however, in respect of the degree to which they bring thematically to our consciousness what heretofore we have only coknown. For this reason, indeed, Christian missionary preaching is "not the proclamation of the hitherto absolutely unknown, . . . but is the expression in concept and objectivity of what [non-Christian hearers] have already accomplished, or could have accomplished, in the depths of their mental being (Rahner, N.

Rel., 155)—not precisely an escorting to faith but an "introduction to its further reflex stages" (Rahner, *Glaubenszugang*, 415; for the interpretation of a point of departure in transcendental philosophy for the grounding of a Christian theology, see Rahner 1976).

Basing and Comparison of Religions

Like the pretranscendental form of onto-theology, so also the transcendental variants of the latter can take on two classical burdens of the philosophy of religion: the task of a justification of religion vis-à-vis atheism, and the task of a critical comparison among religions. This does not mean that atheism is refuted in what it says; rather atheism is reminded that it speaks. And when it says, "There is no God," the transcendental theologian certifies to it that God has no place among the objects that we recognize; but that inasmuch as atheists speak—therefore say "is"—they have already, unknowingly, codesignated the absolute being.

Nor are the various religions criticized in the content of their proclamation. Christianity's preeminence as the "true" religion consists rather in this, that precisely what all religions speak of, Christianity expresses in incomparable explicitness. The non-Christian religions express the human being's openness to God as the absolute being and the self-communication of the divine being to the human spirit implicitly; only the Christian message takes up this relationship expressly as a theme and tells the human being that the divine has "hypostatically united" itself with the being of the human—that is, that in Christ the divine word and human nature have become one, in the unity of a person. But this is the unrepeatable, unique transcendence, and at the same time the express announcement, of what "is given to all [!] in the self-communication of God's Spirit" (Rahner, Transz., 991). As the atheist has unwittingly coaffirmed God, so have the members of the non-Christian religions already spoken of the unification between the divine Word and the human spirit, and thus have been "Christians" without calling themselves such. Thus, they can be called "anonymous Christians" (Rahner, An. Chr.).

A like philosophy of religion justifies Christian believers' commerce with atheists and members of other religions in a peaceable intercourse, which was all but unknown before, without in the least compromising their own convictions. Christians even know themselves to be the siblings of those who, for their part, are unwilling to be the siblings of Christians. Thus, the latter answer enmity with amity, belligerence with solidarity. At the same time, it is true, this focus on the part of the philosophy of religion is reminiscent of the condescending manner of guardians who understand minor children better than the latter understand themselves, and therefore can take charge of their "best interests" over the protests of the wards. But the biblical demand that the people choose between God and idols becomes, especially, the demand to adopt a higher level of reflection. Joshua cried out to the elders of his people: "Now if you are unwilling to serve the Lord, choose this day whom you will serve, whether the gods your ancestors served in the region beyond the River or the gods of the Amorites in whose land you are living; but as for me and my household, we will serve the Lord" (Joshua 24:14).

According to the conceptualization here set forth, however, the Christian is distinguished from the non-Christian in principle, not otherwise than the transcendental philosopher from the naïve believer. After all, philosophers, by comparison with simple members of the religious community, have reached a "further reflex stage" in their understanding of the faith.

Hope as Center and Norm of Religion

Interest in the restoration of clearer alternatives of choice is an important moment in all of the more recent forms of a philosophy and theology of hope. And the criticism leveled against transcendental theology in these terms is directed by and large against the tendency, recognized in our pages, to reinterpret incompatibilities of goal alternatives calling for a choice as degrees of reflection open to a peaceful coexistence.

The classic exponent of this type of philosophy of religion is Ernst Bloch. He claims to find, as the common denominator of all religious tradition, that such tradition keeps troth with hope—a hope that stands over against the given world, seemingly so closed and unchangeable, and therefore hopeless. In the absolute nature of this hope, which knows its superiority to all so-called realities, Bloch sees the foundation of religion's right against irreligion. But the radicality of this hope at the same time counts as the norm of religion. And measured by this norm, Bloch holds, atheism, inasmuch as it holds to the absolute quality of religious hope, is superior to any faith in a God. The no to the world we have must be raised to a radical no to its divine origin—to a protest "against the genesis-pathos of the beginning of such an unsatisfactory world, and against the God who still finds his work 'very good'" (Bloch, *AiChr*, 144).

In antithetic parallel to Karl Rahner's doctrine of the "anonymous Christian," one can grasp Bloch's philosophy of religion as a doctrine of the "pseudonymous atheist." Just as atheists, in Rahner's view, implicitly co-maintain, "in truth," what they explicitly attack, just so, correspondingly, according to Bloch's conviction, believers co-hope, "in truth," what they reject in the literal formulation of their profession: their hope has been directed, without their knowing it, to the defeat of that world that hallows its being and existence through a return to a divine origin. "A withdrawal from God has been the hidden hope of every religion."

This is the standpoint from which Bloch attempts to solve both classic tasks of the philosophy of religion: the justification of religion vis-à-vis irreligion, and the identification of the true religion among all religions. For Bloch, religion's justification consists in this, that it keep faith with trust in the power of hope, under the pseudonym "God." Now the preeminence of Chistianity among all religions consists in this, that, under the pseudonym "kingdom of God," it conceives hope in a "kingdom without God" as the impelling power of history. "The only faith is faith in a messianic reign of God—without God" (Bloch, *PH*, 1413).

In this wise, a "philosophical theology" arises of a new and most paradoxical kind—a hermeneutics of the pseudonym "God," whose true meaning content consists in being the expression of a profession of what is not but will be. The motto of this philosophical theology remains, as earlier with onto-theology, God's self-denomination in the burning bush—no longer, granted, in the "Hellenistic present" tense, but in the future: "I shall be who I shall be."

Evangelical as well as Catholic theologians now mounted an attempt to employ Bloch's understanding of religion as the hermeneutic key for a presentation of the Christian message (see Schaeffler 1979, esp. 118–74). Thus, Jürgen Moltmann interprets Bloch's atheism as an atheism "for God's sake," as if Bloch were only concerned, "for the sake of the inexpressible vitality of the utterly other God," altogether to crush, and shed, "all of those images, traditions, and religious feelings" that would move God into an "illusionary" nearness to the human being (Moltmann 1967, 17). For Moltmann, the criterion for the distinction among religions is the radical character of a promised future, and "the contrary nature of [this future] with respect to what is and what was" (Moltmann, Bze, 251). "Religions of epiphany," in which the God who has always been comes to be revealed, over and again (especially in worship), are to be condemned. Justified, by contrast, is the "religion of promise," for which God is the radically future one. A philosophical theology is such a religion, as well, if contrarily to Moltmann's intention. After all, the thesis that, between the eternity of being and the future of the promise stands a diametrical opposition is not the conclusion but the presupposition of Moltmann's presentation of biblical writings. From the concepts of eternity and future, and thus on a philosophical basis, an opposition is deduced that not only decides which religion is the true one, but also how Christian tradition must be presented—not in the sense of an understanding of Christ in "early Catholic worship," which seeks to bring to revelation, in ever new moments of sacramental presence, the Lord who has been taken up into eternity, but in the sense of a radical trust in the "future of Christ."

Against Bloch, Johannes Baptist Metz has held to the legitimacy of the concept of a redemption, since without the sinner's hope in a redemption all expectation of a future would be shifted to "delusions of innocence," so that those who hope would now understand themselves as executors of a heavenly judgment rightly pronounced upon this "evil world." Delusions of innocence, and the accompanying demonization of any particular adversary, are overcome not through atheistic hope but only through the hope of faith and belief. "The 'God of our hope' is near to us over the abyss of our recognized and acknowledged guilt, as the one judging our decisions and at the same time the one forgiving our guilt" (Metz in UH, Abs, I, 5). Religious hope, and thereby religion altogether, protects itself from atheism in that it renders delusions of innocence, demonization of the adversary, and thereby, last, an ideology of triumphalism, defeatable (see Metz 1973, 127–34). The standard for a comparison of religions, however, is their "critical potency . . . for the societal process" inherent in a religion (Metz, *Apol.*, 275).

A basic category for the understanding of history and society in terms of religious hope is called "conversion." Ferdinand Kerstiens has clarified the meaning of this category for the philosophy of history. He understands "providence" as a "capacity for invention" on the part of a divine love that "provides" ever new opportunities for conversion and responsive love" (Kerstiens 1968, 192). Only trust in a providence thus understood makes possible a responsibility for political morality on a world scale—a trust that eschews all "gilding" of the status quo, but that likewise disdains a destructive demonization of the "evil world," one slated only for decline and demise. No less than with Kant, here too faith in God, in its form, is a postulate posited with a practical interest (for the possibility of political morality), in its content, a trust in the promise of the sinner's justification, and in its function, a resolution of the dialectic of the use of the practical reason vis-à-vis the experience of guilt.

PHILOSOPHY OF RELIGION ON THE BASIS OF PHILOSOPHICAL THEOLOGY: REVIEW OF A JOURNEY AND CRITICAL EVALUATION

The extraordinary variety of the forms of philosophical theologies, and of the philosophies of religion based thereon, could obscure the fact that, with

all of these attempts at variation, a unitary type is at issue. A review of the
path that philosophical theology has traced in its history will make the common elements more clearly recognizable.

Common to the forms of the philosophy of religion set forth here in sum-
mary fashion is the conviction that there are philosophical arguments that
make a special philosophical discourse upon God possible—for example, in
the context of an ontology, a transcendental philosophy, or a theory of
hope. Common, furthermore, to these forms is the conviction that that
reality of which philosophical theology speaks—for example, "the one who
is in an unqualified sense," or "the ground of the possibility of the unfolding of the horizon against which we can encounter objects," or, finally, "the
absolute future, to which we commit ourselves in hope"—is materially
identical with what religious discourse calls "God." Thus, Thomas Aquinas
concludes each of his "five ways" with the observation: ". . . *Et hoc omnes
dicunt Deum*": ". . . And this is called 'God' by all" (Thomas Aquinas,
S. Th. I, q. 2, a.3, c). This material identity gives the philosopher to know
what is being spoken of when religions speak of God. In this manner, philosophical theology both guarantees religious discourse upon God its reference and protects it against the imputation of being deprived of an object.
At the same time, this philosophical knowledge of the reference of all religious discourse upon God contains a norm by which the meaning of this
religious discourse can be measured. Where religions speak of God in such
a way that it is either in dispute or fails to come to clear expression, that
God is "the absolute being," "the possibilitating ground of transcendental
subjectivity," or "the absolute future," there religions are vulnerable to
philosophical criticism.

It cannot be concluded from all of this, however, that only such meaning content must occur that can be concluded analytically from the philosophical concept of God that happens to be in question. Precisely because
philosophers know what they speak of when they speak of God, they also
know that they cannot say everything that can be said of God. Accordingly,
it is not the concern of the philosophers of religion mentioned in this chapter (with the exception of Bloch) to seek to convert religion into philosophy.

Those who understand God as the "one who is in the unrestricted
sense"—those, therefore, who practice philosophical theology as onto-
theology—will conclude that it must be said of this God that God is sole,
eternal, all-knowing, almighty, and so on. They will conclude from God's
eternity that the divine acts, to the extent that they are not observed in
terms of their effects in the world, but "in themselves," as the activity of
an eternal subject, cannot occupy particular positions in time, but take

place in a "perduring now," contemporaneously with all of the points in time of the course of the world. The philosopher will be able to understand that this simultaneity of the temporal human being with the eternal God and the divine activity should be celebrated in particular actions of worship. But nothing can be concluded from this as to what sorts of divine actions belong to the content of worship, or in what form the worship is to be performed. This, and a great deal besides, is unavailable to onto-theological deduction and pertains to the specific content of the religious narrative of the "divine deeds of might," and to the instructions for the actions to be performed in the divine service.

Those who understand God as "the condition for the unfolding of the transcendental horizon"—who, therefore, practice philosophical theology as transcendental philosophy—will conclude that it must be said of this God that God is the nonobjective ground of all objects, the nameless condition of all naming and all that is named, the light that renders all objects visible and yet itself remains invisible (as the optical ray of light for the eye). The transcendental philosopher will further conclude that all speech concerning God is always a discourse at the limits of speech, and that there belongs to religion an ever unstable, but by no means arbitrary, correlation between the command of invocation ("Admonished by saving precepts, and encouraged by divine instruction," is the introductory formula to the Our Father in the Roman Missal) and the taboo of the name ("Thou shalt not take my name in vain"). But nothing can be concluded from any of this regarding in what concrete locus, in a context of individual and societal experience, as related to nature and history for the members of a religious community, a "dawning of the divine name" may have occurred and become the origin of a tradition of religious speech upon God, or how the obligation to transmit the divine name may have been guaranteed in the face of the danger of a magic of the Name, and brought into equilibrium with "falling silent before the nameless one."

Those who understand God as "absolute future," to which we entrust ourselves in hope, will conclude: The self-revelation of this God for the human being—therefore the "truth" of this God—is always primarily the opening of a "way," that is, the enablement of a new manner of praxis, which in turn leads to a new "life." From this unity of "way, truth, and life," the philosopher can further conclude: All speech concerning God, if it is to be adequate to its theme, is far from being "mere theory." It is a speech concerning the one who enables persons to go new ways in the direction of a new life (". . . Who has so done that you could go out from Egypt, out of the house of slavery," Exodus 20:2). But none of this yields an answer to the questions: In which concrete situations and possibilities of action within a concrete religion does the absolute future win presence precisely today? And what concrete opportunities for action does the presence of this absolute future open up to the members of this religion?

The common characteristics of all of the variants of philosophical theology, and the philosophy of religion erected upon them, that we have here sketched, with the exception of Bloch's philosophy of religion, include the following. *Those who know whereof they speak when they discourse philosophically upon God know as well that not everything can be said philosophically that is to be said of God in specifically religious fashion.* Precisely on the basis of a philosophically achieved concept of God, it can be deduced a priori that not all discourse upon God can be deduced a priori. Accordingly, religion, which must also say what cannot be said philosophically, remains the "other," which retains its specificity with respect to philosophy. And this insight grounds the fact that the philosophies of religion of the type here described do not subsume religion into philosophy.

Granted, the philosophies of religion that base themselves on a philosophically achieved concept of God also agree in another respect: while they each have their respective criteria for a critical comparison of religions, the application of these criteria to empirically given religions has led without exception to the finding that only one among them, the biblical, is to be distinguished as the true religion. Onto-theology grounds this view in the fact that only the God of the Bible so arranges a self-manifestation to worshipers that a translation of the divine self-naming at the burning bush as "I am the one who is" was at least possible (in an earlier view, actually necessary). Transcendental theology arrives at the same result through the indication that the relation of being between the divine Word and the human spirit, which bases the possibility of all cognition whatsoever, becomes a theme only in the Christian proclamation, where that proclamation speaks of a unification between divine Word and human spiritual nature in the person of Jesus. Finally, the theology of the future can also grasp God's self-denomination at the burning bush in its meaning, translate God's name in the future ("I shall be who I shall be"), and consequently understand the biblical message as an express profession bearing on an absolute future.

In all three views, the extrabiblical religions are described either as undeveloped antecedent forms of the biblical, so that the unconscious intent of all religions has been oriented to what comes expressly to expression in the biblical proclamation (cf. the doctrine of the "anonymous Christians"); or the extrabiblical religions are described as degenerate or contrasting forms of the biblical faith in the promise. (This is the case with Moltmann's antithesis between religions of epiphany and the religion of the promise, but also with Bloch's confrontation between pagan astrological "lord gods" and the biblical God of the poor, the widows, and orphans, and the promise addressed to them that they will "possess the land.") Finally, pretranscendental onto-theology judges the polytheism of the pagans as religious aberration and emphasizes the formula from the Gospel of John, "God is spirit," in such a way that all extrabiblical religions appear at best as preliminary stages.

In agreement with these data, the representatives of the philosophies of religion here depicted apply strikingly little concern to analyze and to interpret the testimonials of other religions. (In this respect, too, Ernst Bloch is an exception, as he finds the testimonials of utopian hope everywhere in the history of humankind, if nowhere as clearly as in the religion of the biblical prophets and in Jesus' proclamation.) Even where the judgment of the philosophers of religion regarding the other religions is very understanding and pacific, as with the transcendental theologians, this judgment is remarkably sweeping, and without reference to the texts of these religions. Thus, in his articles "Das Christentum und die nichtchristlichen Religionen" ("Christianity and the non-Christian religions") and "Die anonymen Christen" ("The Anonymous Christians"), Rahner can speak purely a priori of the meaning content of the non-Christian religions, without the necessity of an analysis of any historically available self-testimonials on the part of these religions (see Rahner, An. Chr.; N. Rel.; for a criticism of this manner of addressing other religions, see Schaeffler 1982, esp. 80–88). This will become even clearer in contrast with that type of philosophy of religion that we shall now present: the phenomenology of religion and its essential reference to the comparison of religions.

CHAPTER 4

A More Recent Type of Philosophy of Religion

The Phenomenology of Religion

───··◦·◦ꞏ──

THE PHENOMENOLOGY OF RELIGION differs from the philosophy of religion developed on the basis of a philosophical theology not only in individual propositions but mainly in the "consequence" of the steps in its argumentation. With phenomenologists of religion, the concept of God falls not at the beginning but, if indeed it plays any role at all, only at the end of the course of the argumentation.

Philosophy of religion on the basis of a philosophical theology, of which we spoke in the preceding chapter, began with the formation of a leading concept obtained either in ontology or in the theory of subjectivity (transcendental philosophy), or, finally, in philosophical reflection on the future of our hope. In second place, the concept so obtained was identified with that reality that in the discourse of the religions is called "God." In the third place, from the philosophical concept now called a concept of God on grounds of this identification, criteria for an appropriate language about God were drawn up. And only in a final step in the argumentation were religion's statements about itself drawn into focus in order to measure them by this criterion.

The type of philosophy of religion to be presented in the following pages proceeds in the opposite direction. Here at the beginning the testimonials are heard in all of their multiplicity. Then, in second place, reflection follows on that which grounds the comparable character of religious phenomena: we hear of "basic phenomena," or even of "essential structural forms" (*Wesensgestalte*), whose "variations" are expected to render the manifold phenomena of empirically given religions comprehensible. Only last, if at all, is the question posed of the place occupied in the context of religious phenomena by language about God. And in conclusion it is sometimes asked how God is to be conceptualized in order to be able to speak of this reality in a way that this given context of religious phenomena requires.

PHENOMENOLOGY OF RELIGIONS: OUTCOME OF AN ENCOUNTER BETWEEN PHILOSOPHICAL PHENOMENOLOGY AND EMPIRICAL RELIGIOUS SCIENCE

An Observation and Four Questions

The term "phenomenology of religion" was applied by Pierre Daniel Chantépie de la Saussaye in the introduction to the first edition of his *Lehrbuch der Religionsgeschichte* (Textbook of the history of religion; Freiburg, 1887) but was dropped in subsequent editions. Rudolf Otto's *Das Heilige* (The Holy; Breslau, 1917; translated into English as *The Idea of the Holy*) contains only altogether sparse theoretical propositions on the concept of "phenomenology of religion," it is true; to this day, however, it continues to be regarded as the example par excellence of a phenomenological approach to religious consciousness and its objects. Max Scheler has sought to circumscribe the religious act and its object with a phenomenological method (Scheler, *EiM*; see below, pp. 61–71). Gerardus van der Leeuw, in his *Einführung in die Religionsphänomenologie* (Introduction to the phenomenology of religion; in Dutch, Groningen, 1925; in German, Gütersloh, 1925), has set forth the program of a new approach to and treatment of religious phenomena, and in his *Phänomenologie der Religion* (Phenomenology of religion; Tübingen, 1933) has maintained this program in such wise that it is from here on, at the latest, that the expression in his title has become a generally received technical term. Among currently living researchers of religion, Mircea Eliade and Günter Lanczkowski rank as preeminent representatives of the phenomenological school of religions. With the exception of Chantépie de la Saussaye, all of these authors, and many others who call themselves phenomenologists of religion, confess, through quotations, mentions, or mere references, that their orientation is that of Edmund Husserl and his *Ideen zu einer reinen Phänomenologie* (Ideas for a pure phenomenology; vol. 1; Halle, 1913).

From this observation four questions emerge. First, what do the researchers of religion expect from the encounter with philosophical phenomenology? Second, how do they incorporate its methods and arguments into their own thought? Third, by way of what presupposition was this manner of reception conditioned? And finally, what have they gained for their own concern from the encounter with philosophical phenomenology?

Expectations on the Part of Researchers of Religion
from Phenomenology and from the Phenomenological
"Essential Concept" as a Methodological Contribution

In the course of the nineteenth century, advances in philology and archae-
ology, history as a science, and field research had so extensively broadened
the knowledge of religious phenomena and their multiplicity that it seemed
increasingly difficult to gain an abstractive concept of "religion" that would
contain all of those characteristics but only those characteristics that were
observable in each appearance and open to designation as "religious." A
concept gained in this fashion always appeared either too narrow, so that it
failed to embrace all "religious phenomena," or else too poor in content to
contribute anything to the order, let alone the interpretation, of these phenomena. Attempts at a definition of the concept "religion" seemed arbitrary; a nonconceptual collection of material, on the other hand, was
scarcely satisfactory.

Against this background, it becomes comprehensible that scholars of
religion should have turned with such high expectations to a philosophic
method that promised to solve the problem of how it would be possible to
form concepts that would be more than arbitrarily laid-out schemata of
arrangements, but also more than mere sum-totals of impressions occasioned by the examination of a group of manifestations. Philosophical phenomenology had set itself the task of revealing, in the concrete, always
individual manifestations, a form and structure that would permit making
the submitted case experienceable as a case of its own kind, as an example
of a general case—and this in the sense that the given has its essence in the
general, whose example and case it is—and thereby winning its purchase
and stability. It is as this stabilizing structure—and not, for example, as an
artificially isolated complex of individual characteristics described in the
abstract (that is, detached)—that the "essential concept" is to be grasped
that phenomenology sought to expose in the manifestations encountered in
the concrete regard.

Phenomenology had set itself a task reminiscent of Plato's attempt to
seek the essence of a manifestation (the *ousia*) not in a bundle of characteristics but in that primordial form (*paradeigma*) that endows a manifestation
with its foothold in this world (this "participation" being the original meaning of the word *methexis*). However, philosophical phenomenology held
aloof from what seemed to its practitioners would be a hazardous appeal to
the metaphysical hypotheses of a Platonic doctrine of ideas, and so used the
word *eidos* without any connotation of existence, endowing it with the
meaning only of "basic structure," or "essential form" (*Wesensgestalt*).

In this approach to their questions, philosophical phenomenologists encountered the same problem of method as had the empirical scholars of religion. What could not be done by the process of abstraction, that is, the extraction of individual characteristics from a complex, was supposed to be possible to the trained phenomenological eye: a grasp of the "structural law" of each respective religious phenomenon—as prayers, sacrificial procedures, forms of religious community organization, and so on—a law that would make it possible to recognize similar verbal utterances, similar ritual acts, and similar organizational forms, like community structures, in other religions as well. How such a procedure can be managed in the praxis of investigation has its preeminent example in Gerardus van der Leeuw and his *Phänomenologie der Religion* (Phenomenology of religion).

However, the phenomenological concept of essence is to serve as a basis not only for a comparison of phenomena from different religions and cultures but also for a diagnosis of actual defects of structure—a recognition of actually decadent forms and pseudomorphoses of the religions. The goal of these concerns was not to measure such phenomena against arbitrarily adduced criteria, nor indeed arbitrarily to erect one variant of the religious into the standard for all others (for example, Christianity as the standard of all religions), but to read in the phenomenon itself those structural laws that are then recognized in the same phenomenon as decadent.

Concepts of essence as are won by way of the phenomenological method ought therefore to enable the researcher to make a responsible selection of examples and a comparison among them, and the philosopher of religion to create a critical evaluation of the material under consideration.

Reception of Phenomenological Concepts and Suspicion of Their Abusive Application

The authors mentioned at the beginning of this chapter, along with many others, refer to their manner of describing, comparing, and interpreting religious manifestations as "phenomenology of religion." Thereby they use concepts that are known partly from Hegel's *Phänomenologie des Geistes* (Phenomenology of spirit), and partly from Husserl's *Ideen zu einer reinen Phänomenologie und phänomenologischen Philosophie* (Ideas for a pure phenomenology and phenomenological philosophy). However, if we compare the way in which Rudolf Otto, Gerardus van der Leeuw, or other phenomenologists of religion use the term "phenomenology," or concepts like "subject–object dialectic," "epoche," and so on, with the meaning Hegel and Husserl have given the same concepts, we readily gather the impression that concepts whose meaning is clearly marked out in philosophical phenomenology are being used in a very vague sense and therefore robbed of the function that they perform in a framework of the phenomenological method. The phenomenology of religion as actually practiced seems, thus considered, an exemplary case for the application of Husserl's warning: "Unless one has grasped the peculiarity of transcendental focus, and really assimilated the pure phenomenological ground, one may well use the word 'phenomenology,' but not have the thing for which the word stands" (Husserl, *Ideen I*, 216).

Methodological Presupposition: Not Academic Adoption, but Test and Selection

The appearance arises, however, that those researchers of religion who call themselves "phenomenologists of religion" have evacuated of their content this name and other concepts they have found with representatives of philosophical phenomenology, and applied them abusively, only if Hegel's or Husserl's understanding of phenomenology is presupposed as normative. But this presupposition is questionable. Scholars of religion became interested in Husserl (and later in Hegel) not because they wished to orient themselves, in academic fashion, to philosophical authorities, but because their own object of investigation, religion, convinced them that the process of the manifesting (*phainesthai*), and the form and shape of the appearance in which the real manifests itself (*phainomenon*) are in no wise exterior to the thing, but belong to the thing itself. The event of the appearing and the structural form of the appearance are essential for the Holy. As experts in the area of the description and interpretation of "hierophanies," researchers of religion could appeal to their own competence, if they now tested methods and arguments of philosophical phenomenology, case by case, through the application of these to their special area of investigation. Thereby they made their own, on the basis of their own approach to problems, many formulations of philosophical phenomenology.

Considered from the viewpoint of the investigation of religion, Hegel's dictum, for example, "The aspect itself is essential to the essence" (Hegel *Ästh.*, 28), reads as a secularized paraphrase of the religious conviction according to which the *doxa*, the mighty radiation of the divine "light," far from being a secondary "expression" of the divine reality, belongs to God's divinity itself. In Husserl's conviction, the "noemata" (pl. of "noema"— Greek *noēma*, any object "intended": in-tended, Latin, etymologically, "stretched-to"—by an act of knowing, or noesis) or "noematic contents," to which our acts of "noesis" (Greek, a "knowing"—the act by which any subject, or do-er, or know-er, knows or "intends" an object, a noema) are directed, stand athwart these acts, it is true; but this standing athwart, this facing, is nevertheless of such a kind that neither noesis nor noema can be described apart from the interrelation in which they stand to each other. Researchers of religion believe that they know the preeminent example of this correlation: it lies in the interrelatedness of divine epiphany and human eye, divine word and human ear. For it is the conviction of religious human beings that only an eye enlightened by God can grasp God's reality, only an ear opened by God can hear God's word. And thereby even Husserl's "Phenomenological Reduction," by virtue of which "every transcendent positing . . . must maintain its excluding bracket," reads like a later reflex so familiar to religious consciousness: the warning against wishing to search out the divine reality as a transcendent to-be-in-itself, apart from its "epiphany for us."

Thus, researchers of religion were able to certify the pronouncements of philosophical phenomenology on the basis of their own competence. In other, equally important respects for them, they for their own part found themselves endorsed by philosophical phenomenology. Husserl had reduced his "basic phenomenological law" to the formula, "No noeic moment without a noematic moment specifically appertaining to it" (Husserl, *Ideen I*, 232). Thereby he understood, by "noesis," an intentional act—that is, an act directed upon a content with which it stands in a facing relationship. (To cognize always means to cognize *something;* to will means to will *something;* to be deeply moved means to be deeply moved by *something;* to be sorrowful means to be sorrowful about *something.*) By noema, he understood precisely that content upon which a noesis directs itself. And when, in the locus just cited, he speaks of specific "appurtenance," specific belonging, of noemata to noeses, the word "specifically" is intended to indicate that there are noeses (that is, intentional acts) different in kind, and that to these acts correspond noematic contents (that is, intended objects and object references) different in kind. This relation of correspondence is reciprocal. "To each region and category of pretended objects corresponds, phenomenologically, . . . a basic kind of primordially given consciousness, . . . and, in appurtenance thereunto, a basic type of originary evidence" (Husserl, *Ideen I*, 340). The addition of "primordially" denotes here the specific interrelation of three pairs of correlates: that between a specific manner of intentional act and its object; that between specific evidence and the foregoing relation; and that between the object sphere that is "given" and the exclusive source, the noesis and noemata belonging to it. For the religious scientist this means: objects belonging, appertaining, to the particular region of the religious are not to be found apart from their correlation to the specifically religious "basic kind of primordially given consciousness." Or, more simply: The primordial givenness of religious objects is always their givenness for the religious act.

Accordingly, the "evidence with which these objects are given to the religious act is likewise "primordial"—not to be derived from other evidences. With Max Scheler, we have it as follows: "The first certain truth of all religious phenomenology . . . is the proposition of the primordial nature and underivability of the religious experience (Scheler, *EiM*, 170). To seek to ground religious "evidence" on other evidences—for example, on those of scientific or metaphysical cognition—would be as absurd as the attempt to assure oneself of the existence of tones first in a nonacoustical manner, before one is ready to hear them. The demand for proofs of God, or the claim to be able to disprove the existence of God, by way of science or metaphysics, is just as absurd, then, as the demand "that the existence of colors should first be demonstrated rationally, before one sees them, of tones, before one hears them" (*EiM*, 257). A generation later we have Eliade's formula: "to circumscribe a religious phenomenon . . . by means of physiology, psychology, sociology, economics, linguistics, art, and so forth, means to deny it—that is, to procure the escape of precisely what is unique and irreducible about it—let us call it the 'sacred character'" (Eliade, *RuH*, 11).

Regional Phenomenology of Religious Acts (Noeses) and Objects (Noemata)

Scholars of religion concerned with a methodological foundation for their own discipline, and philosophers of religion seeking to describe the structure of the religious act and the manner of being and being-given of the religious object, therefore recognize their tasks where Husserl lays out the program of developing regional phenomenologies from general phenomenologies. Through an elaboration of the specifically structured act-form, and of the "region" of object-contents that is essentially ordered to these acts, each such regional phenomenology constitutes a "science unique on very principle," and circumscribes "the last sense-determination of the 'being' of its objects and the . . . purification of its methodology" (Husserl, *Ideen I*, 148).

But, let us emphasize once more, no obligation whatever is laid on scientists and philosophers of religion to regard Husserl's execution of this program of "regional phenomenologies" as normative. They test this philosophical theory case by case, to see whether and to what extent it is suitable for sharpening the gaze for the peculiarity of hierophanies, for avoiding false sets of interpretative alternatives (for example, the alternatives, "objective," and "merely subjective"), or for facilitating a grasp of hierophanic peculiarities that otherwise appear difficult to understand.

PHENOMENOLOGY OF RELIGION AS DOCTRINE
OF THE APPARITION OF THE HOLY: POSITIONS,
PROGRAMS, AND DEVELOPMENTS

The "Holy" and the Sensus Numinis:
Rudolf Otto's Line of Questioning

When, following Husserl's program, one attempts to generate the "region and category of assumed objects" (Husserl, *Ideen I*, 340) ordered to religious noesis as noemata, one can designate this region, with Rudolf Otto, that of the "numinous," and conceptualize the primary category for the designation of numinous objects as the category of the "Holy" (cf. Otto's title, *Das Heilige*). If, once more in terms of Husserl's demand, one seeks for that "basic kind of primordially given consciousness" (Husserl, *Ideen I*, 340) that is ordered to this particular region of objects, one can, once more with Otto, use the concept of the *sensus numinis* (cf. Otto's title, *Das Gefühl des Überweltlichen [Sensus Numinis]*).

Now, religious noesis is structured by a triple interrelationship of opposites. The religious act always intends its object at once in the manner of naming and grasping, on the one hand, and, on the other, in the manner of feeling. The religious act, then, as the first pair of opposites, combines the moments of rationality and irrationality. Thus, Otto's *Das Heilige* is subtitled *Über das Irrationale in der Idee des Göttlichen und sein Verhältnis zum Rationalen* (The irrational in the idea of the divine and its relation to the rational). Within the acts of feeling are coupled fascination, or the irresistible attraction of the exalted and inspiring, and dread, or stark aversion to the tremendous and awful. This amalgamation of fascination and dread forms the second unity of opposites within the religious act. Third and last, within the acts of naming and grasping are combined two more opposed operations. One is directed toward a progressive clarification of concepts, for the purpose of "countering the 'irrationalism' of teeming, arbitrary discourse with solid, 'sound' doctrines" (Otto, *Hl.*, 72); but the other, equally "intentional" operation is performed in mute silence before the nameless and incomprehensible: "As the 'Utterly Other,' [the Holy] withdraws from all utterance" (ibid., 71).

But all three amalgamations follow a common structural law: they are performed in the consciousness of being under duress, and at the same time in the consciousness of a necessary failure. The fascination of feeling anticipates, sensibly and in sacred terror, the failure of its constrainment to join with the Holy. The consciousness that the Holy, through the fashion in which it shows itself, demands response by way of acclamation of its name, merges with the experience that the same Holy ever recedes into the

Unnameable. The attempts, as well, to convey feeling and naming, the irrational and rational, in the experience of the Holy, are freighted with the awareness of their equal necessity and impossibility.

To this basic trait of religious noesis corresponds a basic trait of religious noemata. The Holy appears as the imperious, as Numen, a word derived from *nutum,* "nod," peremptory sign. But at the same time, as it happens, every human attempt to accede to the demand of the Holy transmits to the human being the experience of already having failed before the Holy. The prophet—and the prophet can stand here for any religious person—answers the sovereign, commanding apparition of the Holy with the double outcry: "Here I am; send me" (Isaiah 6:8), and "Woe is me; . . . I am a man of unclean lips" (Isaiah 6:5).

We cannot here enter upon the circumstance that, in many respects, Rudolf Otto has left his program of religious phenomenology unfulfilled. He has devoted more attention to the noetic side of the religious correlation than to the noematic, and within the religious act has developed the irrational moment more clearly than the rational. It can also only be indicated, without going into detail, that the concept of the *sensus numinis,* as Otto uses it, oscillates between two meanings: the one, which Otto finds attested in Calvin, the other, for which Count Zinzendorf was his informant (Otto, *GdÜ,* 4–10). Rudolf Otto's detailed theories are not the theme of the investigation addressed here (nor is the question whether these theories were fully developed or remain incomplete), but exclusively his questioning, principles of solution, and methods.

Extending the Question: Dialectic of the Hierophany and Historicity of Religion

If we further develop Rudolf Otto's line of questioning, we can say that the phenomenology of religion, that is, the *logos* of the *phainomenon hieron,* the discourse upon the Holy in its apparition, describes noetically that opposition/unity of acts that makes it possible for the Holy, noematically, to be experienced as the Present in the mode of withdrawal, as the Invoked in the mode of namelessness, as the one adjuring human beings in the mode of impossibility of compliance. It pertains to the peculiarity of the "intention" directed upon the Holy that, in this case, noesis cointends its own disintegration. Characteristic expressions for this in religious testimonial are: The eye is "dazzled," "blinded," that is, it sees the failure of its vision; the human spirit comes "out of itself," that is, is itself in the mode of loss of all conscious self-awareness. To this peculiarity of religious noesis, the religious noema corresponds. It is "primordially given" in the manner of withdrawal, retirement. The most familiar example is offered by the Lukan report of Jesus' apparition to the disciples at Emmaus. The disciples "recognized him," but did so precisely at the moment at which he "withdrew from their gaze" (Luke 24:31).

The collapse of noesis and retreat of the noema are thereby experienced not as a kind of disruption of the religious relation but as its structural peculiarity. The Holy can express itself only as that which, as it is often expressed in religious discourse, is greater than can be grasped by us" (Anselm, *Prosl.* 5).

Not infrequently, in the self-expressions of religious consciousness, a meaning is bound up with the description of this "dazzling of the eye" and this "apparition in the manner of withdrawal": both together attest the provisional character of the relationship between the religious act and its object. This relationship is calculated to be surpassed. "Now we see through a reflection, mysteriously, but then [we shall see] face to face" (1 Corinthians 13:12). The awareness of such a provisional character anticipates a future in which the human acts will experience a "metamorphosis," so that the Holy can be manifest to them in new wise. This is the sense in which the apostle Paul admonishes the Romans to hold themselves open for a "metamorphosis" of their thinking, which will at last render them capable of rightly grasping that which is willed by God (cf. Romans 12:2).

To be sure, such interpretations of the dialectic of hierophany are not evidenced in all religions. But they emerge from a generally observable dialectic and tender the opportunity thus to interpret religious phenomena even where religions renounce a self-interpretation of collapsing noesis and the retreating noemata. The structural dialectic characteristic of the reciprocal relationship between the religious act and its object admits of a grasp of the religious relation as provisional, and demanding to be transcended. But therein lies an invitation to grasp the historicity of religion in religious fashion—that is, to derive it not from other historical factors and historicities, but from the peculiarity of the religious relation itself, that is, of the relation between the religious act and its object.

But when the historicity of religions materializes from the structural peculiarity of the relation of the religious act and religious object, then the doctrine of the hierophany, the phenomenology of religion, must stand the test precisely of managing to extract the ground for the fact that religions have a history at all—and the specific religious quality of this history—from the religious relation itself. In brief: A phenomenological interpretation of the history of religion becomes the qualifying test of the phenomenology of religion.

*From the Typology of the Hierophanies
to the History of Religions—Mircea Eliade's Development
as an Example of Altered Tasks Undertaken
by the Phenomenology of Religion*

Mircea Eliade began his scientific religious studies with a strongly typological lens, seeking to designate certain historically invariable hierophanic structures that recurred in the most varied religions. His early *Traité d'histoire des religions* (Treatise on the history of religions; Paris, 1949) may have the term "history" in its title, but he arranges the varied store of religious science not from historical viewpoints but in terms of their now functional, now structural, similarities. In its German translation, his work carries the altogether apposite title *Die Religionen und das Heilige* (The religions and the holy: Salzburg, 1954). The collaborative work *The History of Religions* (Chicago, 1959) is anything but concretely historical in its approach, but rather (in conformity with quite a current linguistic use of the word "history" in English) offers considerations on the methodology of the religious sciences, and is therefore called in German translation, appropriately, *Grundfragen der Religionswissenschaften* (Fundamental questions in the religious sciences; Salzburg, 1963). Only Eliade's late work, *Histoire des croyances et des idées religieuses* (History of beliefs and religious ideas; Paris, 1976– ; in German, *Geschichte der religiösen Ideen* [History of religious ideas; Freiburg i. Br., 1978–]) frankly adopts, with ongoing references to an earlier edition of religious source texts, a historical procedure of questioning. This development seems in no wise coincidental. Precisely the consistency with which Eliade has gone his intellectual route can serve as an example of the fact that the analysis of hierophanies in the identity of their appearance and withdrawal necessarily leads to a historical approach to religions.

In his early work, *Die Religionen und das Heilige* (The religions and the Holy), Eliade argues from the observation that everything that is—"object, action, physiological event, [anything] existing or thought of as existing" can be "transfigured into a hierophany" (Eliade, *RuH*, 33). It is not by way of its objective content, but by way of the manner in which it is given to the religious act, that the hierophany differs from profane reality. It is an essential law of the hierophany that it places this boundary between the sacred and the profane—but there is no essential law determining where this boundary runs: this is precisely a historical question. And it is a task of historical religious science "to seek after the grounds that have made this something, whatever it be, a hierophany, or have brought it about that it cease to be such" (ibid., 33). "For the history of religion is in large part the history of devaluation and revaluation in the course of the manifestation of the sacred" (ibid., 50), or the "revised evaluation of the conventional hierophanies" (ibid., 51).

Now, however it may be that grounds sought are laid hold of that are responsible for the hierophantic evaluation, revaluation (upward), or devaluation of elements of the world of our experience, Eliade is determined to retain the basic principle of the phenomenology of religion according to which the religious act and the religious object can be adequately described only in strict mutual correlation. It cannot, therefore, be a matter of inferring the variation of the religious act from extrareligious premises, the shift in the boundaries between the sacred and the profane from the activity of extrareligious causes. The foundation of the explanation is always "the dialectic of the sacred itself" (ibid., 51)—and therefore not a dialectic adduced on any extrareligious grounds, but the "dialectic of hierophanies," to which Eliade has devoted a separate section of his investigation (ibid., 34–37).

Tightly as the history of religion is interwoven with the general history of society, economics, science, and so on, it can nevertheless be seen and investigated only in its specific religious peculiarity if it is to be grasped from this dialectic of the hierophany. The phenomenology of religion, which must pass the test of producing an adequate interpretation of the history of religion, has therefore found its appropriate approach in the dialectic of the hierophany.

Again, it cannot be the object of the considerations presented here whether Eliade always succeeded, in his ever-renewed attempts, to implement this program. Here there are lines of questioning, bases for solutions, and methods in question. And in this respect, Eliade has beyond a doubt shown the phenomenology of religion the way.

THE QUESTION OF POSSIBILITIES AND BOUNDARIES
OF THE PHENOMENOLOGICAL METHOD IN RELIGIOUS SCIENCE

The Standard to Meet: The Task of an Interpretation of the History of Religions in Terms of the Phenomenology of Religion

It could seem astonishing that one here demands of a phenomenology of religion that it pass the test of an attempt to interpret the historicity of religion and the history of religions from the relation between religious noesis and religious noema. After all, normally one holds religious consciousness to be in large part blind to history. The religious act, it is rightly emphasized, is essentially an act of thought: the religious object appears as a "sacred source," so that religion appears dominated by the thought of a return of beginnings—and therefore contains a cyclical understanding of time, which does not admit of the experience of history. "The myth of the eternal return" seems to be a basic pattern for religious narratives (cf. Eliade, *MeR*).

However, a like judgment seems to fail to do justice to the peculiarity of religious consciousness, and therewith to the possibilities of an investigation in terms of the phenomenology of religion. The Holy, the Divine, is always that at whose appearance human hearing and seeing dwindle away, since the first thing it does is destroy all previous systems of orientation. This is why its apparition, measured against the structural legitimacy of previous experience, is "wonder." And all commemoration and repetition, far from being something that goes without saying, in the religious context is the expression of a struggle with the task of recognizing the "old" God, or "primordial" Sacred in the ever new, strange, and foreign—indeed, dismaying—fashion of the theophany or hierophany. Whether this struggle is to succeed or not is in no wise predictable/foreseeable: and when it succeeds, this in itself is a "wonder"—in the language of religion, it is the "effulgence of the Name." The possibility of recognizing in all manifestations of the Holy the identical God, and of calling this God by one name, therefore remains an eschatological hope. "Then"—namely, at the end of days—"will the Lord be one, and his name one" (Zechariah 14:9).

The tension between the dismaying novelty of every hierophany, and the task and promise of recognizing in the invocation of the Name the old God in a new apparition, produces a specific understanding of religion from its own history. For this recognition succeeds only when that eye and ear whose seeing and hearing have first crumbled, is opened anew in a changed way. And this qualitative change in seeing and hearing has the consequence, in its own respect, that all contents of religious thought and repetitive observances previously handed down are now grasped/seized in a changed way. This is why the history of myths is always at the same time the history of its constant "new redaction": and the history of worship is always at the same time the history of constant "reforms in worship."

If the historicity of religion thus emerges from the religious relation itself—from the way in which the hierophany first destroys the old seeing and hearing, thereupon to have it arise anew in altered form, then it pertains to the tasks of a phenomenology of religion to make the history of religions understandable on the basis of this relationship between religious noesis and religious noema. But if phenomenologists of religion reflect on philosophical theories that could serve them in this task as an aid to interpretation, then such an aid can be less expected from Husserl's theory of the "essential display" than from Hegel's concept of the "phenomenology" that called itself the "science of the experience of consciousness."

Return from Husserl to Hegel:
Dialectic of the "In Itself" and the "For Us"
as Ground of the Historicity of Religion

One of the contents of the store of the science of religion is the observation that, in the hierophany, the "coming to evidence of the Holy in character-istic wise—with its "reservedness"—two elements coincide: the withdrawal belongs to the becoming-present as an inner moment. This finding of reli-gious science is interpreted, with the help of Hegel's phenomenology, as a consequence of the "for us" and the "in itself." Both moments of the object—its being-for-us (apparition) and its being-in-itself (withdrawal)—fall in the event of the apparition itself. What shows itself to the awareness is "the being-for-us of this in-itself" (Hegel, *Phän.*, 78).

What Hegel deduces from the general concept of knowing—in the abstract, as it were—has excellent application to the knowledge of the Holy. One who does not know that the "Holy" is greater than our knowl-edge of it—who therefore fails to experience the difference between its being-for-us and its being-in-itself—knows nothing of the Holy whatso-ever. The property of withdrawal, or retirement, attaching to the Holy belongs to the manner of its givenness. The description of hierophanies thus becomes the preeminent application of a phenomenology understood in Hegel's sense.

Familiar as they are with the testimonials of religious consciousness, scholars of religion know that all names by which the Holy is called retreat again and again into the experience of "un-nameability," but that this expe-rience does not simply snuff out all names by which the Holy is invoked. Rather, they open out to an experience of anticipation of that one Name that shall be manifested at the end of days. In light of such textual testimo-nials, it appears as an aid to interpretation when Hegel stresses, apropos of the dialectic of position and negation, that they "must not converge in an empty nothing," but that, in each case, they generate "a new *Gestalt* of con-sciousness" (Hegel, *Phän.*, 79), to which the object too "offers" itself in a new manner. The alteration common to the consciousness, and to the way in which the object is given to this consciousness as the Withdrawing One, is in Hegel's conceptualization "actually that which is called experience" (ibid., 78). The science of this experience is called by Hegel *Phänomenologie des Geistes*, the "phenomenology of the spirit."

Scientists of religion can refer these declarations of Hegel's to their own field of investigation and conclude: The science of the apparition of the Holy in the *Gestalt* of the Withdrawing One—of the ever new alteration of the religious consciousness on the one hand, and of the manner of givenness of the Holy on the other—is actually what can be called the "phenomenology of religion."

Taking his point of departure from Hegel, Eliade has coined the concept, "dialectic of the hierophanies," in order to indicate how, in the hierophany, the moments of the Present and the Withdrawing are interconnected (Eliade, *RuH*, 34–37). But Hegel's influence is to be felt as early as Scheler, as well, especially in his declarations on the relationship between the human spirit and the divine (Scheler, *EiM*, 190–91; see pp. 65–67 of this chapter).

However, the opportunities for rendering Hegel's concept of the phenomenon and of phenomenology fruitful for the philosophy of religion seem by no manner of means to be exhausted. This holds especially for the connection of the concept of experience with the understanding of history in general and of the history of religion in particular.

In his *Vorlesungen über die Philosophie der Religion* (Lectures on the philosophy of religion; Hegel, *Phil. Rel.*), Hegel himself has shown that his conceptualization of the dialectic of the "in-itself" and the "for-us" has put him in a position to extract the history of religions from the religious relation itself. To the extent that this claim of Hegel is justified—but only to that extent—Hegel's phenomenology is consummately equal to the demand that religious scientists must make on a philosophical method if this method is to serve them as an aid to interpretation in the development of their material.

However, researchers of religion have maintained great reserve with respect to the proposition of the Hegelian method. Underlying this inhibition has not only been the general aversion with which empirically oriented scholars in our century meet all that they call the "pressure," the "coercion," of the "Hegelian philosophical system." Rather, there are specific moments in the relation of the religious noesis to the religious noema whose articulation is such that they are not, *pace* Hegel, available to conceptualization as simple moments in the dialectic of the spirit-coming-to-itself. The "manifestation in the mode of retirement" that is proper to the hierophany seems to be of another sort than the self-awareness of spirit in the mode of *Entäußerung*.

That moment within the hierophany, understood in a religious manner, that especially contradicts an interpretation by way of Hegel's theory of the spirit coming to itself, is the moment of the divine freedom. The "mystery" to which religious consciousness is (reflexively) referred is not simply the inaccessibility of the Unknown but the "unfathomability of a decree," and therewith the free decision of a will that retreats from any attempt of a reconstruction on "grounds." "O the depths of the riches, the wisdom, and the knowledge of God! How unfathomable are his judgments, how unsearchable his ways!" (Romans 11:33).

Religion cannot, therefore, deduce the possibility of the hierophantic experience, but must recount it, since the hierophany is always an unconstrainable event, deducible in advance from no principle, emerging from the decision of an alien, extrinsic will, and causing the Holy to appear as the might of a will (*numen*). But alien freedom, the liberty of another, is not susceptible of subsumption as a moment in the movement in which we come to ourselves: it is an "other-for-us," but not the "other of ourself," an essence referred to us, or, more precisely, referring itself to us. It is not a moment of our own self-reference. That phenomenology that is suitable for an examination of the appearing Holy as a might of a will is therefore not phenomenology of spirit in that sense that Hegel has given this word.

A phenomenology that means to correspond to the noetic-noematic peculiarity of religion cannot, therefore, hark back, without pivotal modifications, to the dialectic of the "for-itself" and "for-us" as it has been developed in Hegel's pneumatic metaphysics. A phenomenology of religion cannot rest content with investigating the dialectic of apparition in general but must extract the specific structure of the dialectic of hierophanies. Accordingly, it inquires into the specific form of the correlation in which religious noesis, on the strength of its special structure, refers to the noema standing correlatively athwart it, whose manifestation and retirement are experienced as an expression as a freedom. This correlation must be described in a manner of investigation that Max Scheler has called the "meaning logic [*Sinnlogik*] of religious acts."

The Religious A Priori and the Meaning Logic of Religious Acts: Max Scheler's Approach to a Phenomenology of Religion

Unlike Hegel and Husserl, Scheler does not work out a doctrine of the general essential laws of apparition, and of the apparition, thereupon to leave it to the empirical researchers of religion in what manner they will seek to apply the conclusions of a general phenomenology to the special phenomenon-field of the religious. He investigates, with philosophical means, the special way in which the religious act, unlike other acts, is referred to specific religious objects, the Holy and Divine. In his *Vom Ewigen im Menschen* (The eternal in the human being), he sets himself the task of describing the "essential connections and essential structures" through which "religious objects" acquire their specific peculiarity, as well as the task of investigating "the immanent act-laws of the religious understanding" (Scheler, *EiM*, 157). In his circumscription of specific religious acts and their objects, he begins with a line of questioning from the

Phänomenologie der Wahrnehmung (Phenomenology of perception), and continues with one from the *Theorie der werterfassenden Akte* (Theory of acts of the apprehension of value).

Perception differs from, for example, simple fantasy in that the object is "intended" as an object that is real also apart from its relation to the object. Belonging to the meaning logic of this act, then, is the positing of a "transcendence" of its (the meaning logic's) objects, a positing of their "being out there," facing all reference to the object. However, these objects can be intended only within this reference, this relationship, to the object. That is, they can be intended only immanently. Now this contradiction, in Scheler's opinion, is to be removed only by way of the postulate that the "being of the object, which obviously transcends human consciousness," must "be utterly immanent to a spirit . . . that is essentially impossible to the human spirit" (Scheler, *EiM*, 182). The perceptive intention is such in its structure that it intends its object as an object not intended only by us. This intention contains a contradiction, then, which Scheler seeks to solve in an understanding of perception as the duplication of another, infinite intending. Thus, his manner of argumentation is not metaphysical but strictly phenomenological: it begins not with the positing of a transcendent being but with the analysis of a particular kind of intentionality.

Now, the hallmark of the religious act consists in its explicit grasp of this unexpressed implication of other intentional acts, especially the act of perception. The act of perception intends its object as the object that has been intended not only by it but by the divine spirit. But it is not accompanied by the consciousness of being a duplication of a divine intention. But this consciousness is precisely the mark of the religious act: "The religious person grasps it as a matter of experience—not through the judgment—that the human spirit is but a reflection"; that it is "'tended,' 'nurtured,' by the spirit of God, 'grounded in it,' 'held by it'" (Scheler, *EiM*, 190–91).

We easily see that, in such considerations, the dialectic of the "for-us" and "in-itself" returns that Hegel has described, and that Scheler's conclusion confirms Hegel's conceptualization to the effect that the human spirit is an apparitional *Gestalt* of absolute spirit. The difference between Scheler's position and Hegel's emerges only in that the former grasps the religious act not as the explicitation of the implicit presupposition of all reality-intending acts but as a special kind of value-apprehending act, whose noematic correlates are the "salvific values." These are qualitatively different from all other values and yet have the function of gathering all values to the unity of an ordering of values. Now, since human beings cannot help calling for an ordering of the values intended by them, they are necessarily steered to a grasp of such absolute or salvific values: "The religious act is necessarily accomplished by every human being" (Scheler, *EiM*, 261).

It is further characteristic of the religious act that it is accomplished with the consciousness of being enabled to do so by its object. In the religious act, the object of this act is posited as that reality thanks to which the act itself is possible. "The object of the religious act is at the same time the cause of its existence" (Scheler, *EiM*, 255). The necessity of performing the religious act therefore implies the necessity with which, in this act, the "vessel," or "vehicle," of all salvific values—God, then—is posited as real. If this vehicle is called "the absolute good," then one can conclude: "There is no choice between having such a good or not having it. There is only the choice of having, in his sphere of the absolute, God—that is, the appropriate good for the religious act—or idols" (Scheler, *EiM*, 263).

The thesis that the religious act exists thanks to its object must be understood strictly phenomenologically—as a description of the manner in which religious noesis intends the religious noema, or in which the noema is "originarily" given to noesis. It is the property of religious "intention" that the act is owing to its object, that it intends its object as its own ground. This conceptualization of Scheler's is confirmed through findings on the part of religious scholarship. For example, the one who prays says to the addressee of the prayer, "Lord, open my lips" (Psalm 51:17).

Scheler goes a step further, however, and thinks he can show that the religious act, which is always already a response to a preliminary act on the part of its object, is, on its side, structurally the anticipation of an ulterior response that it awaits from this object. "Unlike all other acts of cognition, including those of metaphysics," the religious act "requires a response, a counter-act, a re-action precisely from the side of the object at which it aims in its intentional essence" (Scheler, *EiM*, 535). In this wise, the correlation of noesis and noema within the particular sphere of religious acts and objects acquires the particular form of a dialogic correlation. It is clear that a phenomenology of religion that grasps the relation between the religious act and its object as a dialogic and therefore as a personal relation, must ascribe, among all religious acts, a central meaning and importance to those of prayer. Therefore prayer is the preeminent example in terms of which all religious acts will obviously have their specific characteristics.

Phenomenology of Prayer—Problem Indicator for the Dialectic of the Religious Word, and for the Historicity of Religious Discourse

The independence and impossibility of derivation of the religious act, emphasized by all phenomenologists of religion, are nowhere so clear as in the independence and impossibility of derivation of the act of prayer.

The act of prayer can be specified only in terms of the meaning of prayer. And how psychic materials applied or used in this act are combined psychologically–as they are combined, for example, from feelings, sensations, ideas and images, acts of meaning, enunciative expressions, actions—this is of no concern whatever to the religious noetic. (Scheler, *EiM*, 151–52)

The urgency with which Scheler calls for a religious noematics of prayer could suggest that he devotes broad room to it in his investigations in the philosophy of religion. That is not the case. Presumably the reason for this is that, even before the publication of Scheler's *Vom Ewigen im Menschen*, another phenomenologist of religion had undertaken a typology and essential characterization of prayer: Friedrich Heiler, in his *Das Gebet* (Prayer; Munich, 1918; 4th ed., 1921).

Heiler explicitly emphasizes the central position of prayer among all religious acts, and understands prayer, like Scheler after him, as a dialogic relation of the human being to the personal God experienced as present: "There are . . . three moments that form the inner structure of the prayer event: belief in the living, personal God, belief in that God's real, immediate presence, and the dramatic commerce into which the human being enters with this God experienced as present" (Heiler, *Gebet*, 489). By virtue of this sketch of the essential concept of prayer, Heiler is able to describe "types (principal forms) of prayer," in his broadly outlined comparison of religions, and to assign, to each form of the act of prayer, a specific respective manner in which the God prayed to is experienced as present. In his later *chef-d'oeuvre* of religious phenomenology, *Erscheinungsformen und Wesen der Religion* (Forms of appearance and essence of religion; Heiler, *EWR*), he stresses, in agreement with Scheler, that, as in every religious act, so also in prayer, human acting and speaking are response, the word addressed to God is an "echo."

Rudolf Otto had called attention to an ancient Greek Christian hymn in which God is designated as the *panonymos,* the "One with every name," and in the same sentence as the *akleistos,* the "un-invocable" (Otto, *Hl.*, 210–11). Otto accounts this hymn of Gregory of Nazianzus (in Migne, *PG* 37:507–8; erroneously attributed by Otto to Gregory of Nyssa), a typical example of the fact that the divinity is present to the one praying, and to that one's invocation, in multifarious wise, and yet at the same time retires from the worshiper into unnameability. The first thing to result from this dialectic of the act of prayer is the polarity of two types of prayer: prophetic prayer, which responds to the word of God in the word of hymnic address, and mystical prayer, which emerges in silence. These two types of prayer are characteristic for two types of highly developed religions: the religion of revelation and mysticism. Given the preeminence of the religious noema over religious noesis, the polarity of a prophetic religion of the word and a mystical religion of silence is to be referred to a polarity of openness, revelation, and withdrawal within the very Godhead: "But this opposition is ultimately one not of types, but of intradivine poles: of the *deus absconditus* and the *deus revelatus,*" the "hidden God" and the "revealed God" (Heiler, *EWR*, 339). Very God is "the *coincidentia oppositorum* of *logos* and *sigē* ("concurrence of opposites, word and silence," ibid.).

Thus, with the act of prayer and the God to whom this act turns, Heiler demonstrates that dialectic of hierophany that led Eliade from a typology of hierophanies to an interpretation of the history of religion. With Heiler, however, the polarity of God's self-revelation and concealment, of human speech and human silence, does not become the force, the thrust, that exposes the religious relation to the historical process. It remains a mere swing of a pendulum between two forms of piety: "Mysticism and a religion of revelation are the two opposed poles of higher piety, that flee one another in the history of religion, and yet ever converge again" (Heiler, *Gebet*, 283).

The noetic opposition/unity of invoking word and mystical silence, like the noematic opposition/unity of God's invocable presence and nameless inaccessibility, is thus the example par excellence from which the dialectic of hierophany can be read. If the historicity of religion is to be extracted from the dialectic of the hierophany, then the connection obtaining between this dialectic of prayer and the history of prayer is the case par excellence in which the phenomenology of religion must demonstrate its capacity to progress to an adequate understanding of the history of religion. And indeed a multiplicity of hymns, songs, and confessional acclamations give witness that the dialectic of the presence and withdrawal of the God to whom the one praying turns, necessitates a struggle with language that betrays itself in the grammar and semantics of the language of prayer, also demonstrating how this struggle with language has contributed to a historical alteration in prayer (Schaeffler 1978). However, despite intensive involvement with the noetics and noematics of prayer, phenomenologists of religion have until now undertaken no attempt of the kind. This produces a methodological question: Is it a simple coincidence that the connection between the dialectic of prayer and its history has not yet been investigated by religious phenomenologists? Or is this theme, so important for religious scholarship, not accessible with the aid of the phenomenological method? Has the phenomenology of religion not yet exhausted its possibilities in this important respect? Or do we see here a structural boundary of its method?

Unused Potential or Structural Boundary of a Method?

There are grounds for the supposition that it is not the phenomenological method as such that has prevented Scheler, or even Heiler, from taking cognizance of the great number of manners in which acts of prayer are determined, by way of recalling the historical extraction of those who pray and through an anticipation of their historical future. With Scheler, one can speak of a religious conservatism, with Heiler of a religious individualism. The *homo rerum novarum* ("person of revolution") has a very significant right in all areas of the human production of values. Only in the area of religion is this person an essentially contradictory apparition. For here is the 'back to, . . .' here is the essential form of the religious renewal itself" (Scheler, *EiM*, 336). "The ritual prayer formula, the hymn of worship, the liturgical prayer of a community as sacred institution, prayer according to law and for the accumulation of merit—all of these types of prayer are phenomena of paralysis," and the essence of prayer is evinced "only in pure, naive praying, as it lives in simple, earthy 'children of men' and in outstanding, creative geniuses" (Heiler, *Gebet*, 488–89).

However, we must ask: Was it really only a coincidence that Scheler paid so little attention to the anticipatory basic trait of the religious act in respect of his anamnetic, past-remembering direction, and that Heiler could grasp ritual community prayer a priori as a simple "corrupt and paralyzed form" of individual prayer? Or is Heiler's individualism to be reduced to a helplessness on the part of the phenomenological method ever to investigate the relation of noesis and noema otherwise than in individually performed acts? And is Scheler's conservatism a consequence of phenomenology's always being in search of eternal laws of essence, and therefore becomes less sensitive to the dynamics of history?

As a prelude to a decision between these alternatives, let us first pose two questions. Is there a class of intentional acts in which can be read, by way of example, how their individual performance includes at the same time the subject's reference to a concrete, historical group of persons? And do acts of prayer belong to the class of acts sought after? The answer is in the affirmative in both cases. We are thinking of speech acts.

All speaking has a reference to something spoken of, and brings this object, its object, to givenness in characteristic wise. Speaking, then, is an intentional act. But speaking always occurs in a language, and thus causes, in a preeminent way, the connection between individual performance and societal reference to appear: all language belongs to a concrete language community. In this class of acts we have at the same time an example of the structural historicity of intentionality. After all, individual speaking and community language condition each other mutually. No word can be spoken except in a language; no language is real unless it is spoken. The structure of a language (its grammar) determines the possibilities and boundaries of speech and its meaning content (its semantics). But the "use" of language in the currently spoken word has an altering effect on the language of a community and changes the conditions, possibilities, and boundaries of what can be spoken in this language. The reciprocal relationship of language and discourse, then, is the exemplary case for a study of how the relation of act form and object reference unfold historically. Thus, a phenomenological consideration of speech would open the desired access to a phenomenology of history. And what is true generally for the relation of language and history is also true for the relation between religious language and the history of religion specifically. A phenomenological consideration of religious language opens an access to a phenomenology of the history of religion.

But beyond any doubt, the act of prayer falls in the act class of speech. What was said about the reciprocal relationship between language and currently pronounced discourse can be studied by way of example in the dialectical relation of prayer language and prayer act. But if the prayer act, as Scheler and Heiler have so convincingly presented it, is the preeminent case in which the noetic and noematic characteristics of the religious act come to the fore in exemplary manner, then it can be concluded: an analysis of the dialectical relation between prayer language that makes possible the individual act of prayer, and an individual act of prayer, which changes the language of prayer, opens the desired approach to an extraction of the structural historicity not only of prayer but, altogether generally, of religion.

We have shown above that the test of the phenomenology of religion lies in whether it can succeed in extracting the structural historicity of religion. Now we can conclude: the phenomenology of religion can then pass this test if it succeeds in binding an investigation of the intentionality of the act of prayer with an investigation of the language of prayer—that is, if it can succeed in showing how religious language mediates to the speaker a specific form of the reference to specifically religious objects, and how the dialectic of this reference (the dialectic of speaking and falling silent, of nameable presence and nameless retreat of the object addressed) historically thrusts to the fore the relationship between religious noesis and religious noema.

OUTLOOK: THE PROGRAM OF THE PHENOMENOLOGY
OF RELIGION AND ITS MAINTENANCE BY WAY OF
A TRANSCENDENTAL ANALYTICS OF RELIGIOUS LANGUAGE

Husserl's program of a *general phenomenology* contains especially two requirements, which at the same time have found their expression in warnings against an abuse of the word "phenomenology." The phenomenologist must "tread the transcendental soil" and at the same time "annul" any "positing as reality" that would find the object somewhere apart from the reference of noesis and noema, as being in itself. It can be shown that a transcendental linguistic analysis—for example, a transcendental semantics—as Wolfram Hogrebe has presented it (Hogrebe 1974), fulfills this requirement of Husserl's.

A like analysis of language is transcendental: it shows that structural characteristics of language trace out, for the concrete act of speech, conditions of its reference to objects. At the same time, such an analysis of language renounces any pronouncement upon what those objects spoken of may be outside the relation to the intentional act of speech. Instead, it investigates exclusively the "originary manner of givenness" of that spoken of or addressed, for the speaker and in the speech act itself.

Husserl's program of a *regional phenomenology*, again, contains two requirements: The "originarily given acts" of a respective kind are to be investigated on the basis of their structure and ordered to the "originary manner of givenness" of objects of a respective special region. The phenomenology of religion means to be such a regional phenomenology. Accordingly, it investigates the religious act in respect of its specially structured intentionality (its "meaning logic"), and the religious object in respect of its specific manner of givenness (the Holy in the specific kind of its apparition, the "hierophany"). Thereby we see that religious acts and their objects are structured by a specific object-unity, which with Eliade can be designated the "dialectic of hierophanies."

But this dialectic of hierophanies becomes available to experience in the dialectic of the religious speech act and its object, and available to an investigation: this speech act is essentially a speaking at the boundaries of language, and the manner of givenness of its subject is essentially a becoming-invocable at the boundaries of namelessness.

But from such experiences of a speaking at the boundaries of language, of an invocable presence of the Divine at the boundaries of namelessness, there now results the specific manner, for religion, of knowing itself to be provisional, and of anticipating an open future. Precisely here it becomes clear, in exemplary fashion, how the dialectic of hierophanies unfolds to the history of religion. The requirement of a transition from the dialectic of hierophanies to a phenomenology of the historicity of religion and the history of religion will therefore be feasible only when the phenomenological task makes use of the methods of a transcendental analytics, and confronts the latter with the speech of religion.

CHAPTER 5

The "Linguistic Turn" and the Philosophy of Religion as Analysis of Religious Language

———≫•◦•≪———

THE EXPRESSION "LINGUISTIC TURN" has become current for the designation of an event observed in recent centuries—in Germany essentially only in the most recent century—in nearly all areas of philosophy. Problems that have so often concerned philosophy since antiquity, without the centuries-long discussion having led to a consensus, are now to be transformed into argumentatively determinable alternatives, in that not the matters immediately under discussion but the language applied to their debate was made the object of investigation. Here it would be a misunderstanding to think that we are dealing with a simple preparatory test of the "linguistic instruments," which could be distinguished from the actual "discussion of the content," so that, after settling these "preliminary questions" we could finally come "to the matter at hand." The thought underlying the "linguistic turn" rather involves the view that the question of what the objects are to which we relate in speaking is, apart from this linguistically structured relationship, a meaningless question.

The question of the ultimate grounds from which the phenomena of the world of appearances can be derived (the classical question of the *archai*) was thus transformed into the question of the linguistic form of the argumentation, and into the question of the criteria, likewise established linguistically, of whether a line of argumentation can be acknowledged as "adequate." The question of the norms of behavior became the question of the linguistic form of argumentation to be used in the guidance of practice. The question of the conditions and boundaries of knowledge became the question of the conditions for linguistic signs and combinations of signs to relate to something, and of the object to which they refer to indicate something. Above all, the philosophical question of the "essence" or "being" of things was transformed into the question of the experience through which the meaning of words can be established or explained.

In the wake of this "linguistic turn," the philosophy of religion, as well, from a discussion of the question, What is religion? became the investigation of problems of linguistic philosophy: What kind of speech is applied in religious enunciations? And what governs whether these linguistic expressions refer to anything, and denote anything, instead of being as bereft of object as of meaning?

The turn from questions of substance to the question of speech, appositely indicated in the turn from the question of the "essence of things" to the question of the "meaning of words," can be executed on the basis of very different considerations of knowledge theory and knowledge critique. It can be the upshot of positivistic arguments, or it can be that of transcendental philosophy. And its application to problems of the philosophy of religion can, in conjunction with philosophical arguments of both kinds, be based on specific, special theological considerations. And indeed, with the rise and spread of the philosophy of linguistic analysis in general, and the philosophy of religion in terms of linguistic analysis in particular, traditions of positivism, transcendental philosophy, and theology, which otherwise stand in direct mutual contradiction, have cooperated in a particular manner of their own.

POSITIVISM AND THE ANALYSIS OF RELIGIOUS LANGUAGE

At first the influence of the positivistic tradition made itself most clearly noticeable. Questions of metaphysics (for example, of the "essence of things") and questions of religion (for instance, of God's existence and essence), throughout all the centuries in which concern for them flourished, could not be decided argumentatively. Otherwise there would have had to be a consensus among those competent and practiced in the corresponding argumentation forms. The lengthy, unsuccessful effort at a consensus on the part of the experts and those adept at argumentation generates the suspicion, so the opinion now arose, that these questions, and attempts at answers, lacked reference to object and meaning content alike. Unsolvable controversies arise not because the partners say anything different about the same object, but because they struggle over nothing, that is, over chimerical objects, and say nothing about these pretended objects, that is, bring forth merely apparent assertions (see Carnap 1928).

What remains to be examined, then, is the question of how things came to such a pass, with all of these chimerical discussions and objects, and how it is to be explained that the disputants did not notice that this is what they were doing. One of the methods that can be applied in order to solve these two questions consists in analyzing the language applied in such empty discussions.

This method has also been applied to questions of religion. The analysis of religious language, then, is supposed to accomplish two things. It is to show that the propositions formulated in this language are structurally unsuitable for speaking of anything and saying anything, and it is to explain that this lack of reference to reality and meaning content was not noticed by those involved because propositions without reference to reality and meaning content could give the appearance of the consequential or substantial.

Linguistic Analysis and the Suspicion of Meaninglessness in Discourse upon God

When religious persons are asked what they wish to speak about, they frequently respond: In religions, God is spoken of. But they add at once: Of course, the reality denoted by the word "God" is different from anything that we can experience, conceptualize, or express in words. But this seems to be an admission on the part of religious speakers that they themselves cannot say what the word "God" refers to. They use their speech according to rules that rob them of their very reference to any object.

Something similar holds for predicates in religious propositions. With every predicate used in enunciations about God, the religious speaker is constrained to add that it has an entirely different meaning in the religious context than with its use otherwise. "The assertion that God loves us says neither that God experiences certain feelings in our regard, nor that our life is guided in certain relationships that would be reasonably similar to those to be expected of a Good in the dimension of omnipotence" (Crombie 1957, 131).

Through this emphasis on the qualitative dissimilarity between God, on the one hand, and the human being and the world, on the other, so the argument goes, arise those "rule discrepancies" or "antagonisms" of religious speech that evacuate its enunciations of their reference to reality and their meaning content alike (see Crombie 1957). Religious speech uses designators (proper nouns) that fail to fulfill the condition for the use of designators. When proper nouns are introduced, they are supposed to indicate situations in which the person or thing thus designated is identifiable and unambiguously differentiated from all other persons and things. But this is not the case with the proper noun "God." Correspondingly, predicators are used in religious enunciations that fail to fulfill the condition for the use of predicators. Such predicators (for instance, "loves," the verb, or "is almighty") are supposed to be applied when it can be unequivocally stated what is asserted or excluded by its application, and thus what the case must be or must not be—when the application of the predicator in question is justified (when, for example, it is asserted that "God loves human beings"), and when it can be specified what it means to apply this predicate to this "designatum" (for example, what "to love" means when this concept is applied to God). Obviously none of these prerequisites is satisfied in the application of religious predicators.

Now, religion is surely more than a simple maintaining of propositions as true. However, one will have to hold that all other moments of religious life, as well—for instance, divine worship, religious morality, the life of the religious community—have lost their basis, unless the devotees of religion were to formulate enunciations and claim the truth of these assertions (for example, the statement that God has wrought certain deeds celebrated in divine worship). Here it is a prerequisite that these enunciations be signifying—that is, that they speak of something and say something, rather than making fictitious references to fictitious objects.

On the triple premise that enunciatory propositions with a claim to truth are essential for religion, that only signifying propositions are susceptible of being either true or false, and finally, that the enunciatory propositions of religious language do not fulfill the conditions for signifying propositions, the conclusion ineluctably follows that religion is philosophically untenable.

That manner of linguistic analysis in the philosophy of religion belonging to the tradition of positivist thought subjects the language of religion to the suspicion that that language is structurally incapable of referring to anything or saying anything. What remains to be explained, then, is the fact that the nonsignifying character of religious enunciations could have remained hidden for so long to the persons who use such enunciations. The explanation could be sought in the fact that the structure of religious language effects a seduction of thought similar to that alleged by Gilbert Ryle for the language of metaphysics. With the title of his investigation, "Systematically Misleading Expressions" (Ryle 1931), Ryle has broached a theme addressed in a great number of investigations critical of religion and metaphysics on the basis of a language analysis.

A second argumentational approach, however, began with the thesis that religious enunciations are by no means structurally, nor therefore always, nonsignifying. Only, they had lost their signification in the course of their application. Originally, we hear, the proper noun "God" was applied altogether properly, since it was believed that certain experiential situations (hierophanies) could be claimed in which the being so named was identifiable and unequivocally distinguishable from all other persons or things. And the predicates (especially action predicates) applied in enunciations about God were originally applied just as properly. They served for the ascription to this God of events thought to be unambiguously identifiable as deeds of the divine activity (miracles). Only as the critique of religion began to generate doubt even with religious persons whether there are unequivocally identifiable theophanies and miracles, were supporters of religion compelled to maintain that they did not at all mean their statements as the critic understood them so as to be able to contradict them. With the formulation, "I did not mean it that way," believers explain that they are untouched by the particular criticism in question on the part of the nonbeliever.

Wittgenstein has applied this finding to draw the conclusion that includes a self-criticism of the enunciation of unbelief: "When I am asked whether I believe in the Last Judgment or not, in the sense in which religious persons believe in it, . . . and then I explain, 'I do not believe in . . . , then the religious person never believes what I describe" (Wittgenstein, *VuG*, 90). But if what the nonbeliever challenges never coincides with what the believer professes, "then I would not say, 'No, I do not believe. . . .' It would seem to me altogether insane to say that" (ibid.).

Antony Flew, on the other hand, draws a conclusion from experiences of this kind in the sense of a critique of religion: Religious persons constantly insist that they have not meant what the critic challenges; in so doing, they gradually divest their propositions of their original content, to the point that these propositions are, it is true, completely immune from criticism, but only because they no longer have any meaning. "One can completely dissolve one's claim without noticing it. A beautiful, bold hypothesis can thus suffer death, step by step by way of a thousand modifications. And herein, it seems to me, lies the particular danger of the endemic evil of theological propositions" (Flew 1955, 85).

The premise that propositions with a claim to truth are essential for religion, then, has exposed religion to the criticism of the positivists. The latter have declared religious propositions not untrue, but nonsignifying. An analysis of the grammar of religious propositions seemed to confirm this suspicion and at the same time to provide an explanation of why this nonsignification of religious propositions is generally hidden from the eyes of the speaker. Accordingly, it would seem that all of these consequences critical of religion can be avoided only if one gives up the premises that propositions have essential meaning for religion. A more recent type of philosophy of religion in terms of the analysis of language rests on this conviction.

The "Nonpropositional Character" of Religious Language and the Question of the "Autonomy of the Play of Religious Language"

If one conceives of religion as a system of propositions, or if one ascribes to religious propositions at least an essential meaning for religion, then arguments on the part of speech analysis seem to demonstrate the meaninglessness of religion. But a theory that makes all too many linguistic propositions appear as meaningless, arouses the suspicion that it is oriented to false criteria. In this connection, a declaration of Wittgenstein is frequently referred to: "For an error, that is simply too enormous" (Wittgenstein, *VuG*, 98–99). For "whether something is a fault or not, . . . it is a fault in a particular system" (ibid., 95). Thus, what seems an "error" in a system of propositions is too "enormous" not to be noticed. This suggests that the truth of religion may simply not be a matter of propositions. Thus, an assertion that is not to be understood as a proposition is called a "nonpropositional enunciation." And so the thesis was broached according to which enunciations that seem faulty when they are understood as propositions demonstrate their true meaning only in the premise that they have a "nonpropositional" character.

Like Wittgenstein, J. L. Austin was dissatisfied with the conclusions of a positivistic speech-analysis that had led to ever broader areas of language propositions to be judged meaningless. "Constantly, fresh types of nonsense were uncovered. . . . Now, we concede that we speak nonsense; but even we philosophers do so only up to a point" (Austin 1962, 24). A corrective for the obviously falsely posited standard becomes possible when one assumes "that many enunciations that look like propositions or observations are actually not at all, or only partially, pieces of information about facts" (ibid.). Their true meaning does not consist in their transmission of what is outside themselves, but to effect what would not be realized without them. They are manners of "doing things with words" (cf. the title of Austin's lecture series).

Now the philosophy of religion could adopt Austin's theory of word behavior in order to seek the sense of religious enunciations in their nonpropositional function. Here we may notice that Austin had taken some of his examples of "doing things with words" from the language of religion. It is especially a matter of enunciations that are used in the conferral of the sacraments. The statement "I baptize you" does not inform the candidate that he or she is being baptized, but belongs to the act of baptizing. The enunciation "I absolve you from your sins" does not inform the penitent that he or she is being absolved, but belongs to the conduct of the absolution. These linguistic expressions do not inform of facts obtaining independently of them, but are parts of that behavioral connection only through which these facts arise. And if the hearer extracts from these enunciations a piece of information at the same time—for example, learns what is done in baptism and absolution—this is not the primary sense of such linguistic enunciations, but their secondary effect, which in certain limit cases can even be missing. The statement "I baptize you" is, according to the conceptualization of the Christian churches, part of the conferral of baptism even when the person being baptized is an infant, who learns nothing from this sentence. And those linguistic enunciations that belong to the anointing of the sick are, according to Catholic conceptualization, effective even with regard to a dying person who no longer understands them.

Apart from sacramental administration, as well, there can be linguistic enunciations that resemble propositional enunciations but have their actual meaning in other use of language. There are many other instances of the use of language in religious discourse whose truth claim is nonpropositional (cf. Wisdom 1944/1945; idem 1965; Braithwaite 1955; Ramsey 1957). A statement such as "God has created the world" is alleged by positivists to be nonsignifying, since it names an event but at the same time rejects the conditions that must be met if the description of an event is to be signifying: it speaks of an event that does not take place in time and uses a predicate (to "create") whose meaning cannot be indicated, inasmuch as it is applied in a sense qualitatively distinct from all causality that we know in the world. In order to discover the sense of such a statement, it is said, we must ask not what this sentence conveys in terms of information, but what religious persons are doing when they enunciate statements of this sort. They are expressing, for example, their feeling of security in a world that they understand as God's creation; or they are referring to the moral decision to regard the world with reverence, and not use it as a mere means for their own ends; or they undertake the obligation of hope that one is not delivered to the mercy of anonymous powers in this world, but that all that occurs is "meaning" personally, and at the same time points to God's face. (The meaning of this feeling of familiarity has been indicated especially in Wisdom 1944/1945.) But in such feelings, assumptions of obligation, and hopes, a special kind of intersubjectivity is consititued: the community of speech and action of a religious group whose members employ such statements to indicate the ground of their particular form of communication and interaction.

Accordingly, statements like "God has created the world" are understood by certain linguistic analysts (for instance, Wisdom, Braithwaite, and Ramsey) not as propositions but as "doing things with words" in such a way as to ground a particular individual or community way of life.

In this regard, as well, philosophers of religion of the linguistic analysis school were able to appeal to Wittgenstein. Without speaking of specifically religious forms of intersubjectivity, Wittgenstein emphasized generally "that the speaking of language is a part of an activity, or of a life form" (Wittgenstein, *PU*, part 1, no. 23). But since linguistic enunciations are never isolated but always occur or "are used" as a mere part of this kind of comprehensive behavioral connection, of such a "life form," Wittgenstein reduced his rule for the correct understanding of linguistic enunciations to the formula: "The meaning of a word is its use in speech" (ibid., no. 43).

With such considerations, unawares, Wittgenstein was going back to basic conclusions of "historical form" exegesis, which had shown that religious (and other) texts are understood only in light of their *Sitz im Leben*, their position in the life of a community using the language and activities ("doing things") in question. Departing from the linguistic usage of the historical-form school, Wittgenstein has called such a connection of intersubjective activities a "wordplay" (ibid., no. 7). Philosophers of religion could now go back to this theory of a "wordplay"— that is, of the intersubjective behavioral connections within which alone linguistic enunciations receive and maintain meaning—if they meant to counter the positivistic allegation of nonsignification: This suspicion of nonsignification is itself nonsignifying, since it seeks the meaning conditions that are allegedly not met by religious enunciations where they are not to be found, namely, in the alleged relationship of these enunciations to a reality that would be discoverable outside the religious wordplay. What religious enunciations speak of, and what they denote, is to be found only within religious wordplay, and within the "life form" that is their vehicle. Such wordplays and the life forms that are their vehicle can therefore be assessed only in terms of their own laws: they are "autonomous" (see especially Phillips 1965; idem 1968, 253). In a later publication, it is true, Phillips describes himself as an author "who has spoken of religious faith-views as special word-plays, but who has in certain respects had second thoughts about this" (Phillips 1970, 259).

On the Critique of the Theses
of the "Nonpropositional Character" of Religious Language
and the "Autonomy of the Religious Language-Play"

The two theses—that religious language has a "nonpropositional character," and that it represents an "autonomous language-play"—are not identical. According to the language-play theory, there can altogether readily be enunciations that not only speciously seem to be propositions but really are, and that nevertheless possess meaning only within the corresponding "language play." But despite this difference, the two theories have two important characteristics in common. They render religion immune to criticism, since the "suspicion of nonsignification" obtains only when religious enunciations are judged on false criteria. But at the same time, they divest religion of the capacity to make itself understood by those who do not, or do not yet, belong to the religious-language and behavioral community: one must be "playing along" with the language play in question in order to grasp the meaning of the several enunciations, and it becomes impossible to make understandable to a person who does not yet do so, as one "does with religious words," what is at issue.

Against this position in the philosophy of religion, objections have been raised, partly general ones, in terms of religious science, partly specific ones, in terms of theology. The general argument from religious science is based on the indication that those feelings, moral intentions, and positions, hopes, and evaluations that form the true sense of the ostensibly propositional enunciations of religion according to the conceptualization being discussed here, must not be simply presupposed with the members of the religious community. These persons must first be motivated to assimilate them, in a lifelong process of education, and be rendered capable of so feeling, behaving, obligating themselves, and so on, as is held as normative by the religious community. In this process of education, arguments play a role; and these arguments include claims of truth, for instance, of reports of divine deeds, that ground the invitation to hope, to moral commitment, to a feeling of security, and so on. Thus, religion contains actual, and not only apparent, propositional enunciations (against the thesis of the "nonpropositional character" of religious enunciations).

And these enunciations involve the claim that they are true even when the person who utters them does not correspond in his or her behavior to that of which they speak. Thus, the enunciation "God has made the world" is supposed to be true even though those who make it lack the trust, the commitment to God's maintenance and care of creation, that "yes to reality," that could be expected of them if they understood reality as the work of a good God. Indeed, here we find a priority of the factual assertion (for example, "God has made the world") over the expression of feelings, attitudes of will, hopes, and so on. The alleged fact ranks as "greater" than the manner in which the members of the religious community react to this fact in their praxis. The religious "life form" underlies the claim of truth of religious enunciations (against the theory of the "autonomy of the religious wordplay"). And so is verified of all religions what Luther has said of Christianity: "Remove the claims, and you have removed Christianity" (Luther, *SA,* 603; cf. Dalferth 1981, 525).

Now it can surely be objected: Indications of this kind indeed refute the notion of the "nonpropositional character" of religious language but not the thesis of the autonomy of religious wordplay. Even the profession, characteristic of religion, that all of its acts are "lesser" than the divine reality and activity is, as a profession, precisely a religious act, and has its meaning only within the religious "life form" and that "wordplay" (of the comprehensive behavioral and life connection) that brings this life form to expression. However, one must maintain that such a profession of the "ever greater" reality of God, although it is a religious act, nevertheless contains the claim that it speaks of a divine reality that is independent of the manner in which persons relate to it—for example, as "wise" or "foolish," as "chosen" or "reprobate." The claim to truth made within the religious wordplay for the enunciations formulated there does not authorize its conceptualization as being valid only within this wordplay (see Sherry 1972a, 18-37; 1972b, 159–67; 1977).

These general considerations from religious science are frequently combined with arguments that bear specifically on the enunciations of the Christian faith. Christianity is not only a missionary religion—directed to those persons who do not belong to the community of faith. Christians themselves are expected to hear the word of the Gospel again and again, and only thereby to become Christians in the full sense of the word. But to this end, the word must be preached to them, and made understandable. From this, the question arises: Is "understanding" possible only to those who are already "believers" in the full sense of the word? Or must an understanding be transmitted, so that the human being can become a believer?

The theme of faith and understanding, which had stood at the center of the controversy over "dialectical theology" in the first one-third of our century (see E. Brunner 1925; 1928; 1934; Barth 1934; as well as, especially, Bultmann, *GuV*), therefore returns in the present as a theme of the linguistic-analysis school of the philosophy of religion (cf. the colloquium "Faith and Understanding" [Dalferth 1974, 226–57]—underlying D. Z. Phillips's *Concept of Prayer* [1965]). Under the title "First, Understand," Humphrey Palmer represented the thesis, at that colloquium, that faith not only bestows understanding, but prerequires an understanding. He expressed his theological argument in the following way, among others.

> On religious grounds, I regret that characteristic that seeks to divide religion from other life-forms as independent and self-sufficient, immune from criticism and incapable of being evangelized. I should like to participate in no esoteric play to which in principle no observers are admitted. It seems to me

important for the eternal salvation of believer and unbeliever alike, that there be a genuine confrontation between the claims of believers and the objections of unbelievers. (Palmer, in Dalferth 1974, 245)

The claim that religious statements are only understandable to a person already involved in the religious wordplay, already moving within the religious life-form, therefore comes under the suspicion of being a simple defensive claim, which believers mount only when they have no success with their attempt to convince unbelievers. "But religion can scarcely be an island with drawbridges over which argumentational failures can be imputed to the secular world, but which can be drawn when the apologist comes out on the short end of the argumentation" (Palmer, in Dalferth 1974, 247).

The "linguistic turn" of philosophy in general is to be credited with the fact that the methods of analytic philosophy, as they were developed especially in Anglophone countries, have found application in ever broader thematic areas of philosophic thought. From this viewpoint, analytic philosophy stood partly in the tradition of positivist thought, partly in confrontation with this tradition. This holds as well for the philosophy of religion of the school of linguistic analysis. Attempts to demonstrate the "nonpropositional character" of religious language, or to understand it as "autonomous wordplay," are extensively led by the intent to meet those arguments with which it is sought to corroborate the positivist suspicion of nonsignification with methods of linguistic analysis.

On the European continent, however, especially in Germany, a linguistic philosophy has arisen, under the determining influence of Kant, that has made language the object of its investigation under viewpoints of transcendental philosophy, and in this approach—before and after its encounter with analytical philosophy—has tested possibilities of practicing the philosophy of religion as transcendental analysis of religious language.

Both kinds of consideration of language, the transcendental on the Continent and the analytic in England and North America, have long stood side by side without interrelationship. But it was not necessary for things to be this way. That it is possible, from the standpoint of transcendental philosophy, to enter into a conversation with analytical philosophy is clear, especially when one follows the indication of Jan M. Crombie to the effect that the presentation of religious enunciations is not a matter of presenting the images used there through a language free of metaphors. The meaning of the images is rather shown by the fact that "the more we try to understand the world in light of this image, the better our understanding of the world becomes" (Crombie 1957, 143). Without Crombie's being aware of it, this thought forms a transition from the confrontation with the positivist suspicion of nonsignification to a transcendental consideration of language. After all, there is no question here of whether the graphic expressions of religious language designate an unambiguously identifiable object or not, but whether they open new horizons of possible experience against which all other objects to which we relate in thinking and speaking, become understandable in a changed way.

THE "LINGUISTIC TURN" AND TRANSCENDENTAL PHILOSOPHY: ANALYSIS OF RELIGIOUS LANGUAGE BEYOND THE STRUGGLE WITH POSITIVISM

Linguistic Philosophy in Germany under the Influence of Immanuel Kant

No differently than the positivists, who appeared on the scene later, Kant had begun with the observation that, despite centuries-long concern, the questions of metaphysics could not be solved (Kant, *KrV,* A, VII–VIII). In his conviction, the reason for this was that the understanding itself is necessarily "dialectical" in its use (see *KpV,* 192), and that means, with Kant, that it generates contradictions and thereby goes astray. The dialectic of pure reason regards especially those concepts that Kant calls "ideas." In an early writing, Kant describes the ideas as "limit concepts," which "reason demands of itself and places before its eyes by way of anticipation" (Kant, *Diss.,* §1.1).

These concepts, then, describe goals to which reason, and under its leadership, the understanding, must direct their activity: the ordered wholeness of all real and possible subjects of experience (world), the non-contradictory oneness of consciousness (soul), and finally, the totality of what can be expressed and grasped in predicates (*omnitudo realitatis*— God). Unless reason were to demand (*exposcere*) these tasks of itself and set the fulfillment of these tasks before the eyes of the understanding by way of anticipation (*praesumere*), we could not take a single step in our knowledge, since we would not know how we were to proceed with the abundance of the elements of information available (affections of the senses). Only because reason sets the understanding these goals, and because the understanding, for its part, contains the rules according to which it must proceed in the execution of these tasks, do we become capable of erecting a world of objects. Or in brief: Only because the ideas of reason are of purely regulative use, are the concepts of the understanding of constitutive use.

Now, the necessity with which reason traces out for the understanding these goals of the latter's activity (since without these targets neither could

acts of cognition be executed nor would objects of cognition be built) generates the appearance that these ideas designate something that exists independently of us, in itself. "Thus, there is a natural, unavoidable dialectic of
pure reason—not one in which a kind of bungler gets himself tangled up for
lack of cognitions, or which some sophist or other has concocted in order
to muddle reasonable persons, but which ineluctably attaches to human
reason" (Kant, *KrV,* A, 298).

The "endless brawls" of pre-Kantian metaphysics therefore had their
cause in the fact that a *task* that reason sets itself and the understanding was
confused with supposed *objects* that reason would have had before it without itself having had any part in getting them there in the form in which
they had presented themselves. Arguments of this kind, however, mean not
the end of metaphysics but "prolegomena to any future metaphysics that
will be able to come forward as science" (Kant, *Prol.*). For if it is only the
self-set task of reason that makes possible the constitution of objects, then
there are propositions that describe nothing else but precisely those functions of the understanding that are called on to execute reason's tasks.
Propositions that describe these functions of the understanding are then to
be considered as a priori propositions, propositions "from beforehand,"
with respect to any possible object. Now, inasmuch as these functions of the
understanding are described through the highest principles of logic—therefore in Kant's conviction logic has transcendental meaning—it describes
the conditions of possibility of all objects as such (transcendental logic).
And because the actual forms of the ideation of objects, as well, must follow certain laws, if the concepts of the understanding are to be applicable
to the various contents of this ideation, therefore there is, alongside transcendental logic, for Kant, a transcendental consideration of the forms of
ideation, as well—a "transcendental aesthetic."

It was not long after the appearance of Kant's *Critique of Pure Reason* that
J. G. Hamann and J. G. Herder expressed the conviction that the transcendental functions that Kant ascribed to the logical laws of thinking were
ascribable to language instead. It is in language, and not in abstract
thought, that Hamann sees the creative force in a person, through which
that person wins a portion and share in the creation of the world through
God's word (Hamann, UdS, 32). It is in language and its historicity, and
not in the ahistorical laws of logic, that Herder sees the potentiality of all
intersubjectivity and objectivity (Herder, *Metakr.*; cf. Hamann, *MPV*).

Wilhelm von Humboldt has understood his philosophy of language as an
application of Kant's discovery of transcendental philosophy, according to
which we do not find the world of our objects as given, but only build them
through the activity of our understanding. For lack of a transcendental

philosophical method, no philosophy of language arose in antiquity, despite the knowledge of many languages (see Humboldt, *VmS*, 152). Today it has become possible to bring such a philosophy of language to materialization, through Kant's transcendental premise (see ibid., 195). Here it is the formal law of any concrete language, its "build," that determines the experiential world of any given language community. Here, with Humboldt, instead of a transcendental consideration of the once-and-for-all reason-subjects of the same logic, we have the analysis of the differentiation of languages from the viewpoint of the "differences of language construction." (See the two investigations, *Über die Verschiedenheiten des menschlichen Sprachbaues*, and *Über die Verschiedenheit des menschlichen Sprachbaues und ihren Einfluß auf die geistige Entwicklung des Menschengeschlechts.*)

Cassirer's Philosophy of Symbolic Forms and the Philosophy of Religion as an Analysis of the Structure of Religious Language

Ernst Cassirer agreed with Kant that the acts of the subject, especially its ideation and thought, must follow certain formal rules if they are to manage to order the plenitude of subjective impressions in such a way that objects of experience emerge. The forms of these acts, inasmuch as they constitute the world of objects as a whole and the individual objects in it, Cassirer calls "symbolic forms" (see Cassirer, *PsF,* 1:3–17).

Cassirer sought to show, however, that those symbolic forms through which the world of the investigative objects of science is constructed do not make up the only form system of this kind. Another system of ideation forms, concepts of reason, and ideas of understanding is language. And within language there is a specifically structured religious language form: myth (*PsF,* 8–9). There is a specifically mythically structured space-ideation and time-ideation, a mythical understanding of substantiality and causality, a mythical understanding of the "I" and its permanence (see Cassirer's construction [*PSF* 2], following Kant's construction [*KrV*]). These symbolic forms of myth constitute an object world of a special structure, which is distinct from the world of scientifically investigable objects. Cassirer's importance for the further development of the philosophy of religion, then, consists in his having developed the peculiarity of religious objects and their cohesion through a structural analysis of the religious form of language, which he called "myth."

But at the same time, Cassirer has made it clear: Religious language (myth) is merely one of a number of possible complexes of symbolic forms. When a culture has reached a certain level of differentiation (as, for example, Europe), religion is faced with other complexes of symbolic forms, so that religion has become one area of culture alongside other areas of culture. A philosophy of symbolic forms, then, will not only have to investigate the respective specific structures of individual areas of culture, but will have to explain the possibility of their reciprocal relationship, as well. Just as Cassirer approaches the theory of the "autonomy of language play," developed later by analysts, through his thesis that each given complex of symbolic forms structures a "world" of its own, so also his thesis of the reciprocal relationship of the areas of culture anticipates the criticism of the thesis that language play is "autonomous" in its respective presentations. In order to grasp that unity that can unfold into the difference and relationship of areas of culture, Cassirer adduces the concept of "spirit." Only a theory of culture as the multiplicity, rich in interrelationships, of manners in which spirit builds for itself, through symbolic forms, the world of its objects, can keep Kant's mere promise in his critique of pure reason: "The critique of reason thereby becomes the critique of culture" (Cassirer, *PsF*, 1:11).

In any system of symbolic forms, there are transcendental—that is, object-possibilitating—ideation-forms of space and time, correlations of constants and variables (things and characteristics), conditions and consequences. The various systems of symbolic forms (for example, myth and science) are thus structurally distinct from one another, and yet, at the same time, indicate functional equivalencies that make it possible to relate to one another, compare, and critically measure by one another the various worlds that, for example, are built through myth and science. (That the transcendental meaning of specifically religious forms of ideation, and concepts, is verified not only in religious language, but also in religious behaviors, for instance, in worship, is what I have sought to show in my essay "Der Kultus als Weltauslegung"—see Schaeffler 1974).

A Further-Reaching Application of Cassirer's Philosophy of Language

A transcendental consideration of language, such as Cassirer has attempted, can contribute to the solution of those *aporiai* of "analytical philosophy" that are usually described under the heading "subjectlessness." Wittgenstein once formulated: "There is no such thing as the thinking, conceptualizing subject" (Wittgenstein, *Tract.*, 5:631). This was in an important respect an anticipation of the suspicion of "meaninglessness" with which later analysts met religious propositions. Even when they seem to speak purely objectively of sky and earth, of occurrences in nature and society, religious statements deal at the same time essentially with the speaker, with

his or her commitment to, personal confession of, the truths being enunciated. But if "there is" no subject, then religious propositions (and many
another along with them) are without material reference.

The transcendental reference can help one understand more adequately
Wittgenstein's declaration just cited, so that it will not suggest to the reader
the construct, so alien from reality, of a speech without a speaker. Wittgenstein goes on: "The subject does not belong to the world, but is a boundary of the world" (*Tract.*, 5:632). It is "not a part of the world" (ibid.,
5:641). Analogously: "You do not really see the eye" (ibid., 5:633).

The transcendental philosopher can say why this is the case. The eye
does not come into the field of vision any more than the "I" into the world
of objects, since both, each in its way, are structure-bestowing grounds for
being able to see, or conceive, objects grasped. They have, so to speak, done
their work when the object comes before the eyes, and therefore are presupposed by each object—are its a priori. In these terms, the transcendental philosopher will agree with Wittgenstein's proposition: "The 'I' enters
philosophy inasmuch as 'the world is my world'" (ibid., 5:641). But the
transcendental philosopher will contradict the statement: "Nothing in the
field of vision suggests the conclusion that it is seen by an eye" (ibid.,
5:633). The structure of the world serves notice that it is known by an "I,"
as the structure of the field of vision serves notice that it is seen by an eye,
for example, in its foreshortening in "perspective."

Thus, Wittgenstein's assertions concerning the "I" are ambiguous and in
need of explanation. This ambiguity returns with later representatives of
analytical philosophy. Cassirer's transcendental analysis of language can
contribute to a clearer definition of the meaning of the speaking subject for
the world opened up by speech.

Cassirer has shown that the speaking subject's self-understanding by no
means expresses itself only in the use of the word "I." Much more broadly
extensive, and much more significant for language in its overall structure,
is the expression of self-awareness in the moods of verbs (indicative, sub-
junctive, optative, contrary-to-fact, and so on), in the various designations
of spatial structure and temporal succession related in distinct ways to the
standpoint of the speaker, in the construction of sentences, and the like (see
Cassirer, *PsF,* 1:212–48). All of this is verified, and even more so, for myth
as the language of religion (see ibid., 2:185–261).

Going beyond Cassirer, we could see that, alongside the religious narrative form, myth and other forms of language—for instance, the hymn, the
word of worship, declarations of prophets—bring religious speakers to
speech in manifold wise: not preponderantly in the fact that they make

statements about themselves, but chiefly in the fact that the manner in which their world of experience is structured renders this world recognizable as a world of religious persons. Considerations of this kind can fill Wittgenstein's proposition, cited above, with concrete content: "The 'I' enters philosophy by the fact that 'the world is my world'" (Wittgenstein, *Tract.*, 5:641). And precisely in this, the transcendental consideration makes a contribution to the defeat of the "subjectlessness" of analytical philosophy.

The same method of Cassirer legitimates a second application, to which that author himself seems not to have adverted. Modifying Wittgenstein's statements, one could say: "God belongs to the world of religion," but "God enters the world of religion inasmuch as 'the world is God's world.'" Through an analysis of mythic (or, more generally, of religious) language, Cassirer has shown that the space and time of the religious world are by no means homogeneous: their moments and places are qualitatively distinct from one another. But the salient moments and places are not the here and now of the religious speaker. Rather, they are the times and places at which the arrival of the divine, its theophany, is expected (see Cassirer, *PsF,* 2:107-88). And even the connection of constants and variables (things and characteristics), of conditions and consequences, in religious language is determined by the expectation that, through all change of events—of meeting once more the God who has worked "in the beginning" (religious constants), and of experiencing in all events a new dawning of the divine "might and glory" (religious causality). Thus, even if an analysis of religious language, going beyond Cassirer, were to come to the result that "there is" no God, of whom religion speaks, within the world—that is, that God does not occur in this world as a particular object alongside other religious objects—this would not have to lead to the suspicion of meaninglessness against discourse about God. When we regard religious speech as "symbolic form"—as an endowment with shape and mold that builds, from our impressions, objects of a special kind, religious objects—then we see that the God of whom religion speaks determines the structure of religious forms of ideation and concepts, and therewith the religious world as a whole, even when that God might not be met within this world as a discrete object.

As the seeming "subjectlessness" of analytical philosophy could be overcome by the considerations presented above, so those same considerations could overcome its structural "Godlessness," so feared by many critics—that is, its incapacity to focus on religious discourse as discourse about God at all.

A Fertile Encounter: The Understanding of Religion with Kant and in Judaism

Another direction of the philosophy of religion that begins with the analysis of religious language forms has emerged from the connection of the Kantian doctrine of postulates with the Jewish tradition. The ideas of reason, as Kant understands them, not only set the understanding the task of so ordering the fullness of elements of information (affections of the senses) that the world of phenomenal objects arises therefrom; but also, and mainly, they set the understanding the task of making practical judgments—of deciding alternatives of behavior—in order to change the world and even the human being in an effective way according to moral ideas. The world is to be shaped to a "moral world order"; the human being is to become a new, moral person through a "revolution in attitudes." But the third idea, the idea of God, describes, in this connection of Kant's practical philosophy, those conditions that must be presupposed in order to solve the contradictions in which reason would otherwise become entangled in the course of seeking to execute its practical assignments.

The first of these contradictions consists in the double task, on the one side, of maintaining the character pure, and on the other, of effectively doing the good. The first task demands that the moral law be made the only motivating force of one's activity, and therefore that one should take not account of whether the obligation in question is realizable under current conditions, perhaps against contrary forces. The second task demands that one undertake responsibility precisely for the realization or accomplishment of this moral obligation. The two tasks seem incompatible, since the moral will and effective behavior in the world are subject to two structurally distinct laws: "All practical connection of causes and effects in the world, as a consequence of the determination of the will, is directed not according to the moral attitude of the will, but according to a knowledge of the laws of nature, and the physical ability to use them to one's purposes" (Kant, *KpV*, A, 204–5).

The second contradiction consists in the fact that, in order to obey the moral law, a person would already have to have a good will, and in this sense be a good person—while the moral law only has the character of an "imperative" because a person wills the good precisely not out of inner constraint of his or her pure heart, and therefore is not yet a good person, but is only to become one. "Now, how it would be possible for a person evil by nature to make himself a good person, overreaches all our concepts. For how can a bad tree bear good fruit?" (Kant, *Religion*, A, 46).

Neither contradiction, in Kant's conviction, can be solved except under the supposition that there is a God. In this case one may understand the moral law as the command of the one who also prescribes nature its laws, and hence will produce that new moral world order if persons do what they ought. The contradiction obtaining between the law of nature and the moral law becomes soluble "by way of an intelligible author of nature" (Kant, *KpV,* A, 207). Furthermore, if one understands the moral law as the demand of the one who at the same time is gracious to the sinner and thus enables that sinner to undergo a conversion, then one maintains hope in a "sentence of grace" to be pronounced upon one in a state of moral desperation (Kant, *Religion,* A, 95); and this same hope gives one the assurance of being capable not only of self-condemnation but of improvement.

Thus, it is true that we can acknowledge our obligations through pure reason, and without religious foundation. But the contradiction in which the moral idea threatens to do away with itself does not arise before we understand these duties of ours "as divine commands"—as commands of the almighty creator and, at the same time, just and gracious judge. Such "recognition of all of our duties as divine commandments" is, according to Kant's definition, the essence of religion (Kant, *Religion,* A, 216).

This concept of religion on Kant's part has made possible an encounter between his philosophy and Judaism. For Judaism, as well, the center of religion lies not in acts of assent, but in acts of obedience to a command (Tora) that is understood as "God's commandment." And the central asseverations concerning God as creator, deliverer, and redeemer must be understood in connection with the question of how human obedience to God's commandment is possible for a person who has become a sinner amidst a world estranged from God.

There are points of commonality, then, between Kant's understanding of religion and Jewish trust in the God who will open to the chosen people, against all external opposition of enemies (and their own penchant for using the laws of nature for their own purposes), and against all of the internal opposition of a sinful heart, new paths to the execution of the divine commandments. These commonalities make it understandable that Jewish philosophers should have made Kant's manner of argumentation their own in a specific way. (For the following, see Schaeffler 1981a.)

Philosophy of Religion
as a Grammar of Commandment and Prayer:
Hermann Cohen, Franz Rosenzweig, and Martin Buber

The dialectic of reason in its practical use rests on the fact that persons are in need of conversion only because they still lack a good will, but are capable of this conversion only insofar as they already acknowledge the moral law and therefore already possess this good will. This contradiction is soluble if persons understand their duties "as divine commandments." Now they can grasp their guilt as guilt *before God,* and can have hope of being reestablished *by God* "in the task of moral freedom" (Cohen, *BR,* 65). Thus, Cohen apprehends God as the one who renders the human being capable of conversion through the forgiveness of sins; and he understands the human being as the one to whom such forgiveness of sins is promised, and who now can finally become a moral individual. "The being of God would not be available to conceptualization in its perfection unless the forgiveness of sins were to be [God's] own doing" (ibid., 243). But the philosophy of religion must describe the "correlation" between the God thus understood and the human being thus experienced.

Now, for this correlation, the "word" plays a decisive role—more specifically, the word of commandment (of which Kant had already spoken) and the word of prayer (whose meaning for the religious correlation Cohen seeks to present through a detailed interpretation of the liturgy of the Jewish Day of Atonement). More than forty years before J. L. Austin, Cohen called attention to the fact that commandment and prayer serve not to communicate anything that already is but to establish something that otherwise would not be. And decades before J. R. Searle, Cohen had coined the expression "speech act." According to Cohen's conviction, "prayer is the proper language of religion. And all of the thinking of this language, concerning God and concerning human beings, all of the thinking of this correlation, would remain theory, unless prayer were to become the speech act, in which the will becomes vital, with all means of thought" (Cohen, *BR,* 463).

In abiding connection with forgiveness and conversion, this will is directed upon two interdependent aims: upon the "sanctification of the name" (the manner in which the God before whom the sinner stands becomes present-and-invocable; cf. "Before you alone have I sinned," Psalm 51:4)—and upon the "unification of the soul" (the recall of the "I" to the totality, a recall that can succeed only in correlation with God's unicity).

This correlation between the antecedent oneness of God and the totality of the human being that this oneness renders possible, is cited in the two parts of the focal Jewish prayer: "Hear, O Israel: The Lord our God is *one* Lord. And you shall love the Lord your God with *the wholeness* of your heart, with the wholeness of your person, with the wholeness of your forces" (Deuteronomy 6:4–5). Here the unicity of God is the *condition* of all moral efforts at totality. Only because God is already one, can the human being gather his or her forces, in love for God, into a totality. But the "union of the divine name" is at the same time the *goal* of all of the human being's moral striving: only to the extent to which a person succeeds in fusing his or her own life into a totality, through love, does God in the divine oneness become open to experience and invocation for that person. Accordingly, all of the human being's moral service lives by the prophetic promise for the end of days: "On that day will the Lord be one, and his name one" (Zechariah 14:9). Thus Cohen can agree with the aphorism of the fathers, "Let all your dealings be to the name of God" (Cohen, *RV,* 402–3).

Commandment and prayer are distinguished as language behavior, through their grammatical form itself, from all declarative propositions. The declarative proposition speaks of its object in the third person, whether in the personal "he" and "she" or in the neuter "it." It is, as Cohen's younger friend Franz Rosenzweig says, a "he-she-it sentence." Perhaps we should be more precise: the declarative sentence, even when it is formulated in the first person ("I am a person") can be adopted by another speaker without alteration of its meaning and then enunciated in the third person ("He is a person."). This does not hold for commandment and prayer. The commandment, "the imperative, . . . does not abandon the circle of the I and thou" (Rosenzweig, *SE,* 2:126). And from the "I" and "you" of commandment we have the "I" and "you" of prayer: "In the place of the divine "I," which only God can utter, the divine name must come, which even human beings and the world can bear in their hearts" (ibid., 2:185).

Commandment and prayer are the examples par excellence of those speech acts in which the correlation between "I" and "you" materializes. The introductory formula of the commandment runs, "I am the Lord your God" (Exodus 20:2). The prayer of a person in need of the forgiveness of sins in order to become capable of conversion, begins with the confession, "Before you alone have I sinned." And to this confession of sins the speech act of forgiveness responds: "I forgive you, as you have said" (Numbers 14:20). Each of the passages cited contains the personal pronouns "I" and "you(r)." In combining these passages in such a way as to characterize the event that leads to the forgiveness of sins and conversion, Rosenzweig concretizes Cohen's positions on speech acts. It is Cohen's theory of conversion in terms of the philosophy of religion that has shown Rosenzweig the way to his philosophy of the "I" and "you."

Only in this connection of historical philosophy does Martin Buber's thesis become understandable: "The 'I' stands divided between the 'I-thou' and the 'I-it.'" Or again, "There is no independent 'I,' but only the 'I' of the 'I-thou' and the 'I' of the 'I-it'" (Buber, *IuD,* 79). The speech act in which the correlation between God and the human being is accomplished, the "I" and "Thou" of commandment and prayer, constitutes not only the world of objects (as throughout Kant's transcendental logic, as well as in Humboldt's transcendental consideration of language); first and foremost it constitutes the speaking "I" in a new quality of morality and religion. Only in the gathering to the divine "Thou" in its unicity does the human "I" find that totality of heart, of person, and of forces spoken of in the central Jewish prayer. "The basic expression I-Thou can only be spoken of with one's whole being. The basic expression I-it can never be spoken with one's whole being" (Buber, *IuD*, 79).

Thus, to the Kantian constitution of objects in acts of ideation and conceptualization is added, in the philosophy of religion of Hermann Cohen and his disciples and friends, the constitution of the subject in speech acts. The subject so constituted is irreplaceable, since no one can undergo conversion as the representative of someone else. Accordingly, Cohen has emphatically spoken of the "moral individual"; but Rosenzweig has espoused the "private subject," over against philosophy's anonymous reason (Rosenzweig, Urz. SE, 359). But this individual or private subject becomes, precisely through the speech acts of commandment and prayer, a member of the community. And the community understands itself as *locum tenens* of a future, universal language community of all persons, indeed, of everything that lives (see Rosenzweig, *SE*, 3:46). At the end of days, the last verse of the last psalm will reach fulfillment: "Let everything that has breath praise the Lord" (Psalm 150:6). The express manner in which Cohen and Rosenzweig orient themselves to prayers from the community liturgy in order to develop their philosophy of the "I and Thou" is clear: This philosophy defends the individual, to be sure; indeed, it even defends the "private subject" against its dilution into a simple moment of the supraindividual reason. But it is not "privatistic"; it remains referred to the community, its history, and its service to a future humanity.

Further-Reaching Applications of Cohen's and Rosenzweig's Theory of Religious Speech Acts

J. L. Austin has posed the question of what conditions must be fulfilled if speech acts are not to be "unsuccessful." J. R. Searle has described these conditions summarily with the indication that, in order to be effective, speech acts have need of an institutional framework—an intersubjectively acknowledged system of rules X, having the consequence that a behavior Y has the value of Z (see Searle 1969). The liturgical language of prayer, as well, investigated by Cohen and Rosenzweig, obviously presupposes such an institutional framework. For a general theory of speech acts, however, prayers for forgiveness and prayers of praise seem important because they not only presuppose the intersubjectively regulated connection of acts but actually contribute to its original materialization. Following this indication, the relation between speech act and institution will have to be determined otherwise than it did with Austin and Searle.

Rosenzweig has emphasized, in his considerations on the prayer of praise, the dative case as an essential element of the language of prayer. The Jewish celebration of the Sabbath, like the daily Divine Office of priests, monks, and nuns, begins with the psalm: "Come, let us sing *to the Lord*, shout joyfully *to the rock* of our salvation!" (Psalm 95:1). Rosenzweig comments: "The dative is the connector, the gathering element— . . . the point . . . at which all givers can join" (*SE*, 2:178–88). His use of the word "giver" plays on the fact that the word "dative" comes from the Latin *dare*, "to give." The speech act of thanksgiving, in which the speaker transforms his or her life from a life "for self" into a life "for God" opens at the same time the community-founding perspective, the common outlook on God's glory, to which the thankers surrender themselves in common. From the commonality of the prayer of praise, community arises. The concrete language community, then, with its concrete rules of speech, is here neither reduced to a simple conventional agreement, nor grounded on the legitimate authority of a legal instance, but is understood as the result of precisely those speech acts that at the same time represent the essential task of this institution. After all, the prayer of praise is not only the ground of emergence of the community; it is also its central communitarian task.

Now, although Cohen does not go into this explicitly, the community-founding dative also governs that confession of sins that stands at the beginning of conversion, and, in Cohen's conviction, indicates the moment of the birth of the moral individual. "Before you alone have I sinned," the psalmist prays. Were persons' guilt only guilt before themselves, their confession of guilt would be the expression only of a self-alienation, in which do-ers fail to recognize themselves in their deeds ("Even I don't understand how I could have done something like that"). Were sin only guilt before other individuals, and ultimately before humanity, then the confession of sin would be a special form of that "triumph of the species over the individual" that Feuerbach has described and has held to be the source of the religious misunderstanding: the individual acknowledges that only the human race can claim ultimate right. The human being who recognizes his or her own sinfulness exclusively before humanity, understands the moral law as the obligation to act only as a representative of the human race, as a moral "consciousness *simpliciter*," as *volonté générale*. Only when a human being knows herself or himself to be guilty "only before God" (*tibi soli*) can she or he hope to become capable of morality and yet not be extinguished as an individual. "The individual opens up to ethics in humanity. But the religious God . . . must be loved by persons, and indeed by each individual as such" (Cohen, *BR*, 80). "God's good in the specialty [that is, in the deed reserved to God alone] of the forgiveness of sins is the emblem of the moral world inasmuch as its members are individuals" (Cohen, *RV,* 251). The dative, "to you alone," which qualifies the confession of sins makes this speech act at the same time the source of the religious community in which the individual is neither isolated nor subsumed into an abstract generality. "Thus has arisen the community, as the sole corresponding unit for the sole task of religion" (Cohen, *RV,* 230).

Another lesson of Cohen and Rosenzweig for a general theory of speech acts can be learned. Between speech acts made possible by an institution, and institutions made possible and constantly renewed through these speech acts, obtains a mutual relationship of conditioning that can be read in the grammar of these speech acts. For a special theory of religious speech acts (and therewith for a philosophy of religion that participates in the linguistic turn), we can gather from Cohen and Rosenzweig the indication that not only does the world of religious objects constitute itself in the use of religious language, but the subject as such comes into being only in the implementation of religious speech acts. The correlation, implemented especially in the confession of sins and the prayer of praise, between the human being and the God who loves the individual and at the same time gathers the community—indeed, ultimately, humanity—in the praise of the divine name, at the same time reconciles the individual with the partial and universal community, instead of dissolving this individual anonymously in humanity or sacrificing him or her to the species.

PHILOSOPHY OF LANGUAGE AND THEOLOGY OF THE WORD: THE LINGUISTIC TURN IN THE ENCOUNTER OF PHILOSOPHY OF RELIGION AND CHRISTIAN THEOLOGY

After initial hesitation, the theologians have embraced the linguistic turn of the philosophy of religion and have thereby contributed to the preponderance, in the field of the philosophy of religion, of publications today that deal with the analysis of religious language. Precisely in this field, an intensive conversation has materialized between philosophers and theologians. This is understandable from the special theme of Christian theology. If Christ is revered as the Word made flesh, and if faith, which alone renders blessed, comes from hearing, then the doctrine of the divine Word, and the human word in its service, must be a central theme of Christian theology. But a theology of the word is especially apposite to the encounter with a philosophy of language.

Following is an indication, however brief, of three theological positions: we sketch them in order to show the manner in which theology, too, has embraced (alongside the positivistic and transcendental philosophical tradition) the linguistic turn. Here it cannot be the task of our considerations to evaluate these positions from a theological viewpoint. Instead, our aim will be to show how the results of such a theology can have importance for the philosophy of language in general and a linguistically oriented philosophy of religion in particular.

Theology as the Language Doctrine of Faith: Gerhard Ebeling

Gerhard Ebeling understands the word that God "brings to expression" in a manner that can be called transcendental. After all, this word does not bring to our knowledge a new object or set of facts, but alters the conditions under which all objects, be they only imaginable, become visible and understandable to the human being. "God's word . . . is not a light that, so to speak, streams forth God, but is a light that streams forth from God. . . . Thus the world acquires a new face for us" (Ebeling 1959, 255).

The transcendental character Ebeling's understanding of the word is also made clear by the fact that this author (here, not far from Rahner's position) sees the divine address to the human being at work wherever human beings experience it that the reality surrounding them concerns them, even when these persons know nothing of a particular, biblically attested address on the part of God. "The world, as the reality that concerns us, as it has always already come to expression, is already call, already question, even when not understood" (ibid.). In the encounter with the real, human beings, by virtue of that encounter itself, are constantly the summoned and the questioned, and this in such wise that "in their character as speaking beings, they are not in their own control" (Ebeling 1966, 57).

The human capacity for language—and this means, at the same time, human beings' humanness—must always be called forth anew. The enablement for language must come athwart the human being, must "oc-cur," ever and again. This is the "ground situation of the human being as word situation" (ibid., 54). And, in Ebeling's interpretation, it is the meaning of the word "God" to address human beings in their basic situation—indeed, to awaken them to their basic situation (ibid., 54, 61, 62). The word "God" designates the bestower of a "bestowal of speech . . . overlaid on the forces that render one speechless" (ibid., p. 74).

Thus understood, the word "God" designates an "already"—thus, an a priori of human existence, inasmuch as the latter can be understood as "capacity, summoned forth, for language." A central problem of Christian theology is the question of how the "word of God" relates to the word "God" in this understanding—thus, the biblically attested address of God to human beings, transmitted in the community of believers, and therefore by no means a priori, but involved in history.

> The word "God" is not an unambiguously biblical word, let alone a Christian word. It shimmers in all religious hues. Its use for the word that the Bible attests as the word of God is an endless struggle over the word "God." So understood, the word of God is the endless de-divinization of the word "God." (Ebeling 1966, 86)

Without the word "God," Christian preaching would be speechless and could no longer indicate what it speaks of and what it says. Thus, a hermeneutics of the word "God" is necessary in order to counter the allegation of meaninglessness leveled against religious language. However, the ever–a-posterioristic preaching of the word of God must not be transformed into a simple reminder to human beings of their a priori, of the conditioning of their capacity to speak at all, that is designated by the word "God." The old question of how a general philosophy of religion relates to a specifically Christian theology (and whether the concepts "general" and "specific" are applicable to this relationship at all), thus returns in Ebeling as the question of the relationship between the "word 'God'" and the "word of God." And one can say that Ebeling's formulations describe the shape that the old problem of the relation between the philosophy of religion and Christian theology has adopted, since both have made the linguistic turn (not meaning that this problem in the shape it has acquired today can be formulated only in Ebeling's fashion).

The suggestion for a solution that Ebeling develops rests on the thesis that the human ground situation of being summoned to speech, and being ever and again summoned to speech by reality, is basically flawed. The "'language of the world' is a formalized code for the speech-jumble of the world" (Ebeling 1971, 230). The language of faith, and with it "God's word," is necessary in order that language in general (whose ground of possibility is called by the word "God") may become once more precisely capable of what it is supposed to do: make it possible for there to be responsible, understandable, and communicating discourse. And thus we see that "the language of faith, for its part, means to be a language enabler—namely, a language help for life" (ibid., 226).

Ebeling expects from a theological doctrine of language such as he would seek to develop it, "that it make an important contribution to the doctrine of language in general" (ibid., 224-25). Were we to attempt to stipulate more exactly what this contribution could consist in, then the following indications could be given.

1. As Aristotle himself established, the capacity for speech is the distinguishing characteristic of human beings. This capacity for speech is like a window on reality. But at the same time, speechlessness is an ever-threatening danger. The capacity for speech can be acquired, can be lost, can change. Thus, it is contingent and has a history. The analysis of the "human ground-situation as word-situation"—that is, as a situation in which the human being is challenged to the capacity of speech by concrete challenges—therefore makes it legitimate to connect the transcendental reflection with the analysis of human historicity. (On another basis, the connection between historical and transcendental reflection is dealt with in Schaeffler 1976.)

2. Through its structure, language or speech prescribes conditions that any discourse must meet if it is to mean anything—if it is to refer to anything. Language is the a priori of discourse. Just as a thought can refer to no object when it violates the laws of logic—for example, by self-contradiction, so also can a discourse refer to nothing if it violates the laws of grammar—for example, the syntactic rules of sentence structure. But language is not an eternal a priori; rather, it acquires form and shape in the manner in which it is "used" in discourse. But discourse is possible only as discourse "in a language." Thus, as Ferdinand de Saussure has shown, there arises a reciprocal conditioning relationship between language and discourse (see de Saussure 1916, esp. intro. to chap. 3). This reciprocal relationship is constitutive of the human capacity for speech, and thereby of transcendentality in all of its forms. But nowhere can it be studied more clearly than in the example of the relationship of tension between the religious word and religious language—concretely, between the "word of God" as proclaimed. and that language that makes the "word 'God'" available. (On the historicity of the relationship between religious language and the religious word, see Schaeffler 1978.)

3. If we follow Ebeling's search for the sense of the word "God," attempting to name that ground that founds the contingent capacity for speech and therewith the human being's transcendentality, we are met with

the structural difficulties of any transcendental discourse: transcendental address must speak, and it thereby presupposes the capacity for speech; but it attempts to speak of what is presupposed by any ability to speak as its possibilitating condition. Plato himself knew that, on the same grounds, he could speak only in comparisons of the "sun" that communicates to objects their cognizability and to the understanding its power of cognition (Plato, *Pol.* 506Dff.). Discourse upon God is necessarily discourse at the limits of speech (see van Buren 1972).

Situations of Address—Experiences and Narratives—Theological Summary Formulae: Ingolf U. Dalferth's Efforts in the Area of a Speech Logic of Faith

Under the title *Sprachlogik des Glaubens* (Speech logic of faith; Munich, 1974), Ingolf U. Dalferth has selected certain "texts of analytic philosophy of religion, and theology, bearing on religious speech," and published them with an introduction of his own. "Speech Logic of Faith" would likewise have suited as a title of his *Religiöse Rede von Gott* (Religious discourse upon God; Munich, 1981). Decisive for Dalferth's position is the fact that he answers the question of the reference and meaning content of speech about God in an exclusively Christian sense. He emphasizes that "what 'God' means cannot be elucidated without recourse to Jesus and the experience of him by particular persons as address" (Dalferth 1981, 481). "God [is] identifiable only in the occurrence of the address experienced in Jesus" (ibid., 600).

With this, not only the pertinence but also the meaning content of discourse upon God is now decided. If "the referent intended by 'God' in Christian discourse is established through the Christian experiential situation, then through the same, in a manner, it is sketched out what predicators can be predicated of God" (ibid., 626). "Christian discourse upon God"—nor does other discourse than the Christian enter Dalferth's considerations—"is in this sense the recital of a multiplicity of experiences that persons have had with the subject of the address experienced in Jesus" (ibid., 666).

On these grounds, the question that was so important for Ebeling goes by the board: how "the word 'God'"—relates to the Christian "word of God." Or, stated more generally: For Dalferth, the question no longer exists of the relationship between the Christian faith and religion as it presents itself outside Christianity in its multiple forms. The conversation with philosophy—and specifically, with analytical philosophy—is not necessary, in Dalferth's conception, in order for Christians to gain an informed knowl-

edge of what they are speaking of when they use the word "God"; rather an
analysis of religious language serves only to preserve speech upon God from
the "bewitching of our understanding through the media of our language"
(Dalferth 1981, 15; cf. Wittgenstein, *PU*, part 1, no. 109). Christian discourse upon God requires reflection on language in order to escape this
beguilement; but it needs neither this reflection nor any other form of philosophy in order to be certain of its object and of the content of its enunciation.

True, Dalferth's formula, according to which "with [the word] 'God,' a
relationship is struck with the subject of the address experienced in Jesus"
(Dalferth 1981, 669), and all predications applied in discourse upon God
are "'zur Prädikation geronnene Erzählung," does not definitively solve the
problem of pertinence and meaning content. What does the concept "subject" denote, and in what sense is the word "address" applied, when the
intent is to speak of a subject that is distinct from the perceived speaker (in
this case, distinct from the human Jesus)? And what does it mean when the
subject of the address experienced in Jesus is called "God" and nothing
else? Many in Jesus' audience could know that, "in Jesus," they were
addressed by the spirit of post-prophetic Judaism, by the religious genius of
humanity, or even by the experience of futility and the strength of hope of
all victims of political and religious oppression in the history of humanity.
The word "God" obviously serves, with Dalferth, to lay out a multifaceted
experience in a unitary concept. But it would be presupposed, to this purpose, that the word would already be accompanied by a pertinence and
meaning content (if only in a form thus calling for correction). Otherwise,
it could no longer be claimed why and in what sense, in one's presentation
of the address experienced in Jesus, one's discourse is really upon God and
not upon something else.

For a concern with a philosophy of religion in terms of the linguistic
turn, Dalferth's undertaking is instructive in a number of respects:

1. First, it shows that the old question of whether the Christian faith is
a religion, or the end of all religions, returns even in terms of the "linguistic turn." The attempt to render the language of Christian faith fully independent of the language of religion (and of the religions!) would rob of its
language the Christian discourse of faith. For if it is claimed that the word
"God" wins pertinence and meaning content exclusively through a reference to the Christian ground situation (the situation of the address experienced in Jesus), then it becomes incomprehensible why, for the
presentation of this ground situation, the word "God" is used and not
some other word. And what holds for the word "God," we could show,

holds as well for other words used in the language of Christian faith, and
in other religions—for example, "to worship," or "to expect the coming
salvation," or "to be certain of the presence of this salvation despite all
appearances to the contrary."

2. On the basis of the observation that, in the effort to evince the preeminence of the Christian faith proclamation, Christian theology can risk
depriving precisely this proclamation of its language, the philosophy of religion is confronted by certain questions: Is there, shall we say, a form of religious speech acts (for example, the "elimination of strange gods") that
comports the danger that the implementation of such an act will result in
the cancellation of the very language in which alone it can be implemented?
Is the language of biblical faith, which refuses strange gods the designation
"gods," and foreign religions the character of "true religion," an example
of such self-annulling religious language? Does the confession of Christian
faith, inasmuch as it begins by contesting a reference and meaning content
of the word "God" apart from specifically Christian connections, in a second step render a reference and meaning content of this word undiscover-
able in specifically Christian connections as well?

If this is the case, then by annulling religion as such, the Christian faith
would end by annulling itself. A theory of this kind would be the form
assumed by a theology of the "death of God" when reformulated in terms
of the linguistic turn. (Paul M. van Buren comes to a like conclusion [van
Buren 1963].) Here Dalferth explicitly indicates that, with special methods
of the analysis of religious language, he comes to conclusions very similar
to those of J. A. T. Robinson's *Honest to God* (Robinson 1963).

Praise of God as Language of Faith, and the Doxological Origin of Speech concerning God: Geoffrey Wainwright and a New Foundation of Systematic Theology

If the Christian discourse of faith is not to be defined through a method of
presentation that will deprive it of its own language and thereby destroy it,
then it is advisable to observe this language of faith where it seems least
threatened by the danger of speechlessness: in the praises of divine worship.
Goeffrey Wainwright has undertaken an attempt to determine the reference
and meaning content of religious discourse through an analysis of the language of divine worship (Wainwright 1980). Wainwright's fundamental thesis runs: "The language of divine worship transmits the object upon which
theologians reflect. Without this object, theological discourse would have
no reference" (ibid., 21). Even the theology that develops its own scientific

language but finds its pertinence only through its reference to the language of divine worship is, "on its own level, doxological in a strict sense" (ibid.); that is, it is a discourse (*logos*) in the service of the apparition of the divine glory (*doxa*). It performs this service in that it "uses, in a dialectical reference, both Christian language and the language of the broader human community" (ibid., 3).

The point of departure of Wainwright's investigation, which he refuses to understand as a specific tractate in liturgical science but calls a new foundation for systematic theology, forms a concise analysis of religious speech acts. To the latter belong especially adoration, confession (as *confessio peccati* and *confessio laudis* alike), and supplication. All of these speech acts presuppose a specifically religious relation of the speaker to the God to whom that speaker turns and are at the same time directed to the active implementation of this relation. This relationship—Wainwright calls it the "relation of [public divine] worship" (ibid., 16)—is theologically described through the doctrine of the human being as the image of God, therefore through a theological expression that, for its own part, becomes understandable only in connection with divine worship and the meaning of the image in that worship. Christian discourse upon God, the human being, and the world presupposes this basic relationship: the human being speaks and acts in the world as God's image.

We cannot here undertake to report how, from this point of departure, Wainwright attempts a new approach to the most important themes of classic Christian theology: the doctrine of Father, Son, and Spirit, of the church, scripture and doctrinal tradition, of the one church in many communities, of the necessity of the *reformatio perpetua*, of the relationship of faith to the world and the ethical implications of this relationship. In his earlier work *Eucharist and Eschatology*, Wainwright had undertaken a trial run, as it were, of how from the viewpoint of divine worship even a theological teaching of the expectation of eschatological salvation can be formulated anew. Our own concern here will not be the fertility of Wainwright's thesis for theology, but will be its significance for a philosophy of religion in its linguistic turn. In this respect, we may make the following observations:

1. Wainwright's point of departure in public divine worship is peculiarly suitable for constituting a bridge between analysis of, on the one hand, speech acts, and, on the other, propositions as such. After all, adoration, proclamation, and other forms of speech used in divine worship employ the grammatical form of the proposition ("You alone are holy, you alone are the Lord, you alone are the most high") and raise the claim of truth for these propositions, but are primarily intended to accomplish an act. In such

enunciations, neither God nor human beings are told what sort of object that God is of whom the praises speak. Instead, persons making this prayer, by speaking these words, place themselves in a relationship to their God and to others making the same prayer. Or better: such persons accept for themselves a relation which they believe has already been bestowed from God's side. Analysis of an act-intention and of the claim of a preexisting truth no longer form, in an investigation that takes its point of departure in the analysis of the language of divine worship, any a priori exclusive alternatives.

2. Precisely this connection between claim to truth and intent to act, of proposition and speech-act in one and the same linguistic enunciation, affords an opportunity to shed light on what is specific in religious discourse and its linguistic form. With those exemplary propositions that are customarily used by representatives of analytical philosophy ("God is almighty," or "There will be a last judgment," and so forth), it becomes far less clear whether we are really dealing with religious enunciations or only with enunciations upon religious objects. The language of divine worship leaves no doubt.

3. Wainwright's investigation shows further that specifically Christian content, as well (for example, Christology and the doctrine of the Trinity, ecclesiology, and eschatology), can be subjected to the analysis of its linguistic utterances, which in their form can be observed also in non-Christian religions. Adoration, proclamation, profession, and so on, are no Christian monopoly in their form of speech. Precisely this observation opens the way for a renewed conversation between the philosophy of religion and theology—a conversation that with other analysts of religious language had threatened to be deprived of an object—a fructification of the conversation for both parties.

4. To be sure, one question is in need of further discussion. A point of departure in the language of divine worship occasions the danger, mentioned earlier, that religion's speech and life form may draw apart, as merely one among many speech and life forms, into an "autonomous language play" of its own. Now, in order to hold the language of divine worship open to encounter with the speech of the world (which, after all, is also spoken by the believer, outside the divine service), Wainwright has pointed to the religiously interpreted relationship to human world service in the divine service itself (see "The Earthly Task," in Wainwright 1980, 23–28). However, it would surely have to be more exactly determined how this special, religious service to the world (at hand in an exemplary manner in the prepa-

ration of bread and wine as the matter of the sacrament of the Eucharist) relates to the human being's workaday world. It is obvious that the daily praxis and speech of the hunter and gatherer, the shepherd and the farmer, found relatively easy access to the praxis and speech of divine worship, but that the daily praxis and speech of industrial labor seem to present certain difficulties to their adoption in the action and speech of divine worship.

5. Wainwright's attempt to establish reference and meaning content of speech upon God through "pertinence to divine worship" permits not only a nexus between his findings and the considerations in the area of philosophy of religion of Cohen and Rosenzweig on the language of commandment and prayer, but also a confrontation with more recent findings of the theological discussion in France and Germany. It appears as no coincidence that, instead of the theme "speaking of God," it is the theme "to call God by name" ("nommer Dieu"), since Paul Ricoeur injected it into the discussion (Ricoeur 1977), that has occupied philosophers of religion and theologians (cf. the joint work edited by Bernhard Casper, *Gott nennen* [Naming God; Freiburg and Munich, 1981]). The doxological invocation of the divine name (or of an abundance of names for the divine excellence and glory) seems an especially promising approach to problems of the philosophy of religion in function of its linguistic turn.

CHAPTER 6

Philosophical Theology, Phenomenology of Religion, Analytics of Religious Language:

A Review of Three Methodological Approaches to the Philosophy of Religion, and a Systematic Outlook

———❖———

COMPARATIVE REVIEW AND CRITICAL EVALUATION

THREE OF THE METHODOLOGICAL POINTS of departure developed by the philosophy of religion in the course of its history have made especially fertile questions possible and have led to especially rich results: the points of departure in a philosophical doctrine of God, phenomenology, and philosophy of language. This becomes especially clear in a comparative review. Such a review can show, at the same time, that each of these starting points offers specific possibilities, but comes up against its own specific boundaries. Thus, no one of them can replace the other two. It is understandable, accordingly, that the philosophy of religion should be practiced in such different ways. However, at the same time, the question arises: Could the philosophy of religion not broaden its possibilities, fine-hone its methods, and come to better-founded results if it could manage to splice these three methods together?

Examination of the Types of Philosophy of Religion in Terms of Their Preferred Thematics

The two oldest types of philosophical inquiry into religion rested on the attempt to specify the special character of philosophical thinking as over against that of religion. This occurred in two ways: Religious thought and

106

action could be conceptualized as the expression of a "prerational consciousness"; or else one could undertake to transform religion into philosophy. Both manners of philosophical commerce with religion have been practiced from the first appearance of philosophy until today.

The first starting point is applied especially to findings of religious ethnology—therefore to the description of cultures that have not yet reached the development of a philosophical or scientific thought. There religion answers questions and fulfills functions that in cultures with a developed philosophy and science have become tasks of so-called rational thinking. Philosophy and science then contemplate, in these cultures, their own prehistory.

The second starting point serves above all as a self-corrective to philosophy and science, once a first disappointment with "rational thought" has entered the scene. This holds especially for the phase of an awakening criticism of ancient sophistry; but it is applicable as well to the time that followed the triumphant advances of the modern Enlightenment (that is, to the intellectual turn of the late eighteenth and early nineteenth centuries), or to the present, in which a unidimensional scientific thinking has come to an obvious crisis. In situations of this kind one sees that an all too cavalier criticism of religion easily loses important thematic fields from view and is helpless in the face of tasks that ought not to remain unperformed in the interest of individuals and society. Then it lies in the interest of philosophy and science themselves to allow themselves to be reminded of these thematic fields and these tasks by religion. Granted, the goal of the effort then remains, to incorporate these thematic fields and tasks into the philosophical and scientific effort and thus, in this respect as well, to install philosophy and science as the "heir" of religion.

The fertility of both starting points is beyond question. The first, the gaze of philosophical and scientific thought on its "prehistory," transmits to philosophy and science a consciousness of their own historicity and contingency: philosophy and science were not always, and have not arisen everywhere. The second point of departure, the attempt to take over from religion questions and insights that have not yet become accessible to philosophy and science in the course of their development until now, can protect philosophical and scientific thought from impoverishment of content and can open to it heretofore closed fields of question and investigation.

Just as apparent, of course, is the methodological danger inherent in both approaches: The latter never describe religion except as the "other from philosophy"—that which contrasts with themselves, be it as their "prehistory," be it as the fund of that "legacy" that philosophy and science mean to inherit after the "death of God." Religion is not asked what it itself wants to say, but only how it can help the philosopher and the scientist, who take their distance from it and thereby gain their self-understanding, to a clarification of precisely this self-understanding. The viewpoint under which religion is here regarded appears defined and narrowed through an interest that does not include that of religion's very themes.

The three other types of philosophy of religion set forth in the present investigation seek to avoid this danger. This holds for the philosophy of religion on the basis of a philosophical theology, as for the phenomenology of religion and the various approaches to an analysis of religious language.

The first type—*the philosophy of religion on the basis of a philosophical theology*—seeks to determine the *specificum* of religious thought, speech, and action from the viewpoint of their content: Religious persons think of God (and of all else only insofar as he or she grasps it in its relationship to God), speak of God (and of all else only insofar as, in all that can be spoken of at all, they proclaim the mighty deeds of God or hopes in God's salvific deeds as redemption from the experience of an unsaved reality), and relate in their actions to God (and to all else only insofar as they seek to fulfill God's will therein). But philosophers, so they think, can only know what religion unalterably says if they have antecedently grasped, in philosophical wise, what the object of discourse is when God is spoken of. In the terminology of more recent philosophy of language, one can express this approach to an understanding of religion thus: A philosophical doctrine of God is first accredited in its own competence of *reference* to all religious thinking, speaking, and acting—and only thereby becomes capable of grasping the specifically religious *meaning content* of this theory and praxis. Only in that it has learned to speak philosophically of God does such a philosophy of religion hope to be capable of asking, thereupon, what religion—in its peculiarity as over against philosophy—can say of this God.

While philosophical theology, and the kind of philosophy of religion based on it—takes its primary orientation in the central *content* of religion—in the God-relation of religious thinking, speaking, and acting—by contrast, the newest type, *the philosophy of religion according to the "linguistic turn,"* seems primarily interested in the form of religious consciousness, as this form is "legible" in the grammar of religious language. This turn from content to form seems to many observers a regrettable impoverishment in philosophically relevant content. The clearer it becomes that religious and philosophical discourse are structurally distinct from each other, the less likely it looks that religion will have anything to say that philosophers too should have to take account of in their own efforts of clarification of questions and acquisition of fruitful answers. Religion, which speaks its own language, would have nothing to say to the philosopher, who moves in structurally different linguistic connections.

But above all else, this manner of consideration seems to lead to a bracketing of religion's claim to truth. One who asks primarily not what religion says, but how it speaks, can leave to one side the claim of truth alleged by religion precisely for the content of its enunciations. For that matter, persons whose interests lie here can prosecute their investigations even if persuaded that religious discourse speaks of nothing and says nothing. After all, even then it remains a specifically structured linguistic enunciation, whose formal singularity can be investigated.

But even the investigator who wishes to raise no "suspicion of meaninglessness" of this kind can still interpret the structural difference between religious and philosophical discourse in the sense that what we have are (at least) two "autonomous language plays," which, while, granted, they do not criticize each other, do not learn anything from each other either. The one question that then seems left open is whether the same person can alternately participate in distinct "language plays" (for example, that of science and that of religion), and consequently can simultaneously or successively exist in two structurally distinct "ways of life."

Thus the danger arises of losing, through an exclusive interest in form, the capacity for a dialogue with religion having a reference to content. To be sure, this danger has a greater chance of besetting the philosophy of religion "in terms of the linguistic turn": the chance of allowing religion to express itself without philosophical transformation in its religious peculiarity. The history of those philosophies of religion that have been undertaken on the basis of philosophical theologies has shown that a philosophy of religion antecedently assuring itself, through a philosophical concept of God, of the *reference* of religious discourse has already decreed its decision as to the *meaning content* of religious thinking, speaking, and acting. After all, a like philosophy of religion makes it necessary to interpret this meaning content in such a way that it remains possible to ascribe the content of religious enunciation as predicate to the God already grasped as subject. For example: If we are convinced on philosophical grounds that the concepts "God" and "being" are interchangeable, then we must interpret all religious enunciations "ontologically," and conceptualize all religious praxis as "stepping beyond (categorical) being to being itself." And the question poses itself: Are we not thereby already prejudicing our understanding of religion in an irrelevant and at the same time uncontrollable (by us) manner? The analysis of religious language, on the other hand (and its apposite methodological doctrine or "analytics"), precisely in that it provisionally "shelves" all problems relating to content and is interested exclusively in the form of religious speech and action, avoids this danger of an irrelevant preconception.

Weighing the pros and cons (the dangers) of these two types of philosophy of religion, we seem to see the *phenomenology of religion* as the necessary synthesis of a content-oriented and a form-related consideration of religion. The basic phenomenological principle according to which noesis and noema strictly correspond permits one to define, through an analysis of the form of the religious act (its "logic"), at the same time the specific manner of its object reference (its "sense"), and the essential structure of its objects (its *eidos*—Greek, outward appearance). The phenomenology of religion as "sense logic of the religious act" and "eidetics of the religious subject" avoids the one-sidedness of purely content-related philosophical theology and purely form-related analytics of religious language.

It is therefore comprehensible that precisely representatives of the empirical religious sciences should have preferred to take advantage of this kind of philosophy of religion in casting about for a philosophical basis for their own disciplines. On the one hand, the phenomenological method has permitted them to go beyond the gathering of purely empirical facts and to formulate questions of essence, thereby securing criteria for the selection and assessment of the material with which their investigations deal. On the other hand, a point of departure in the form of the religious act and its "logic" makes it possible to avoid the foreign infiltration of religious phenomena by preconceived philosophical notions (for instance, philosophical concepts of God).

Examination of the Same Types of Philosophy of Religion in Terms of Their Methods

In terms of its *thematic center of gravity*, then, the phenomenological type wins out. While philosophical theology concentrates in the main on the content of religion, and linguistic analysis looks to the formal characteristics of the religious act, phenomenology connects questions of content and form in a methodologically mediated unity.

The picture changes, however, when, instead of comparing these types of philosophy of religion in terms of their thematic concerns, we consider them in terms of their *methods*. E. Husserl himself, the founder of philosophical phenomenology, discerned the risk of phenomenology's degeneration into a simple enumeration of examples, unless it remains *consistently transcendentally oriented* (see Husserl, *Ideen I*, 216). The strict correlation of noesis and noema is available to our grasp and retention only when it becomes clear that all objects of our theory and praxis are only constituted by the acts of perception, thinking, and willing—that, consequently, these acts are not to be analyzed as psychologically describable conditions of our experience but are to be reconstructed from the peculiarity of the object-field constituted in them. The structure of the religious act is mirrored in the eidos of religious objects.

We see the like when we weigh the pros and cons of a philosophy of religion after the linguistic turn. A linguistically oriented philosophy runs the risk of entrapment in a simple positivistic substitution (that knows in advance what kind of enunciations are "meaningful") and an a priori relativistic theory of the "autonomous wordplay" (that holds all wordplays as equally valid, none as open to criticism). It can escape this danger only when the consideration of religious language is connected with transcendental methods, somewhat after the fashion of Cassirer's or Hermann Cohen's philosophy of language.

Both the phenomology of religion and the analysis of religious language, then, in order to fulfill their tasks, have need of the transcendental method. But not even the application of transcendental methods to religious phenomena is immune to dangers of false methodological orientation. The specific possibilities and dangers of a like transcendentally oriented philosophy of religion are nevertheless discovered not so much by phenomenologists or analysts as by the representatives of a specific kind of *philosophical theology:* the discourse upon God in terms of transcendental philosophy. Thus, with respect to a sharper consciousness of method, the nod must go to philosophical theology over the phenomenology of religion and the analytics of religious speech.

The danger just mentioned, inherent in a transcendental consideration of religious phenomena, consists in this, that it can be constrained, on the basis of its methodological point of departure, to contradict a priori, on a central point, religion's self-understanding, without examination of possible contrary arguments. Granted, the philosophy of religion obviously must have the right to judge religious convictions as without an object, or false. But in the case before us, there is the danger of pressure, generated by its method, to claim to know that religious consciousness is in error even before the confrontation with this consciousness has so much as begun. After all, transcendental philosophy rests on the claim that the acts of regarding, thinking, willing, speaking, and so on, belong to the conditions that alone constitute the objects given to them as objects. Thus, Kant could say that reason prescribes the laws of the objects of experience. But although this holds for the acts of *religious* regarding, thinking, willing, and speaking, the conclusion seems to be that the reality to which the religious person is related is constituted only through this person's religious acts. But this claim seems a priori a-religious.

After all, the religious person may very well grant that sacred places and signs, sacred actions in sacred times, indeed the whole world into which such places, times, and actions are inserted, gain and maintain their specifically religious character only where they are "seen with religious eyes" or "interpreted in religious concepts." What for the religious person is a hierophany, for the profane person is perhaps an unexpected natural phenomenon, or a societal crisis. As soon as this interpretation is applied to the central religious reality, however, to God, now religious persons will refuse to recognize that whereof they speak in the interpretation of transcendental philosophy. This interpretation seems to amount to this, that even the God spoken of in religious terms, celebrated in religious actions, and conceived of in religious terms, emerges as this specially religious reality only from the religious act as such. But for the religious person this would be a preeminent form of "idolatry."

As a cautionary example, Kant, the founder of the more recent transcendental philosophy, is again cited. Kant is constrained through his manner of argumentation to the following conclusion:

> It sounds dubious, but is in no way reprehensible, to say: each person makes a God—indeed, in moral terms . . . must make one, in order to reverence, in God, the one who has made God. In whatever fashion one being is recognized and described as God by another, or indeed would like to appear as one himself (if that is possible), he must first of all join this conceptualization with his ideal, in order to judge whether he is authorized to hold and reverence it as a divinity. (Kant, *Religion*, B 257, n.).

God understood in terms of transcendental philosophy is, as Kant himself admits in this locus, a "self-made god." But then it appears a foregone conclusion when Feuerbach, who expressly appeals to Kant's transcendental reflection, comes to the thesis that, where religious persons think they speak of God, in reality they are speaking of themselves, since a self-made God is nothing other than the divinity of the human subjectivity itself, projected outside and become the object.

The danger of a transcendental consideration of religion appears especially evident, then, where the central content of religion itself, God, is to be understood transcendentally. On the other hand, a transcendental consideration of religion also affords specific advantages. These consist primarily in the opportunity to grasp the old concept of God's transcendence in a new way, through considerations of the kind just presented, and thereby to avoid two shortcomings of the traditional concept of transcendence.

The first deficiency in the traditional manipulation of concepts consists in this, that it makes it necessary first of all to constrict in some way the concept of the "world" (that is, the totality of what is and can be), in order thereupon to be able to hold that, "beyond" the world, something or someone (the Holy or the Divine) possesses a special kind of reality. "World," then, appears as that part of reality that is immediately accessible to our experience, understanding, and thinking; the "transcendent" (that beyond the world) is now to be that part of reality that does not show itself to us directly yet operates in a determining way upon the part of all reality that is given to us—for example, through creation, preservation, specification to and attraction to an end, or indeed through special acts of wondrous interference in this connection of events. But in this fashion the boundary between the "world" and the "transcendent" is defined by way of the relationship with the human power of cognition. Where "the world" ends and the "transcendent" begins for reasoning subjects of an entirely different kind, in case there were to be such elsewhere in space, would not be understandable by us human beings. Thus, the concept of transcendence would become relative.

The second flaw in this pretranscendental consideration of God bears on the concept of religion. Religion as the human being's relation and bond to the Holy and divine (and thereby to the "transcendent") would have to be understood as a relation that, at least in our ordinary experience, remains inaccessible. But in such an understanding religion would be relegated to the sphere of extraordinary, "supernatural" events—for example, theophanies and wonders—and the danger would arise that any connection between "supernaturally revealed truth" and "naturally experienced life" would be lost.

These deficiencies can be avoided if the concept of "transcendence" is understood in a transcendental sense. If the "world" is not the sum of the realities presupposed by our acts of regarding, thinking, willing, and speaking but the totality of objects that are only constituted through this activity on the part of the subject, then all that does not proceed from our subjectivity, but is precisely made possible by that subjectivity, will be "transcendent," as opposed to the world. The "transcendent" will then be not just another part of reality, that only for us (because of the boundedness of our cognitional faculty) does not belong to the realm of what can be experienced and cognized in the everyday, while for another, superhuman consciousness it could altogether be a part of "this being's world." Instead, if it is understood transcendentally, the "transcendent" will be the ground of possibility of the subject's being enabled to perform its acts of the constitution of objects. So understood, religion as the relation to this ground of possibility of human transcendentality is as "natural" to the human being as the capacity is natural to the eye to find that light reflected in all of the colors and forms of the visible world that renders these colors and shapes visible. Correspondingly, we have the finding of religious science that, for the religious person, everything can be a hierophany, not only the extraordinary and unusual. Everything available to experience also reveals to a person that "source of light" to which every "manifestation" whatsoever owes its potential.

Thus, a comparison of the three bases of the philosophy of religion in terms of their methods has led to this conclusion: For the establishment of a *phenomenology* that goes beyond a simple recital of empirical findings, a transcendental method is indispensable. Just as indispensable is this method if *speech analysis* is to get beyond the fruitless struggle between the positivists and the language-play theoreticians, of whom the former come up with an ever further-reaching "suspicion of meaninglessness," while the others blur the pursuit of truth and thereby can no longer discuss the possibility of an encounter among various kinds of language play and manners of life. A transcendental approach, then, is indispensable, both for phenomenology and for the analysis of religious language. But nowhere are the dangers, as well as the opportunities for an application of transcendental methods to religious phenomena, so clearly front and center as where the attempt is made to use such methods in order to indicate the matter of discourse when God is spoken of—where, then, a *philosophical discourse upon God* is attempted that utilizes transcendental methods.

Therefore one may suppose that, in the doctrine of God as maintained in transcendental philosophy—this newest form of philosophical theology to date—and in the philosophy of religion founded thereon, a heightened consciousness of method has been developed; but it is reserved for the future that the transcendental doctrine of God should produce thrusts to a further development of the phenomenological and linguistic-analysis methods that will be conscious of its methods.

How these impulses of renewal could look will be indicated in our closing systematic view. First, however, we must show that, despite the preference cited above for the methods of transcendental philosophy, the analysis of religious language, too, can make its own irreplaceable and indispensable contribution to a renewal of the philosophy of religion.

The Same Types of the Philosophy of Religion
with Respect to the Specification of Criteria of the Religious

The philosophy of religion relates, by way of interpretation, explanation, and criticism, to a complex of phenomena that occurs in the life of individuals and communities and is empirically observable. The philosophy of religion need not "invent" religion: it finds religion as a given (even though many philosophers of religion adopt a project of going beyond, and ultimately replacing, this "empirical" religion with a "reasonable" one).

But if the point of departure is to be the empirically given, then it is necessary to circumscribe, with as much certainty as possible, that area of phenomena to which the interpretation, explanation, and critique of the philosophy of religion is to relate, and in terms of which it must justify itself. The philosophy of religion needs a criterion for a decision whether a phenomenon can count as "religious" (and therefore belong to its area of competence) or not. However, the acquisition of such a criterion has turned out to be unexpectedly difficult. The pre-concepts of "religion" that do not *emerge* from considerations of the philosophy of religion, but are *given*, since they already govern the choice of the phenomena that count as important, have always shown themselves too broad or too narrow.

Too broad, for instance, is a concept of religion that qualifies all phenomena as "religious" in which in any way an ultimate grounding or an ultimate value comes to expression. Here, any metaphysics (even when it understands itself as emphatically irreligious), or any certitude of value-preferences, would have to count as "religion" (even when it is a matter of the praxis of atheists). Too narrow, on the other hand, would be, for instance, a concept of religion that would regard phenomena as "religious," and therefore in the purview of the philosophy of religion, only when it brings to expression a relation of the human being to a transcendent God. Both the concept "God" and the concept "transcendent" are ordinarily used by philosophers in such a way that most of the beings revered in the religions do not fall under this concept. The "gods of the religions" are, for example, neither almighty nor eternal nor bodiless. And they appear, in the conviction of the members of most religions, as altogether "natural" in relations of daily experience, and in this sense by no means "transcendent." Thus, assuming a philosophical concept of God in the philosophy of religion, the result will be that, in such a regard, most of the phenomena occurring in the religions could simply not count as manners of the "relation to a transcendent God," and consequently would not be "religious phenomena." And so a philosophical theology, even when it uses transcendental methods, usually turns out to be unsuitable for erecting criteria that would make it possible to distinguish religious phenomena from the profane.

Precisely this task is supposed to meet the demands of the phenomenological "essential concept." It is to serve to delineate a "class" of acts, and a corresponding "region" of objects, that thereupon can be presented to a given science or group of sciences as a field of themes. According to this program, the "essential concept" of the Holy would make the "class" of religious acts and the "region" of religious objects distinct from other acts and objects with sufficient certainty.

Rarely, however, do the methods of phenomenology lead to the desired result. The question of the "logic of meaning of religious acts," and the corresponding "basic manner of the given of religious objects," is only answerable when two conditions are met. First, acts must be indicated that can count as examples of the specifically "religious act." Second, these acts must be of such a kind that their "meaning-logic"—that is, the structural peculiarity on which their relation to a specific object-region rests—can be unambiguously gathered from them. Not all examples brought forward by the phenomenologists of religion fulfill both requirements at once.

For example, sacrifice counts as a typically religious act. It would be a good example of a religious act, if only its immanent logic were not so ambiguous. Is it the attempt, as Alfred Bertholet holds, to enter into a relationship of giving and receiving with otherworldly powers (Bertholet 1942)? Or is it, as Gerardus van der Leeuw suggests, a technique for making available and releasing the cycle of life-promising powers (van der Leeuw 1920/21)? Or is it, as Thomas Aquinas supposes, not a goal action at all, but an action of expression (Thomas Aquinas, *S. Th.* II-II, q. 81, a. 7)? The variety of such interpretations of sacrifice entails a multiplicity of conceptualizations as to how the religious act, for which sacrifice will serve as a particularly good example, is structured, and what sort of reality is "basically given" to this act and consequently is to be addressed as a specifically religious reality in which, then, the "meaning-logic" of the religious act and the "kind of being" of religious objects are to be seen.

In contrast to sacrifice, with its many ambiguities, there is another group of acts that play a role in religions and whose "sense logic" seems altogether unambiguous. We mean acts of evaluation, which are distinguished by the fact that, on the one hand, they bear upon "highest values," and, on the other hand, gather all other "classes of value" into a "realm of values" (cf. Scheler, *EiM;* and Spranger, PPR). Religious persons, by a gift of self to the God they "love above all things," submit, for the sake of that God, all that is in any way experienced as a value or an anti-value to the unity of a supreme cluster of values. But are such acts of evaluation, and of the organization of a "realm of values," of a specifically religious nature? Are there not also expressly secular manners of relating to values and of the hierarchization of values, indeed manners of relating that are out and out hostile to religion? Of course, one can find a language usage that calls all of these acts "religious," and any life determined by such acts "religion." In that case, where these acts are performed in a tendency subjectively deprived of religion or even inimical to religion, one can speak of "unconscious piety," perhaps even of "substitute religion." But such language procedures are forced; and it is methodologically dangerous to base the philosophy of religion on a concept of the "religious act" that needs such forcing.

Thus, sacrifice is doubtless a religious act, but one of scarcely transparent meaning-logic. The relation to values and the hierarchization of values is of a clearly transparent meaning-logic, but its religious character is not unambiguously open to observation. It is understandable, then, that phenomenologists of religion like Max Scheler and Friedrich Heiler should have turned their attention to a third group of religious acts, whose religious character seems evident, and whose meaning-logic at the same time seems unambiguous: acts of prayer. Here, as we have shown above, once more within the phenomenological school, the attention of philosophers of religion has been directed to an especially revealing group of linguistic utterances: the language of prayer. It is held that, in the language of prayer, the act-structure and the relation to reality of the religious act will be studied in exemplary fashion.

Such investigations on the meaning-logic of prayer build the bridge between the method of the phenomenology of religion and the method of the analysis of religious enunciations. And if, as we have shown, even as important a phenomenologist of religion as Friedrich Heiler has not escaped the danger of arbitrary interpretation and evaluation, then the supposition suggests itself not that it is his choice of examples that is unhappy but that the apposite methods for an analysis of the language of prayer were not yet available to him.

This means, for the interrelationship of the three methods here described that, owing to its special manner, act-structure, and object-relationship, by way of the "basic phenomenological law," the phenomenological method wins a preeminence with regard to a choice of themes. As for method, the doctrine of God in transcendental philosophy is to be ascribed a preeminence, since without the transcendental method neither can phenomenology and linguistic analysis reach their appointed goal. But the analysis of religious speech, especially the speech of prayer, wins a preeminence when it is a matter of obtaining criteria on which the religious act and its meaning-logic clearly distinguish themselves.

Three Approaches to a Solution and the
Question of Their Connection

The reflections set forth immediately above could occasion the impression
that their purpose would be to accord equal rights to each of the three types
of philosophies of religion that have been particularly considered in this
investigation, and therefore to ascribe to each of them a preeminence, from
a particular viewpoint, over the other two. A concern for a balance of this
kind could, it is true, stand as the expression of a pacific attitude, and—
more importantly when it comes to scientific considerations—an unpreju-
diced readiness to learn. However, such an aim would be open to the
suspicion that necessary decisions were being sidestepped by way of a non-
commital "both . . . and." The simple reflection that the various approaches
to a philosophy of religion were of equal worth, and that each had priority
over the other two in a different given respect, and would be a question of
viewpoint, is in itself without consequence for the concrete effort to formulate and to solve problems by way of a scientific approach. To this purpose, it is necessary to bring the three approaches into mutual connection.

In quest of such a convergence, let us begin with a purely schematic formulation. Transcendental methods as have been developed—precisely on
account of the especially clear experience of their difficulties and dangers—
from the *trancendentally conceived philosophical doctrine of God,* appealing to
examples whose particular religious trait can be developed through an
analysis of religious language (especially the language of prayer), finally prepare the prerequisite for an adequate formation of the themes addressed by
a *phenomenology of religion.*

The examination presented here of questions, assumptions, and methods of the philosophy of religion has a descriptive character. Its intent is to
facilitate a survey of what, in the efforts of philosophy to gain an understanding and an elucidation of religious phenomena, has been accomplished in the past and is under discussion in the present. It would not be
within the framework of such a presentation to attempt here to develop our
own conception of the philosophy of religion or to suggest pathways for its
further development. But the results of the critical comparison just
attempted do call for at least a basic systematic evaluation. On the one
hand, it would be unsatisfactory to rest content with the twofold observation that it is not enough simply to distinguish from one another the various questions, premises, and methods of the philosophy of religion, and
that it is necessary to connect them with one another. On the other hand,
the program formulation that we have now offered, whose purpose is to
indicate how such a connection could look, is all too formulaic and

schematic. And so we must attempt, in a final systematic outlook, to impart somewhat more content to this programmatic formulation.

A SYSTEMATIC VIEW

A comparison of the questions, premises, and methods of the philosophy of religion has shown that both philosophical phenomenology in general (and in particular the phenomenology of religion) and the philosophical analysis of speech (and in particular of religious language) need transcendental methods if they are to accomplish their task. On the other hand, it has become clear that the application of transcendental methods to religious phenomena comports special risks, which appear especially when transcendental philosophy fails to develop a concept of God. Such a concept of God seems a priori—that is, antecedently to an argumentational confrontation—to contradict the religious understanding of discourse upon God. The God of the transcendental philosophers seems to be a "self-made God"; the God of the religions, on the other hand, is a "real" God, independent of all human activity, whose free will determines whether and how the human being can become active.

Should we rest with this immediate confrontation, then a philosophy of religion that makes use of transcendental methods could present the religious discourse upon God only in such a manner as would have it at the same time withdraw from its object, the real God. Philosophy of religion on the basis of theology in terms of transcendental philosophy would then fall back into an older form of philosophy of religion, one that we had believed was moot: philosophy of religion as an attempt to transform religion into philosophy (see above, chap. 2).

Whether this consequence can be avoided will therefore appear where, on the basis of transcendental philosophical discourse upon God, the attempt is made to lay out religious language concerning God critically, but without transforming it into philosophy. After all, a philosophical presentation will have to be *critical:* therefore it cannot be a matter of unquestioningly making the self-understanding of religion the judge of philosophical theories of religion. Often enough, philosophy enlightens the religious person regarding certain self-misunderstandings. But a philosophical teaching of God, also and precisely when it makes use of transcendental methods, will have to remain *hermeneutic;* nor, then, can it be a question of leaving unobserved the peculiarity of religious acts and the special structure of religious language. Precisely the phenomenology of religion has warned against this, and rightly. Philosophers withdraw themselves from the object of their reflection if they think that they can engage the reality of which they would speak outside the relationship between noesis and noema. Philosophers of religion must not think, then, that they know the reality of God apart from the relationship between the specifically religious noesis and the specifically religious noema. Rather, their task consists in making the meaning-logic of the religious act understandable; and correspondingly, when the philosophy of religion makes use of methods of speech analysis. Even here its task consists not in translating the language of religion into the language of philosophy but in making the specific intentionality of religious language understandable.

Philosophy of religion on the basis of philosophical theology (and in a particular way on the foundation of a speech upon God in terms of transcendental philosophy) has the double task, then, of a criticism of religion and at the same time an exposition of religion in its self-presentation. It contains a hermeneutic proffer to religious consciousness to understand itself better in its own meaning-logic and intentionality, and to become critically attentive to dangers of its own possible faulty composition.

Transcendental Doctrine of God as Hermeneutic Proffer to Religious Consciousness

The moment the attempt is made to make religious consciousness a proffer of its self-presentation and its self-understanding, it must be taken into account that religious persons resist such an attempt. This resistance is by no means irrelevant to the attempt of a speech upon God in terms of transcendental philosophy, as if the philosopher knew how to speak of God better than did the religious person. Rather, such resistance makes it clear of what kind the religious act is—how it is distinguished from the act of philosophical reflection and argumentation, but especially, in what manner that reality of which religious persons would speak confronts them in their specifically religious acts. Those seeking to speak of God with the method of transcendental philosophy will have to take this resistance on the part of religious persons into account, in order critically to assess whether they have not already, through the choice of their methods, failed their task of speaking of God.

Religious persons fear that, through a transcendental understanding of religion, and especially through a concept of God in terms of transcendental philosophy, the living God, who demands worship and obedience, the God to whom the devout turn with petition in need and danger, who forgives them their sins and from whom they hope for forgiveness, will become a product of reflection, or an idea mirroring random mental objects. The philosopher of religion who would make use of transcendental methods must be prepared to accept these fears on the part of the religious person as a call to critical self-examination. Nevertheless, this philosopher can attempt to answer these critical inquiries with the following counter-questions:

The religious person speaks of a God who demands "worship and obedience"—one to whom a person can turn with the "petition for deliverance from need and forgiveness of guilt." But what the concepts "worship and obedience," "petition and trust," mean, when these acts refer not to earthly powers but to God, is by no means clear without explanation.

Neither is religious consciousness a priori immune to illusions here. Faulty forms of religious theory and practice in history sufficiently evince this. Thus, it is indeed at least worth examining whether it is not also, and precisely here, in the sense of religious awareness, that a proffer of interpretation could be helpful—one that would assist the religious person to understand these concepts in a transcendental sense. "Worship" or "adoration" would then be that act in which persons regard their being, all of their capacities in theoretical and practical reference to the reality of the world, their capacity for contemplation and thought, for speaking and acting, as owing to a reality independent of themselves. Religious persons will say that they confess this reality as the "light of their eyes," or understand it as the power that has "smoothed the path for their feet." These expressions from religious language obviously denote the enabling conditions of religious theory and practice. A transcendental understanding of God could help toward a clearer view of how such an enablement of human "seeing" and "walking" is to be conceived.

Religious persons tell us that obedience to God's command delivers them from worldly constraints. But it remains to be asked how the distinction is more precisely to be grasped through which this liberating obedience is distinguished from submission to worldly powers. An especially typical example of a religious understanding of the connection between obedience to God and deliverance from worldly powers is to be found in the verse introducing the Ten Commandments: the Lord, who binds the children of Israel in obedience to his commandments, calls himself the deliverer, who "has led you out of Egypt, out of the house of slavery" (Exodus 22:2). Obedience, in a religious understanding, does not consist *primarily* in this, that the God revered as deliverer withdraws once more a portion of the freedom bestowed, and in this area requires the submission of the human will to his command; rather, in all of its areas, human life is to be the adequately practical response to the fact that human beings have been set free, and that it is God who has set them free. Obedience in the religious sense, if this interpretation is correct, is an expression of the will to understand one's own freedom not as "naturally given" but as a "freedom of deliverance," to be referred dynamically to its own ground of possibility, its "deliverer."

But what the concept of a "delivered freedom" denotes, in turn, is by no means an evidence before the fact. Neither in this respect is religious consciousness a priori immune to self-deception. It is at least worth examining, then, whether it would not also be in the meaning of religious consciousness, and precisely here, that a helpful interpretation could be the suggestion to understand "delivered freedom," "freed freedom," transcendentally, that is, as the surmounting of that dialectic into which reason in its practical use, according to Kant's conception, is entangled, or as that "restoration to moral subjectivity" of which Cohen has spoken.

And when the religious person stresses that the living God is something other than an idea or a product of reflection, that God in the overwhelming and liberating divine reality is not constructed or invented but experienced, still the difference between this religious experience and all worldly experiences must first be more closely defined. Is it not at least the proffer of an interpretation that is worth examining, when the transcendental philosopher points out that worldly experience brings respectively this or that object to cognition, while in the resolution of the dialectic of reason an "opening of the eyes" is experienced that consists in this, that the human being is granted to see all that is in a new light? Is it not precisely the distinguishing mark of the "divine light" of which the religious person speaks, that this light "enlightens every person who comes into the world" (John 1:9), so that all that is (not exclusively striking religious objects and occurrences, then) becomes visible for the human eye in a manner not to be constructed a priori? Is that experience, then, to which religious persons appeal in order to distinguish their living God from all products of reflection and ideas, really so basically distinct from that "transcendental experience" in which persons experience their own transcendentality (that is, their capacity to relate *constitutively* to objects contemplated, reflected upon, and dealt with, in all these respects) as a *contingent, bestowed capacity?* And does it really gainsay the proffer of a transcendental interpretation when the religious experience here is so construed that in it not a sacred or divine reality would also be grasped, "alongside" the objects in the world, but in the new "light" of God the world and all that it envelops would appear in a new way before human eyes?

Such counterquestions will not suffice, for transcendental philosophers striving to propagate a transcendental concept of God, to silence the criticism that will be directed against them in the name of religious consciousness. But they will have prompted, by way of counterquestions of this kind, a new departure in the conversation between religious and philosophical consciousness. And in the course of this conversation, they will be able to heighten their own consciousness of method, in a manner that can be helpful to them in their concern for the underpinnings of a philosophy of religion. Only this heightened consciousness of method makes it possible for the two other methods of a philosophy of religion—phenomenology and the analysis of religious language—to continue to be relevant.

Heightening of the Consciousness of Method in Transcendental Philosophy with Respect to Concern for a Concept of God in Terms of Transcendental Philosophy

The attempt to make a philosophical speech upon God possible with methods of transcendental philosophy provokes the criticism of religious persons. Even when transcendental philosophy answers the like religious criticism of philosophy with a philosophical criticism of religious consciousness, it still remains to be determined whether the former cannot learn something from this conversation. Not only the philosopher may be in a position to issue a warning as to self-misunderstandings on the part of religious consciousness: religious consciousness, as well, can at times recall transcendental philosophy to self-critical insights that are very apposite to the matter of transcendental philosophical argumentation, but that are not infrequently lost sight of by its representatives.

When religious persons express the suspicion that God understood in transcendental philosophical fashion is a "homemade" God, then they are reminding the philosopher that transcendental reflection is in error when it thinks it *creates* the possibilitating conditions of human transcendentality instead of *finding* them as the preliminary conditions of all of its reflective acts.

Even Kant's argumentations could have occasioned the insight that ideas are indeed the necessary, but not always the sufficient, conditions for the construction of the world of objects. Those objectives at which the understanding must aim, if it is to erect from the material of sensory impressions the ordered whole of objects and object relationships, do not of themselves guarantee that, in their contemplation and thinking, their willing and behavior, human beings will also be up to the task set before their eyes by the idea. And the limit of this "can" is not only of a psychological, empirical nature, but of a transcendental one: reason, which sets itself its own tasks, inasmuch as it fashions objectives or ideas, thereby demonstrates its autonomy, it is true, but in the same process necessarily gets into contradictions with itself—has, as Kant says, "its own ever-present dialectic"

(Kant, *KpV,* A, 192). Nor can reason once more, as is the case with the ideas, demand the resolution of these contradictions of itself by way of anticipation (see Kant, *Diss.,* §1.1). The human being can only hope that the dialectic of the use of reason will be resolved.

While ideas are target images in which reason contemplates its own task, the postulate designates a content of hope whose fulfillment reason cannot guarantee as a part of its own accomplishment, but must indeed presuppose if it is to undertake the accomplishment of its own tasks. Were it to be definitively entangled in its self-contradiction, it would extricate itself as reason. The doctrine of this hope-content, however, right back to Kant's critique of practical reason, forms the central content of a philosophical doctrine of God that employs transcendental methods. The moment, then, that the attempt is made to sketch such a doctrine of God by the use of transcendental methods, transcendental philosophy is reminded of its own, momentarily forgotten insight that reason must *hope* for all that lies before its capacity of accomplishment by way of enablement.

A transcendental philosophy that forgets its dialectic, degenerates into an ideology of self-defense. Whatever may happen, everything is a priori "reduced" to an immutable, long in hand, apparatus of forms of views, concepts, and ideas. Against a transcendental philosophy that misunderstands itself in this fashion, the suspicion is frequently cited in more recent times that it is like the porcupine that calls to the hare (that is, to the experience acquired slaving away in the "furrows" of life) at the end of every trek down a furrow, "I'm still here!" and thus spares itself the effort of taking cognizance of the content of experience in its variety and unsystematization. A transcendental philosophy that undertakes the attempt to develop a doctrine of the postulates of reason and, therein enclosed, a philosophical doctrine of God will thus be reminded of the dialectic of reason that was of course discovered by Kant, but that was all too often forgotten again by other transcendental philosophers. And it will further have it pointed out that human reason remains directed to experiences in which this its dialectic is resolved in unpredictable wise, inasmuch as the postulates of hope are satisfied in a way in which the human being could not have necessitated.

A transcendental philosophy that does not distinguish between the tasks that reason sets itself and the hopes that it cannot itself fulfill becomes willy-nilly a utopianism. The latter transforms the postulates of hope into "demands" on the world, which, where they cannot be employed as material for the realization of reasonable objectives, must be destroyed. The postulates of hope then appear as justification for a praxis that would execute judgment on this evil world. This transformation of postulates of a hope directed upon God into demands that can be made against an "evil reality" are addressed by way of example in Bloch's *Atheismus im Christentum* (see Schaeffler 1979, esp. 289–99).

However, a transcendental philosophy that, because it identifies postulates of hope with ideas of the understanding, misunderstands itself as a theory of "judgment upon the unreasonable world," runs the risk of losing its relation to reality in theory and practice. After all, such a transcendental philosophy cannot be brought to self-correction by anything it encounters. It will register any opposition placed in the way of its objections by the world of experience only by observing the latter in its own judgment upon the "stupidity of the facts" and the "evil relations of the times." A transcendental philosophy, on the other hand, that strives to develop a transcendental philosophical concept of God will be reminded of the postulates of hope and thereby be preserved from such loss of the capacity for experience and be capacitated to self-correction.

Considerations of the kind here indicated lead to this: Not only can transcendental philosophy make religious awareness a critical-hermeneutic proffer that will warn it of self-misunderstandings and preserve it from the same; but religious awareness, as well, can fulfill such a critical-hermeneutic function vis-à-vis transcendental philosophy: warn it of self-misunderstandings, and remind it of its own, but occasionally forgotten, insights. Transcendental philosophy, then, in its endeavors to acquire a philosophical concept of God and thereby join conversation with religious awareness, can acquire a heightened awareness of its own methods.

But then it will be in a position to give continuing methodological indications both for the analysis of religious language and for the phenomenology of religion. Precisely this, after all, was called for above, at the end of our retrospective comparison. As we brought the three most important questions in religious philosophy and attempts at a solution into conjoint focus, transcendental philosophy (especially in its application to the problematic of philosophical speech upon God) was to contribute to the necessary heightening of methodological consciousness; while the analysis of religious language was to serve to uncover, in utterly clear examples of a religious sort, a "meaning logic of the religious act" and its corresponding "manner-of-being-given of religious objects" that would permit the acquisition of criteria for the delineation of that area of investigation to which religious science and religious philosophy relate. Transcendental methods, applied to examples whose specially religious peculiarity could be assured through the analysis of religious language, as was observed in the formulation of that program, first prepare the presupposition on the basis of which, in a phenomenology of religion, the reciprocal relationship between religious noesis and religious noema can be denoted, and the modifications of this relationship across the entire breadth of religious phenomena can be studied (see above, p. 118).

Methodological Indications for the Analysis of Religious Language

The peculiarities of religious language, to which repeated reference has been made in more recent times, include especially the following three. First, the language of religion is self-involved: that is, it is so structured that it enables and requires speakers, in each enunciation upon God, the world, and all objects, to speak of themselves. Second, in religious language, in a manner not easy to grasp, are linked enunciations that raise a claim to truth and speech acts that mean to be efficacious. A third peculiarity of religious language, less intensively investigated up to the moment, bears on the peculiarity of religious narrative, especially where religious propositions find their place in laudatory invocation of God. Here the one who prays frequently emphasizes, on the one hand, the unforeseeably new, fully surprising, incomparable with all previous experience, nature of the theophany and hierophany, and yet in this report of apparitions of God or of the Holy includes all theophanies and hierophanies in an ordered narrative connection. In what follows, we shall attempt to indicate how transcendental methods can contribute to making this triple characteristic of religious language understandable.

In any enunciation made by religious speakers, they also speak of themselves. They cannot speak of God without at the same time saying that they were known to this God. They cannot speak of the world without at the same time saying that, with everything that can be seen, they see the glory of their God shine forth. This "self-involvement" in religious enunciation can readily occasion the conclusion that religious language is lacking in a capacity for objectivity, so that in this language it cannot be said how things really are, but only how speakers evaluate the content of their experience.

The manner in which religious speakers also speak of themselves in everything they say, brings to expression that they endorse what is said, that they stake their salvation or reprobation on their determination that "God be glorified in everything" (1 Peter 4:11), that they oblige themselves to ends that according to their religious experience are binding. From this it can readily be concluded that all enunciations of religious language are "disguised speech acts"—that they are by no means intended to inform the hearer of what is, but are intended to place speakers in a relation to God, to the world, and to their fellow human beings such as is to be realized only through this speech act.

Transcendental considerations upon the dialectic of reason in its theoretical as in its practical usage, as well as upon the postulates of hope, can contribute to overcoming a situation characterized by potentially hasty alternatives—the seeming contradiction between "self-involvement" and objectivity, between enunciation and speech act as a false contradiction.

When speaking of God and the world, religious persons must *at the same time* speak of themselves, since the new "dawning of the divine glory" has at the same time opened their eyes anew. Only a new eye and ear become able to grasp the new light and word of the Holy, since any hierophany is of such "novelty" that it makes all previous thinking and willing appear as "old." But religious persons *cannot speak of themselves alone,* however important their determinations, appraisals, and acts of self-obligation might be for them, since the light that has "removed the veil from their eyes" appears as a foreign light, enlightening persons "from without and from above": after all, only such a light, that does not dawn from one's own interior, can endow religious persons with clear sight, in a new way, for the reality of the world. And in this new light, according to their own convictions the being of things opens up.

A hermeneutics of religious texts that makes use of transcendental philosophical methods can evidence, then, both why, in all that they say, religious persons must speak of themselves, and why they can never speak of themselves alone. They must speak of themselves because they speak of the condition that makes them capable of their new manner of seeing and understanding. Yet they cannot speak exclusively of themselves because they speak of a condition that must already have become effective with themselves, before they could see and understand in the way to which their enunciations upon everything that they encounter testify. And they can never speak only of themselves because the efficacy of this transcendental condition is evinced by the fact that their gaze upon all things and persons in the world is "illuminated": their understanding at last peers through the given in its connections. Transcendental reflection, which shows that religious persons must at the same time speak of themselves, but can never speak of themselves alone, and why these conditions are imposed, thus overcomes the supposed contradiction between "self-communication and objectivity."

The case is analogous to the relationship between speech acts and enunciatory propositions. Religious speech always has the nature of a speech act, because religious persons (to borrow a term from Cohen) must enter actively into the "correlation" offered them with the newly shining light, in order to be illumined by this light. Only in that they owe the opening of their eyes to this light, only in that they attune their thinking and acting to the source of this light, and with their words (*logos*) confess the glory (*doxa*) of this light doxologically (to speak with Wainwright), do their eyes grow bright, does the real show itself to them in such a way that the Holy can dawn upon this reality. But the enunciations made on this occasion by religious persons are not mere "disguises" for those speech acts through which these persons enter into correlation with their God. Rather, these expressions announce what has been shown to them in the light of the newly resplendent divine glory. Hence religious statements, like statements of any kind, lay claim to truth, instead of only enfolding a hope in reality; for the divine light, like any light, shines only in that it makes visible what enters into the area of its radiance.

A hermeneutics of religious texts that makes use of transcendental philosophical methods, then, can evince why in so many cases religious language is both enunciation and speech act. Religious language is enunciation because it seeks to communicate how the world looks when seen in the light of divine truth. It is also speech act because the subject who has come to see and understand the reality of the world in this way materializes only in active execution of a "correlation of divine and human freedom." The speech acts of commandment and prayer, of which Cohen and Rosenzweig have spoken, the speech acts of the promise of the grace of divine forgiveness, which make it possible to overcome the self-contradiction of practical reason, and of doxology, which is the response to the dawn of the divine glory, finally constitute that religious "I," who is capable of the religious act and receptive to the "primordial givenness" of the world of objects grasped in religious fashion.

In twofold form, then, transcendental methods make characteristics of religious language understandable that otherwise present special difficulties for an interpretation: the tension between commitment and objectivity, and the double characteristic of speech act and enunciation.

The case is similar with the peculiarity of religious narrative, otherwise so difficult to understand. It belongs to the structural peculiarity of the language of prayer that it characteristically emphasizes the unpredictability of those events that it narrates. In the moment in which the hierophany occurs, it overspills all expectation, indeed, all conditions of the heretofore imaginable: "As the Lord turned [to us] and worked the turn for Zion [the return to Zion], we were as persons dreaming" (Psalm 126:1). But it is just as characteristic of the language of prayer that those who are praying can once more appeal, in all of these turning points of their lives, to the one Name through which they identify the God of the currently experienced, overwhelming new "mighty deed" with that God upon whom their forebears have called and upon whom their last descendants will call: ". . . As it was in the beginning, is now, and ever shall be, world without end [from age to age]" (cf. the standard conclusion at the end of every psalm in Catholic worship). That it is possible precisely through the invocation of the divine name to establish the unity of a narrative connection even beyond the boundaries of the "ages" becomes even more clear in the cry found in the Jewish morning prayer: "Praised be the Name in which dawns the glory of his reign, . . . henceforward and unto all eternity."

This twofold characteristic of religious language, as well—on the one side the confession of the unforeseeably new, and on the other, in retrospect, the invocation of the old name—can be made understandable through a hermeneutics that makes use of transcendental methods. What is brought to expression here is the experience of the contingence and historical variability of the human capacity for experience.

Because in the hierophany a new kind of context of possible experience has materialized, the content of this hierophany at first seems impossible to human thinking, like the content of a dream. But because the speaker, in the event thus experienced, recognizes once more the divine power that has turned out to be efficacious with that speaker "from age to age" (that is, in the transition from one comprehensive connection of the speaker's experience to a different, and differently structured one), the speaker can also call the God of the fathers by name in gratitude in the new experience. And precisely thereby does the new event become a part of a narrative connection in which the speaker recognizes personal history. Thus, the address by name of the God whose presence is always experienced as "unheard of" (as different from everything simply known and handed down) connects the present theophany with the narrative of past mighty deeds of the same God, and with the tradition that can be handed on from parents to children, "from generation to generation."

On the Question of Criteria of the Religious

Our retrospective comparison of questions, premises, and methods of the philosophy of religion has yielded the following. Philosophical theology, especially when it makes use of transcendental methods, can be expected to produce an especially keen consciousness of method. The analysis of religious language, however, bids fair to offer especially clear information on how criteria can be established as to whether a phenomenon has a specific religious character (and hence falls in the area of investigation of religious science and the philosophy of religion), and whether it corresponds to the "meaning logic of the religious act" (or the *eidos* of religious objects), or whether it must be judged to be an aberration of the religious.

And as a matter of fact we have seen that a hermeneutics of religious language practiced by way of a transcendental method can lead to such criteria of the religious. The connection of three pairs of seeming contradictions belongs to the peculiarity of religious language: the connection between personal commitment and the claim of objectivity, the connection between enunciation and speech act, and the connection between a profession of the unforeseeably new and the ability to produce a narrative connection. An application of transcendental methods has made it clear that it is a matter here not of coincidental peculiarities of religious language but of consequences of the specific manner in which the religious act is related to its most important object: to God as that ground of enablement by which human beings are aware of their ability to perform their religious acts.

Thereby is acquired not only a criterion for the selection of religious phenomena but also a standard for their evaluation. Neither a subjectivism without obligation to objectivity, nor an objectivism without subjective self-commitment, neither a system of mere enunciations without the character of act, nor a system of speech acts without a claim to truth, can be evaluated as a religious expression in the unrestricted sense of the word. Precisely the third criterion, however, seems to be of special significance: Neither a sheer stereotyped tradition without profession of the unforeseeable novelty of the hierophany, which overspills all expectations, nor a confession of the sheer wondrousness, which overspills all narrative connections, can rank as genuinely religious. The latter is always the combination of shock at the "unheard of" and the repeated capacity for the transmitting narrative. This becomes especially clear through an analysis of religious language; but the criteria acquired here are applicable as well to phenomena of the religious other than speech.

With reference to religious speech, one can say: What is *only* new renders one speechless; what is *only* old renders experience in seemingly a priori foreknowledge superfluous. Religious speech can be spoken only where persons are neither mute nor incapable of experience. It is essentially speech of a praising narrative that attests experiences that have transcended all previous contexts, but that at the same time orders these experiences in a comprehensive narrative pattern.

Precisely this characteristic of religious language challenges the transcendental philosopher to a particularly great extent, since it belongs to the special tasks of transcendental philosophy to specify the conditions of possible experience. Religious language testifies to the capacity of an experience of a special kind: the capacity for historical experience. This capacity presupposes that persons, in their speech, not slip into an alleged foreknowledge of what is shown them (in the case of religion, then, the apparition of the sacred and divine). But it likewise presupposes that they not fall mute indefinitely before the incomprehensible, but are able to fit it into the narrative connection that they conceive as their history.

Understood in religious terms: To speak of God always means to recount the history of the divine mighty deeds. These cannot be deduced from a presupposed concept of God, but are always astonishing and surprising, requiring a revision in theory and a conversion in practice. But they can be recounted. They yield, in retrospective consideration, a connection: after all, "his goodness abides for everlasting, and his faithfulness from generation to generation" (Psalm 100:5).

An interpretation of religious language undertaken by means of transcendental philosophy can seek to elucidate this capacity for the religious consciousness of historical experience. The history of the transcendental problem, in its development from Kant to the present, has led to this, that the conditions of possibility of experience are no longer (or at least not only) to be sought in immutable forms of contemplation and thought, but precisely in that these forms, in the encounter with paradoxical content, nevertheless, in a second step, appear once more in a new, now specifically historical, form (see Schaeffler 1982, esp. 35–48). Religious narrative calls by name precisely that reality to which human beings ascribe, in thanksgiving, both the shattering and the reconstitution of their capacity for contemplation and thinking, both their "blinding by the overwhelming light" and the "reopening of their eyes."

But if the peculiarity of religious naming and narrative is thus understandable transcendentally, if the relationship of religious consciousness to its proper ground of possibility is expressed therein, then a criterion for the evaluation of religious expressions is available here.

A transcendental hermeneutics of the speech of religious narrative can remind religious persons that the "glory" they claim to have seen is only really the divine glory if it fulfills two conditions: if it makes not only itself but everything that is, visible in a new way and opens new paths into the world for the human praxis that has become caught in the aporias of the dialectic of practical reason; and if that "light" that, in the moment of its apparition, was unforeseeably new is evinced in retrospect to be identical with the a priori of all human theory and practice—or, to express it in religious terms, with that light that already shone upon human beings as they were formed in the womb (cf. Psalm 139:13), with that opening of the ways that had already occurred before a person could take the first step along such ways.

In the absence of the first condition, the apparition of what religious persons call "glory" (*doxa, gloria*) occurs only for themselves—instead of rendering all of the real visible, in astonishing fashion, in a new light—then this apparition has been only an empirical, and not a transcendental, experience. Or, to put it in religious language: then it has been a worldly, and not the divine, light. In the absence of the second condition—if what the religious person calls the "dawning of the divine glory" is not found, even in retrospect, to be identical with the "light that has ever shone"—then we have those religious dualisms on which the unity of the "I," the coherence of the world, and the unicity of God are all shattered. Then the new-dawning God does appear as victor over the evil demons that have dominated the world until now, but not as the one God who holds the world in divine hands from its beginning to its end. Persons who experience their "rebirth" in the dawning of the divine light then no longer recognize themselves as who they have been. But the abiding world, into which the new glory of God has shone, now seems destined to pass away, and thus to make room for a future world of goodness.

In this theological, anthropological, and cosmological dualism, to put it philosophically, the one, comprehensive context goes by the board in which alone it would be possible "to spell out apparitions, in order to be able to read them as experience" (Kant, *Prol.*, A, 101). Or, in religious language: Dualisms of this sort make it impossible to speak of God, who has appeared in the novelty of the astonishing divine apparition, simultaneously in such a way that human beings recall in praise the mighty deeds this God has wrought "with the fathers," and that they are sure of the fidelity of this God for coming generations as well.

The one who became speechless in the experience of paradox, without subsequently acquiring once more the capacity for narrative; those whom the brilliant coming of the hierophany only withdrew from the world, without, in a second step, making the entire world of experience understandable in a new manner; those whom the unforeseeably new element in the theophany has so alienated from all that has ever been, and been experienced, that they can no longer, in a second step, produce a connection in which they recount the history of the divine deeds at the same time as their own history and future; these persons are incapable of religious speech. They may grasp religious texts allegorically as picturesque raiment of the testimonial to the unnameable; they may grasp the content of religious tradition as antithetical representation contrasting with the present world, and as projections of the hope of an altogether differently structured future; but they have in any case lost the capacity to grasp themselves from their history and to "spell out" the apparitions of radical historical change in such a way that they allow themselves to be "read as experience" in a historical sense. However, this is more than a mere linguistic failure. With the loss of the ability to understand oneself historically, the ability is simultaneously lost to speak in religious wise of that God to whom human beings owe precisely their capacity for historical experience. The loss of the speech of religious narrative signals the collapse of the relation between the religious act and its object, between the human *logos* and the divine *doxa*. Whether and to what degree acts and objects, noeses and noemata, have a religious character is determined by the capacity for a simultaneously reminiscent and hoping doxology.

Methodological Indications
for the Phenomenology of Religion

What we have just said is also an indication of the manner in which the programmatic formulation that was ventured at the end of our comparative review can be implemented. Methods as they were developed from the philosophical doctrine of God conceived in transcendental fashion, applied to examples whose specially religious characteristic can be developed through an analysis of religious language, present the premises for an adequate handling of those themes that a phenomenology of religion poses itself. A transcendental hermeneutics of religious language, especially the doxological language of narrative, permits a closer specification of the specific relation of religious noeses and religious noemata. This is evident at once in its most important application: the phenomenological interpretation of the hierophany.

It belongs to the structural characteristic of the hierophany that it is characteristically individual and exclusive and at the same time universal. In the presence of the Holy, when it appears, "the world sinks away" (exclusivity). And to this peculiarity of the religious noema the religious noesis corresponds: the religious act is always first a "dying to this world" in order to "live for God alone." Furthermore, the apparition of the Holy is never simply one case among many, but is always unique and incomparable in its kind (individuality). Correspondingly, on the side of religious noesis, the religious act is always accomplished in such a way that the person's entire existence is concentrated in this one moment. The "now" of the religious act is not a segment of the temporal course of one's life but a unique, precious hour before which time sinks away.

But despite this exclusivity and individuality, in the apparition of the divine light the overall connection of life and the world is at the same time understood in a new way, so that religious persons have the impression of only now grasping in its true being everything that is (universality). This status of the Holy corresponds, on the side of the religious act, to the fact that it includes the whole of reality in the encounter with the dawn of the Holy: "The heavens declare the glory of God, and the firmament proclaims the works of his hands" (Psalm 19:2).

This peculiarity of the hierophany, this connection of its exclusive, individual character and its comprehensive, inclusive one, becomes understandable through a reflection in terms of transcendental philosophy. When the light begins to shine that fundamentally transforms the conditions for the experience of the reality of the world, then there is nothing in the old world of objects or a prioris that can make this event of the hierophany explainable and understandable. Hence, for religious persons in the moment of the hierophany, "the world is dead, and they die to the world." But neither is there anything in the world, either in the "old world" (in the old, reliable connection of experiences) or in the "new world" (in the newly established context of understanding) that for the religious person would not be reflected precisely by this light of the new apparition of the Holy. Precisely because the religious experience has a transcendental character, it is at once exclusive and individual, and inclusive and universal.

The considerations, in terms of transcendental philosophy, upon the dialectic of reason, as well, especially in its practical use, and the insight into the difference between ideas of reason and postulates of hope yield methodological indications for the phenomenology of religion. These indications bear especially on the danger that a phenomenological consideration might fail to take acccount of the specifically historical character of religion. The basic phenomenological law according to which acts and intended objects correspond to each other precisely will all too easily occasion the notion that the relation between religious noesis and religious noema is altogether free of tension, so that there would be no call to alter these acts structurally and thereby to experience the objects in an altered way. The phenomenological "view of being" then leads, on the contrary, to the insight into the "eternal laws of being of the religious," and the phenomenologist may raise the claim of being able, when confronted with disturbances of the religious act or vagueness in the manner of presentation of religious objects, to recall religion from its "false being" into its "true being." "Back to," then, as Scheler held, is the essential law of the history of religion.

A transcendental philosophy, on the other hand, which takes in hand the *dialectic* of reason in its theoretical and practical use, and grasps as *hope content* the resolution of the contradiction into which reason is necessarily transformed, can deliver phenomenology from such a nonhistorical manner of regard. In this case, the "fundamental phenomenological law" takes the following shape. The strict correlation between noesis and noema requires that the old form of thought and regard shatter on the qualitatively new content of the hierophany (since new wine cannot be poured into old flasks), and that to the consciousness of having seen a "new light" corresponds to the experience of the opening of one's eyes "in a new way." Objects—be they, for that matter, sensory apparitions or mental apprehensions, be they presented to the eyes in fantasy and dream or grasped as goals of activity—belong to the "region of being" of specifically religious objects only when they are signalized precisely by the fact that they are first experienced as that "blinding light" in the presence of which the human ear and eye "lose hearing and seeing," and that, in a second phase, in the same objects that "illuminating light" is reflected in which all of experiential reality presents itself to a person in a new way. Intentional acts—be they, for that matter, acts of regard and thought, of feeling, or of willing—are only "religious" acts when they are so performed that they are exposed to their own breakdown on new objects, to entrust themselves in hope to the reestablishment of their intentionality through the same object. Thus, in its structure, the religious act bears the stamp of hope in the experience of collapse: but the religious object is that which "kills and restores to life." This structural characteristic is demonstrated by religious acts and objects across the whole gamut of differences among act forms and object spheres. The objective declaration, "It is the Lord who kills and brings to life (1 Samuel 2:6), and the subjective declaration, "I die not, I live and praise the deeds of the Lord" (Psalm 118:17), are strictly correlative to each other in the language of religion—the application case par excellence of the correlation between noema and noesis in the area of religion.

Dialectical Relation between
Religious Noesis and Religious Noema

Our comparative survey of the various questions, premises, and methods of the philosophy of religion has shown us that the philosophy of religion on the basis of philosophical theology (especially in the form of transcendental philosophy) enjoys a preeminence with respect to a heightened consciousness of its methods; the analysis of religious language is better suitable than other forms of philosophy of religion when it comes to the development of criteria for the selection and evaluation of religious phenomena; however, the phenomenology of religion has priority over other forms of the philosophy of religion with respect to the capacity adequately to interpret, with regard to their form and content, the abundance of religious manifestations that are to be described in the religious sciences and interpreted in the philosophy of religion. The phenomenology of religion accomplishes this by showing the specific relation between the religious act and its object.

Correspondingly, the problem sketch that formed the transition from our comparative survey to a systematic perspective was the following. Methods of a doctrine of God in terms of transcendental philosophy, applied to examples whose specifically religious peculiarity can be worked out through the analysis of religious language, finally provide the premises for an adequate development of the themes addressed by a phenomenology of religion (see above, p. 118). We have already spoken, in this systematic perspective of the fine-tuning of the consciousness of method in transcendental philosophical discourse upon God, as well as of criteria of the religious acquired through an analysis of religious language. In conclusion, we asked whether an approach to a philosophical phenomenology of religion can really be gained, as expected, along this path.

Now, it would surely be outside the framework of a handbook to wish to show in detail in what manner a phenomenology of religion corresponding to this program wins access to the entire breadth of its themes. However, the considerations presented here have led to a clearer grasp of the structural peculiarity of the correlation between religious noesis and the religious noema. Employing formulary language, we could say that this correlation is of a dialectical nature. As we have shown above, the dialectic in question is the object of a phenomenological description of the hierophany: The noematic content of the religious act, the Holy, presents itself in the mode of withdrawal (cf. Luke 24:31, cited above, in which, precisely at the moment that Jesus "opens the eyes" of the disciples at Emmaus, he "withdraws from their gaze"). But religious noesis—religious contemplation, naming, and grasping—anticipates its own undoing (see the hymn of Gregory of Nazianzus, cited above, who calls on God as the "possessor of every name" and at the same time the "One beyond invocation"). But the withdrawal does not extinguish the presence of the Holy: consciousness of an incapacity adequately to see and to name the Holy has not annihilated the religious act. "Negation"—the experience of the inadequacy of the religious act with respect to its object—is "thrusting negation," driving negation, which lends the relation between religious noesis and noema its historical dynamics (see above, pp. 68–69).

However, this thrusting, propelling dialectic ought to be not only described by a phenomenology of religion; it ought, at the same time, to be *interpreted philosophically*. This is accomplished through considerations of transcendental philosophy that Kant's doctrine of the dialectic of pure reason in its theoretical and practical use subject to further development. The religious act is always an act of hope, addressing a reality before which persons experience themselves (their regard, thinking, and activity) as basically denying themselves, but of which at the same time they expect that, in the passage through its collapse, it will again produce its subjectivity. This interpretation of religion as a connection of postulates of hope can now serve a philosophical phenomenology of religion as a guide. What Rudolf Otto has described, in psychological categories, as an amalgam of terror and fascination is understandable transcendentally as the connection of two experiences: the experience that, in the encounter with the Holy, the form of human self-understanding and understanding of the world collapses, and the second experience, that human beings can commit themselves in hope to that "ever greater" truth and reality of the Holy—to be graced, where their own capacity for an accomplishment of regarding, thinking, and grasping ends, with a transformation of their entire existence. Not only the grammar of religious language but also the characteristic element in religious activity especially in divine worship, religious community, and that community's historical self-understanding, is defined through this dialectic, which cannot be resolved otherwise than through the fact that religious subjects commit themselves in hope to the Holy and Divine. A phenomenology of religion that would avoid slipping into a collection of material, devoid of concept, and avoid deforming religious apparitions precipitously into philosophical concepts, can, in this dialectic of a horizon of experience in terms of a collapse and historical restoration, find something like a basic law of the "meaning logic of the religious act" and of the "eidetic of the religious object"; but the multiplicity of the nature of religious apparitions can be grasped as a plenitude of modifications of this specifically religious correlation of noesis and noema.

In the framework of the considerations presented here, we had to be satisfied with only a few examples, by way of a first approach, of how the interplay of three methods of the philosophy of religion might look: philosophical theology in the particular form of a teaching of God in terms of transcendental philosophy, the analysis of religious language, and the phenomenology of religion. The analysis of religious speech offers the philosopher of religion the example par excellence on which the structural peculiarity of the religious act and its content can be studied. The phenomenology of religion warrants the philosophy of religion its theme: the characterization of the religious act-sphere and object-sphere in all of the breadth of their multiplicity, but especially the "strict correlation" between religious act and religious object. But the transcendental method, honed fine in the encounter of the particular advantages and dangers of a transcendental theology, is apt for preserving phenomenology from a slide into a sheer listing of examples, while the analysis of religious language frees it from imprisonment in false alternatives.

This interplay of methods had to be at least indicated, unless the typology of philosophies of religion presented here was to content itself with positing premises and manners of argument that in this area have been addressed, in the course of history, in mere, unrelated propinquity. A further systematic presentation of how a philosophy of religion might look that combines the methods named in the manner indicated is not the task of this investigation. The latter has limited itself to a description of questions, premises, and methods of the philosophy of religion such that an orientation to this most multiform area of investigation will become possible.

Supplementary Material
for the Second Edition

———»·0·«———

FOUR ELEMENTS, ESPECIALLY, in societal development, affecting the tasks of the philosophy of religion, have altered since the appearance of the first edition of this book: (1) the accelerating secularization process, (2) a contrary process of the sacralization of certain areas of culture, especially politics and environmental ethics, (3) a sharply intensified intercultural encounter, including a religious encounter, and (4) the rise of "new religions" on various parts of the globe. In connection with all of these developments, there has arisen (5) a hesitation within theology as to orientation, which bids fair to proclaim a new requirement regarding the latter.

The Secularization Process as a Question
to Be Addressed to the Philosophy of Religion

The process of secularization, observed to be under way ever since the eighteenth century, has acquired a new depth and extension over the course of the last decade. Growing parts of the population "don't miss anything" if they fail to be led in the formation of their lives by Christian convictions and values. Only a portion, presumably the lesser portion, of those persons ascribing no meaning to the specific content of Christian tradition turn to other religious communities. For the quantitatively preponderant part of those who—with or without a formal departure—turn from the churches, religion across the board appears as the superfluous relic of a bygone time.

In view of this development, a first alteration has occurred with regard to the function of *criticism of religion.* If, beginning in the eighteenth century and continuing down to the middle of our own, this criticism has stood in the service of the emancipation of religious traditions and institutions, today the struggle with the overpowering influence of those traditions and institutions seems to be bereft of an object. The criticism of religion has lost its once mighty adversary and has become a method for rendering understandable the process of secularization, which is essentially closed off, on the basis of its own foundations. And since it thus makes understandable only what has long since occurred in societal reality, its propositions acquire a popular plausibility that no longer need be reached through the rigor of argumentation, verging as it does on the obvious.

Our average contemporaries claim to have known long since what they can look up in Feuerbach: religious enunciations transmit no information about God or the gods, but only about those persons who sketch such images of God or the gods: these persons, unbeknownst to themselves, relate, in the medium of their religious conceptualizations, to their own being, and only thus become conscious of this being of theirs. Granted, it no longer seems plausible today to take the "projections" or "externalizations" through which what is in the human being is turned outward, or projected on high, and deduce them from a metaphysics of spirit, as Feuerbach has done. (The central explanation here was: spirit must contemplate itself in its productions before it can be recognized as their author.) Popularly, on the other hand, it seems obvious that the production of such images arises not from a metaphysical but from a psychological necessity: in the depths of the soul, a power for the production of primitive images (archetypes) is at work, which, in all of the differentiation of their variations and combinations, return in the basic makeup of the dreams of individuals and the religious traditions of peoples. Carl Gustav Jung's theory of the "collective unconscious," and of the "archetypes" generated there, belongs no less to the popularly received certitudes of the criticism of religion than does Feuerbach's "theory of projection." And since it corresponds to general experience that there are maturation crises in the psychic development of the individual that can generate psychic illnesses, Sigmund Freud's concept of religion, as well, in which the latter is the expression of such a crisis of maturation, seems altogether plausible: the "malaise in culture," which today does guarantee manifold freedoms, but which at the same time means the deprivation of security, generates in maturing persons who have wrested free of the real, earthly father, a longing for new forms of personal acceptance; and the more their environment denies them this experience, the more readily they are inclined to commit themselves to religious assurances affording them the prospect of now being the adult child of a heavenly Father. Thus, religion appears to be an affair of those who have been psychically wounded in the transition to adulthood. This explanation for the survival of religion

SUPPLEMENTARY MATERIAL FOR THE SECOND EDITION

even in enlightened societies appears today all the more plausible in that, among other things, it makes understandable the increasing popularity of sects that draw their membership from youth. At the other end of the spectrum, but just as self-evident today, is the acceptance of the Marxist theory of ideology. Even one who does not accept Marxism as a theory of socioeconomic relations and their development is inclined to "unmask," as an expression of the social will to power, the claim to authority on the part of religious traditions and institutions, to the extent that these mean to be anything more than a help in the process of psychic maturation.

Now, self-evidences of this sort repeatedly awaken the critical attention of philosophers. Convictions that count as so unquestionable in a society that they seemingly no longer need to be discussed at all repeatedly arouse the suspicion that, instead of solving problems, they relegate them to oblivion. The *philosophy of religion*, in this situation, becomes the critical scrutinizing of such popular "evidences" of the criticism of religion. Thus, the philosophy of religion first faces the question: Is the general reception that the criticism of religion has found really owing to the strength of its arguments, which over the course of time have been grasped by ever wider circles of the population? Or has the criticism of religion—just as "then," when it was by no means obvious but required detailed argumentation in order to win popular assent—been not so much an ensemble of argumentations as rather the reflection of the secularization process already factually under way at the time? And if this process has owed its constancy and progressive acceleration not to the arguments of the critics of religion but to the growing familiarity of ever broader circles of the population with scientific and technological rationality, which factually leaves no room for religion, then the question arises whether this development has not reached its limit today.

As for the evident crisis of the specific manner of rationality on which contemporary science and technology rest, first of all the general philosophical question arises whether other forms of the critical examination of claims to validity might be possible. And specifically, the philosophy of religion must examine whether such forms of criticism and examination of claims to validity, forms distinct from scientific and technological procedures, have perhaps been developed precisely in religious connections. Religion, thus understood, would be not the expression of a prerational consciousness but the form of externalization of a specifically structured critical rationality, distinct from technology and science (see R. Schaeffler, *Religion und Kritisches Bewußtsein* [Freiburg and Munich, 1973]). Argumentation of this kind wins new currency in the situation of today and sets the philosophy of religion the task of indicating alternatives to the scientific

and technological form of rationality, now in its crisis, through a rehabilitation of nonscientific forms of thought. In this context we find, for example, the arguments for the rehabilitation of myth that Kurt Hübner has
presented in multiple form (see Kurt Hübner, *Kritik der Wissenschaftlichen
Vernunft* [Freiburg and Munich, 1978]; idem, *Die Wahrheit des Mythos*
[Munich, 1985]; as well as the festschrift dedicated to him, *Kritik der Wissenschaftlichen Rationalität* [Freiburg and Munich, 1986]).

On the other hand, the rejection of irrationalisms that now, in the crisis
of contemporary science, appeal to religious traditions, becomes a prioritar-
ian task of the philosophy of religion, which must ask: In the societal conditions of today, is religion really no longer anything but an overcompensation
that makes the awful burden of contemporary rationality bearable to so
many persons? Or does it fulfill, in responsible wise, accessible to rational
justification, certain inescapable tasks that scientific and technological
thought cannot solve? The investigations of Niklas Luhmann (*Funktion der
Religion* [Frankfurt, 1977]) and Heinrich Lübbe (*Religion nach der Auf-
klärung* [Graz, 1986]) suggest this direction. And the documentations published by Willy Oelmüller of conferences on the theme "Wahrheitsansprüche
der Religionen" (Claims to truth on the part of the religions) are likewise
devoted to the question of what sort of claim to truth, and therewith of
demands of rationality, religion can fulfill in the technological and scientific
age. It is the common goal of this manner of endeavor of the philosophy of
religion to defeat the "bad" self-understanding of a criticism of religion that
has forgotten its problems, and which thinks it has gotten beyond the problem of religion, but at the same time, precisely in the age of the criticism of
science, to come to grips with the attempts to legitimate anti-intellectual
tendencies of the most diversified kind with an appeal to religion.

In brief: With regard to the fact that the critique of religion in a secularized society seems to have become a self-evidence, and, on the other hand,
with regard to the fact that the scientific and technological rationality that
has seemed until now to legtitimate this critique of religion has come into
crisis, the question results: *Does religion imply a specific rationality of its own,*
which has been missed by the classic criticism of religion and that, on the
other hand, forbids an appeal to religion for that irrationalism that not sel-
dom arises out of an ennui with scientific and technological rationality?

Secularization of Politics and Environmental Ethics,
and the Need for a New Orientation of the Philosophy of Religion

The secularization process has indeed led to religion's (and especially
Christianity's) loss of meaning for public, as increasingly for private, life;

but it has failed to entail the "dying out" of religion awaited by so many authors. In a countercurrent to the retreat of religion as a special area of culture, with its center in institutionalized divine service (that is, with emphasis on discipleship) and its radiation into art, science, politics, and morality, other areas of culture, until now ranking as "profane," have seen a growth of their "sacred" quality.

In the decade of the seventies, it was not infrequently politics whose alternatives were set before our eyes with the religious pathos of the choice between salvation and reprobation, along with the attempt to resolve these alternatives. Socialistic programs, especially, came forward as the legacy of what was designated, for instance with an appeal to the biblical prophet Amos, as "prophetic socialism," or, invoking (Deutero-)Isaiah and his words on "beating swords into plowshares," proclaimed as "prophetic pacificism." That this was a matter of the secondary sacralization of politics as an originally profane area of culture was clear, along with other evidence, from the fact that the political problems thus endowed with religious values were not developed from religious contexts, or by specifically religious arguments; rather, their plausibility was induced from other sources. The secondary application of religious concepts and images of certain programs in political ethics was preponderantly owing to the claim to indisputability with which the political confrontation was loftily stylized into a conflict between the servants of the coming reign of God and the hosts of the "princes of this world" (with examples especially in the works of Ernst Bloch).

In the eighties, the "environmental" movement took on religious traits in increasing measure. In part, for instance, under the concept of preservation or stewardship of creation, it laid claim to a Christian terminology, without being disturbed by the fact that the expression *conservatio mundi* originally was the designation of an activity of God, whose creation of the world continues as an ongoing maintenance of the world through the ages. In part, the environmental movement blamed the biblically proclaimed "de-idolization of the world," the prohibition of cults of fertility and death, and the associated demonization of the numinous powers of blood and soil, for the loss of reverence for nature, and recommended, as an escape from the ecological crisis, the rehabilitation of the divinities of nature, among them especially such as exhibited a maternal characteristic. Here again we are dealing with a secondary sacralization of an important domain of culture, namely, of the ethics of behavior toward extrahuman reality. The goals and programs of environmental ethics are not developed in a religious context; rather, previously established evaluations and behavioral injunctions dictate the criterion on which it is decided which religious traditions are to count as worthy of appreciation and how they are to be understood.

A sacralized environmental morality has gone hand in hand with various approaches on the part of an equally sacralized feminism, which either seeks to replace the "patriarchal biblical religion" with a rekindled reverence for the archaic mother-divinities, or indeed, in the form of a "feminist theology," would like to uncover in the biblical tradition itself the hidden traces of an archaic unity of reverence for the "maternal nature of God" and the "sanctification of nature." But in many of these forms of feminism as well, be they presented in terms of religious history or even of theology, the option for the sacred dignity of the feminine is not so much the *result* of investigation into religious history or theology as it is the *guiding viewpoint* to which the selection, appraisal, and presentation of the elements of tradition in question are a priori subordinated. An altogether plausible interest in the promotion of woman in society sketches out in advance the goals of this kind of feminist investigation.

For the philosophy of religion, the duty emerges of developing criteria for an assessment of the manner of application of elements of religious speech, and therewith for the use of a religious claim or religious threat of catastrophe for positions in the area of political morality. Here new meaning attaches to the tradition of a philosophical critique of ideology that reaches us from antiquity itself. At the same time, of course, this critique misses its mark if it implies a mistrust of ideology as such.

Ideologies, in the understanding of the word now become classic, are always at hand when claims to the weapon of truth are used that secure for a particular group a competitive advantage in its struggle with others, because they cause their adversaries to appear as devotees of the lie, while allies are now seen as comrades-in-arms on the side of truth. The one acknowledging the claim to truth thus presented thereby submits to the "stipulated goals" of the one who introduces this "truth." In particular, if the matter at issue involves truth claims of a religious sort, then, say the critics of ideology, the will to submission is absolute: the adversary—in the previous case, then, the "bourgeois reactionary" who opposes "prophetic socialism and pacifism," or else the "representative of the interests of a profit-oriented economy," who misappropriates the "sanctity" of nature and thereby occasions the curse of the ideologues—is declared not only a disciple of the lie but an accomplice of diabolical powers: this agent's privation of all opportunity to cooperate in the organization of societal life then becomes a matter of immediate service to the Holy. Political struggle thus understood, be it in the service of the socialist revolution or of the environmental rescue of nature, acquires characteristics of a "holy war."

Clearly, the phenomena of the sacralization of politics or environmental ethics, just described, must summon the philosophical critic of ideology to the field. To be sure, in this connection, as well, the adage is valid, "Qui nimium probat, nihil probat"—who proves too much, proves nothing—that is, an argument so general that it is seen to base something obviously false, contains a fallacy that renders it unsuitable for a grounding even of the obviously correct. If the criticism of ideology is universalized (for instance, in the sense of the reproach, "Speak of truth, and you have nothing in mind but subjugation"), then it destroys any possibility of dialogue, in which even adversaries trust that the other could have something true to say. And if, specifically, the theoretical ideology-critique of religion is universalized (for example, in the sense of the reproach, "Claim to reveal and accomplish the will of God, and you demonize your adversary, and gain immunity from all criticism of your views and intentions"), this kind of critique of religion destroys the premise of responsible theory and practice altogether. After all, the latter rest on a confidence that we encounter the form of apparition and presence of the absolute in the provisionality of a content of human opining and willing that is ever needful of criticism—an absolute that can never be available to us otherwise than in its worldly "image." Without this basically religious trust in the presence of the divine, in the ever inadequate phenomenal form of what persons opine and will, human theory and practice would fall ever and again into the exclusive alternatives of dogmatism and skepticism. It would be dogmatism to equate what we can recognize, and practically realize, with the absolutely true and good. It would be skepticism to contest, knowing the difference between them, all relationship between the absolutely binding and its ever provisionally encountered form.

The question for the philosophy of religion, in this situation, will be the following. How is it possible, with regard to religion—and especially with regard to the sacralization of various areas of culture—to bring the theory of ideology critically into play without falling, in a universalized mistrust of ideology, into the skepticism that regards as impossible all solution of theoretical and practical problems and thereby yields the field of theory and praxis to the partisans of an uncritical dogmatism? But this question is the model for another: What kind of relationship, in the religious understanding, obtains between the absolute, against which all human attempts at knowledge and creativity must be measured, and the forms of its apparitions, always needful of criticism? Are there specifically religious occasions and procedural forms for a self-criticism of religion? And can criteria be extracted, from the specifically religious form of this self-critique, that would legitimate identification, as degenerate forms of the religious, of the sacralization of ethics and politics that posits the absolutization of anyone's own views and procedures? The question of the possibility of a critique of ideology that is not to collapse into a ruinous universalization of mistrust of ideology thus leads to the question of the bond, characteristic of religion itself, between the claim to unconditionality and self-criticism—the question of the conditions of this bond and of its consequences for the appraisal of religious (or pseudo-religious) phenomena (see Schaeffler, *Religion und Kritisches Bewußtsein* [Freiburg and Munich, 1973]).

In brief: With regard to the sacralization we observe of particular areas of culture—especially politics and (environmental) ethics—and, on the other hand, with regard to a radicalizing critique of ideology that would be raised against any claim to theoretical truth and practical obligation, the question arises: Is it possible to discern in religions (if not indeed in all presentations of the religious) a potential for the linkage of confidence in the absolute nature of the true and the good with the self-criticism of all human cognition and volition? And can an indication be gathered, from this specifically religious form of criticism, as to how a critique of ideology would be possible that does not, on the basis of an immanent logic of its own, press on to a universalization of mistrust of ideology, and therewith generate a skepticism that renders any responsible theory and praxis impossible?

Intercultural Encounter and Dialogue of the Religions

While Europe has the problems consequent upon secularization to deal with, we find in other parts of the world a revitalization of domestic religions, frequently in the twofold demarcation of an opposition to Christian mission and European secularism. Not only Islam, Hinduism, and Buddhism, but African tribal religions as well are undergoing in their respective lands an appreciable renaissance. Islam and Buddhism, for their part, are developing new missionary activity as well in Europe and America. Here it is clear that this re-strengthening of non-European religions has ties with a new sense of self-worth in non-European cultures, which discern an effective means for their liberation from European dominance in those religions that have arisen within such cultures or have found their form therein.

Simultaneously, through migratory movements, new religious minorities are arising in the lands of their immigration: Hindus in Africa, Muslims in Europe and North America demand acknowledgment of the self-determination of their religious cultures, and at the same time seek to be recognized as enjoying equal rights as members of the society of their new countries.

All of these phenomena lend new significance to the old question of the *relation of religion, culture, and society*. Is religion so much the expression of a given culture that the adoption of religions stemming from other cultures necessarily destroys the original culture from the inside out and subjects a

person to a foreign "imperialism of culture"? (Here it is of secondary significance whether this adoption is planned and executed through mission
or, from the side of the receiver, occurs through unprovoked imitation.)
And conversely: Does every attempt to "inculturate" a given religion in a
culture to which it has been foreign involve the loss on the part of this religion of its specific character? For some years now, in the sense of a negative
appraisal, we have heard of the "Hellenization of Christianity": the attempt
to "inculturate"this originally Jewish religion into the Greco-Roman world
is supposed to have led to a falsification of the proclamation of faith, which
only today can be discerned and corrected. On the other hand, today we
hear, from missiologists, in a positive sense, of an "Africanization of Christianity," representing the hope that the Christian faith can be delivered
from its original involvement with a given culture, be it the Jewish or the
Greek, and precisely thereby manifest its "transcultural meaning." Protests
against religious "cultural imperialism" presuppose that a very close relationship obtains between religion and culture, so that a given culture cannot be transmitted without its traditional religion. Discussions on the
paths of "inculturation," on the other hand, presuppose that religion and
culture are distinct, if related, quantities. The difference between them
grounds the "transcultural" meaning of this concrete religious tradition or
that one, which is supposed not to be restricted to a given culture. On their
relationship, conversely, rests the charge to give religion its respective context in the culture of the land of its origin as well as in that of possible mission countries.

The question of the relation of religion and culture involves the question
of the relation of culture and society, the moment—especially as a consequence of migratory movements—there appear minorities in a society that
lay claim not only to a free practice of their religions but at the same time
to cultural self-determination. Freedom of religious practice was first understood as an individual freedom, while participation in societal life was oriented to the capacity for participation in the general culture. (Hence the
importance of access to schools and colleges for religious minorities, as
well—for example, Jews in Germany, who, without surrender of their religious singularity, have sought to demonstrate their full membership in the
German cultural community and therefore also in German society.) But
now we have the aspiration of a "multicultural society," with the claim not
only to religious autonomy, but to cultural autonomy as well: Not only religion but also cultures, in their respective peculiarities, ought to become, it
is said, instead of a common concern of society at large, the affair of particular individual groups within society. And as the state must maintain
neutrality with regard to religious differences, so now society is to maintain

neutrality vis-à-vis cultural differences, to limit itself to the assurance of space to these differences, and, in case of conflict, to offer procedures for a peaceful settlement.

The philosopher of religion is concerned by this development, in part only called for thus far, in part already operative, under the following viewpoints: In an extensively secularized society, what is the duty of a culture in terms of society at large? If society must behave neutrally with regard to religious differences, to what extent does culture inherit, as a factor for integration in this society, functions that previously fell to religion? Is the price of religion's exoneration from the tasks of the cultural integration of society as a whole (a consequence of the secularization process) this: that now the unity of culture must accomplish what no longer can be accomplished through the unity of religion—the shaping of a *forma mentis* that binds together the members of a society over and above all content-differences in their views and intentions, and thereby renders them capable of dialogue? And what does it mean for such a society if, after the unity of religion, the unity of culture, too, offers room for a multiplicity? Or in brief: Does the unity of religion facilitate the formation of multiculturality (for example, the shaping of culturally specific forms of Christianity), while a secularized society is radically threatened by the loss of its cultural unity? And what does it mean for the relationship between religion and society when, within a secularized society, religions, or partial phenomena of the religious, acquire the identifying characteristics of appurtenance to this or that partial cultural society?—when, for instance, it becomes necessary for Arabs in a West European country, even those "alienated" from their religion, to take part in certain religious celebrations of Islam in order to have themselves recognized as members of a particular partial cultural community. The relation between religion and culture, then, precisely in a society at once secularized, and tending more and more toward the multicultural, calls for a new determination.

In brief: In view of the growing intensity of the encounters between religions and cultures, the old question of the *relationship of religion, culture, and society* wins new currency. More specifically, this question bears, on the one hand, on the conditions of the "transculturality" of certain moments of individual religions (that is, their importance beyond the cultural circle in which a given religion has arisen or has developed its special fertility), and on the other hand, on the conditions of the "inculturation" of religions in societies to which they have not originally been native. More recently, the question bears on the relation of religion, culture, and society—especially in terms of the social status of religious communities within secularized societies, first of all the status of religious minorities to the extent that they claim not only freedom of religion but also, bound up with the same, their cultural autonomy.

"New Religions" and the Question of Criteria for the Distinction of the "Genuinely Religious" from "Pseudomorphoses of Religion"

The procedures of selection and combination that characterize the "new religions" are to be distinguished from the encounter of concrete religious tradition communities, and the resulting problems of the interreligious dialogue and multiculturality.

A Strange Involvement with Elements of Tradition: Eclecticism, Syncretism, Allegorization

We have spoken above of the sacralization of certain positions of political morality, which can be studied with special clarity in the position of supporters of the "environmental movement." Now we discover that precisely this movement can be connected with attempts to reach back, behind the biblically grounded "de-idolization of the world," to archaic forms of religion that would be "nearer to nature." The intended service to the future and the criticism, bound up therewith, of the present are thus connected with the attempted revival of a distant, indeed archaic, past. It is a matter of an argument form observable again and again in the history of religion: To reach back to origins is to deprive the present of legitimacy ("It was not so in the beginning") and facilitates the call for a radical revision of relationships in preparation for a future that is the object of religious hope. At first this future was merely promised, while the accomplishment of this promise, in the claim of the herald, is now at hand. The concept coined by historians of religion in another connection, "regression in the service of progression," can be applied to these forms of recent religious archaism.

To be sure, the archaisms on whose strength the "new religions" call into play certain elements of the ancient East, or indeed of Native American, or, finally, of the Hindu worship of nature divinities, against conceptualizations of the Jewish-Christian-Islamic God of history entertain a characteristic selective element. Whatever the emphasis on a rehabilitation of reverence for the "Magna Mater," generally speaking, fortunately, there is little inclination to rehabilitate the temple-prostitution originally bound up with it. And with all high consideration for the Native American worship of the sun, one scarcely wishes to return to the practice of human sacrifice, based in the myth of the sun that died and rose again. Finally, an equally high esteem for Vedic poetry ordinarily does not lead to an imitation of those forms of radical asceticism through which the Hindu "holy man" seeks to attain to enlightenment and thereby prepare for the liberating unification of the individual atman with the all-pervading Brahman.

And not only the content contexts, from which the individual words and rites are drawn, are omitted, but the social contexts as well: the introduction of such elements of religious conduct in the life of concrete religious tradition-communities is regarded as nonessential. In connection with the "new piety," it occurs that a person will recite passages from the Rig Veda with religious reverence without seeking to become a member of a concrete Vedic community. Another may ring a Hindu temple gong, or operate a laman "prayer wheel," and interiorize, with each turn of the wheel, the sacred text, "O thou mystery of the gem in the lotus blossom"—"*Om mani padme hum*"—but not participate in other religious words and behaviors of the Hindus or lamans. Or one lights, on eight successive winter evenings, the eight lamps of the Jewish Hanukkah menorah, or recites, as day begins to dawn, the prologue of the Gospel of John with its celebration of the life that is the light of human beings, but does not think of applying for candidacy in a Jewish worship community or a Christian church.

Thus, here verbal and behavioral elements from various religious traditions are severed from their context and brought into new associations, in which they take on a new meaning. This behavior frequently gives the appearance of the arbitrary and occasions the suspicion that it is a matter not of new forms but of degenerate forms of religious conduct. At all events, the question posed by the philosophy of religion as to the criteria of the discernment of the "genuinely religious" from its "pseudomorphoses" wins, through phenomena of this kind, new currency. The problem for the philosophy of religion, occasioned by such behavior with partial components of various religious traditions, bears first of all on the relationship between element and context and thus the relationship between religion and history (which latter is always the history of concrete tradition communities).

The Question of Adequate Criteria of Evaluation

With regard to the phenomena just described, hasty judgments are to be avoided. Both the use unrelated to their original contexts of elements of foreign traditions and the selective appropriation of elements from other religious traditions, occur so frequently in the history of religions that one suspects that this procedure, which contradicts all rules of today's hermeneutics, must have a specifically religious ground. Examples of usage foreign to its original context would be: the incorporation of individual verses of a hymn into a psalm altogether different in content and form; the application, suggested solely by its words, of a prophetic utterance to the context of a proclamation of altogether different context; the retention of a rite in a completely altered worship context. All of these manners of application of verbal and behavioral elements can be termed "allegorical," since the retained element betokens continuation, while its meaning is always different, in the new context, so that it "says something else"—*alla agoreuei.* Examples of a selective incorporation of elements from foreign traditions are: the reception of a foreign god into one's erstwhile indigenous pantheon; the ascription of a narrative found in another community to one's own ancestors or eponymous hero; the redactional alteration and hence reinterpretation of songs used in worship, which have been found in a foreign cultus and are now to be sung in one's own worship. In all of these cases, a selective adoption occurs whereby one's own tradition determines the criterion of selection; and it occurs with the intent of assimilating the foreign traditional element as a medium of a new understanding of one's own tradition. The procedure is therefore at once eclectic and syncretistic.

The sheer fact that the "new religions" endow texts and rites with an altered meaning (that is, make allegorical use of them), and that they deal with elements from various traditions in eclectic and syncretistic fashion, is therefore in itself no sufficient grounds for judging them differently and more negatively than other religions, with which such phenomena likewise occur. Such a judgment is to be rendered only when it is possible, first, to determine the specific sense of allegorical procedures of interpretation, and eclectic-syncretistic procedures of incorporation, and then to decide the boundaries beyond which such procedural manners cease to be religiously meaningful—and only thereupon to ask whether these boundaries are transgressed by the "new religions."

Here we can observe that both the allegorization of one's own tradition content and the selective appropriation of elements from foreign tradition connections have their function in the reflection of religious tradition communities on their own history. The allegorical use of elements of one's own tradition reflects, as could and should be shown in individual cases, an awareness of the identity of the tradition community and the recall, constitutive of this community, of the diversity of its historical periods, and resulting diversity in the conditions of reception. The selective assimilation of elements of foreign religious tradition, however, is an expression of the constitutive meaning that can attach to interreligious encounter for the history of a given religious tradition community itself. Neither the allegorizing of one's own tradition content, nor the reception of selected content from abroad, therefore abandons the connection of one's own tradition history. There is a difference here from the procedure of interpretation and reception maintained by an enlightened philosophy of religion, which seeks to extract the "core of eternal, reasonable truth" from its "accidental historical habiliments"—or again from the procedure of interpretation and reception practiced by the members of "new religions." The latter goes beyond the discovery of a stock of primitive symbols, which would mediate religious experiences without essential reference to the concrete tradition communities in question and their history.

Indeed, to the extent that the members of "new religions" even involve themselves in an argumentational grounding of their procedure, they will say that it is a permanent task to distinguish and to deliver the true core of religious traditions from abusive shapes and forms, and that this is valid even for religions originating in earliest times. These are never handed down to us in their original purity, we hear, but always in their historical form, and this form calls for a critique. Not their dull or trivial reproduction but only their critical appropriation permits their guiding fund of truth to emerge for our time as well. But to this end it is necessary to let such texts and actions "speak for themselves," without attending to those special meaning contexts that have overgrown them in their respective tradition communities in the course of history. And this procedure, we are told, serves, for instance, not for the rejection of Judaism, Christianity, and Islam, in favor of restored nature religions, but for the liberation, even in the monotheistic religions, of the true, spiritual core from its historical, seductive, superficial accretions. But precisely then, it is hoped, the commonality of the religions will become clear, which have come into contrast with one another not through their "true core," but through the expression of their historical overgrowth.

And so, with all the basic difference between the enlightened, rational religions and the "new religions," which incline more to irrationalism, their assessment depends on the same question: To what degree is it essential for religion that the normativity of religious content at the same time constitutes concrete tradition communities and their history? Beginning at what frontier does the attempt to leave behind the history of such tradition communities, together with all of their "historical accidents," lead to a depravation of the religious act and its specific intentionality?

In brief: In view of "new religions," new currency accrues to the question, on the part of the philosophy of religion, as to the manner of acquisition of *criteria for the distinction of the "genuinely religious" from its "pseudomorphoses."* In this connection, two problems primarily emerge for the philosophy of religion: To what degree is it essential for religion to develop a *consciousness of its own history* (a consciousness that can also be expressed in allegorizations of its own fund of tradition and in the appropriation of elements of foreign tradition)? And within what bounds is the attempt legitimate, within religious traditions, to overcome the "historically accidental" in favor of the "eternally valid"?

Questions for the Philosophy of Religion
on the Part of Theology

Finally, we can point to a need for orientation that has arisen through developments in church and theology in time of crisis. These developments too have occasioned new expectations of the philosophy of religion.

1. The process of advancing secularization concerns the churches in Europe in a manner that threatens their very existence. They complain of a decline in church attendance, their waning influence on publicly accepted values, and recently, a decrease of their members' participation in public affairs. Withdrawal from the church, and especially a decrease in the number of baptisms, suggests that this development will prevail. It is a condition of existence for the churches that they manage to hand on their faith tradition to each coming generation; and, conversely, this faith tradition can be preserved only if it has witnesses in every generation. Thus, as early as the beginning of this century, Alfred Loisy could rightly say: "The church is as necessary for the gospel as the gospel for the church" (Alfred Loisy, *Das Evangelium und die Kirche* [Paris, 1902], 139). This task—to preserve the life of the church through the transmission of the gospel, and at the same time to enable the church to transmit its proclamation through the preservation of the life of the church—encounters increasing difficulties in a secularized society. And in this connection, the *theological* question is unavoidable: What *understanding* of the Christian faith can and should be transmitted to the coming generation? But this theological problem implies, as we are about to show, problems such as can be elucidated and resolved only through *arguments to be maintained by the philosophy of religion*.

After all, in view of the danger that, in Europe at any rate, the continuity of the handing on of the faith could be interrupted, it becomes more urgent to attempt to interpret this proclamation anew. Within the Christian churches, this consideration is not in last place as a reason why an ever more intense controversy is being waged over a right understanding of each one's respective tradition of the faith, and over a praxis corresponding to this understanding of the faith. This shows that it is not only content that is at stake but, especially, the criteria on which a theological theory at once adequate to the faith tradition and conducive to its transmission is to be distinguished, along with a moral praxis, from a falsification of the proclamation of the faith or a seduction of consciences respectively. Neither the canonical rank of texts, nor traditional confessional formulae, nor the positions of institutionally accredited authorities are above question and acknowledged as authoritative by all involved—that is, even by members of the faith community who dissent from content. And only under this presupposition would there be sufficient guarantee for the common ground of a criteriology by which diverging opinions could be evaluated. The contrary seems to be the case: content-oriented controversies over the right understanding of faith enunciations, or norms of activity extracted from the same, are reproduced in the struggle for or against the obligatory character of certain criteria. "Directions" within the Christian churches and communities are distinguished not least of all by their respective answers to the question of "what counts as an argument." What is the relative importance for argument of the appeal to a biblical text? What obligation for the faithful attaches to the expounding of the Bible by theological experts? Can one appeal, in the appraisal of a given doctrine, to the consensus of the faithful? And here, is it the agreement of the generations over the course of centuries that is meant, or is it the assent accorded to a given theology by the majority of Christians living at the present moment? What is the importance, in this connection, of confessional declarations or conciliar acts?

The question, which we broach here, of a criteriology for the evaluation of theological debates and ecclesial "directional battles" (which latter are not always waged on the basis of theological arguments) also renders a problem inescapable for the philosophy of religion: Of what sort is that reality with which a religious enunciation must "be in agreement" in order to be "true"? What does it mean, in the specifically religious connection, to "be in agreement"? What, in the religious context, is at stake depending on whether or not an enunciation is acknowledged as "true"? (What is the relative value of "enunciatory truths" in a religious context?) And what are the possible procedures of certification of truth—thus, procedures of argumentation—adequate to specifically religious truth? (See R. Schaeffler, *Das Gebet und das Argument: Zwei Weisen des Sprechens von Gott* [Düsseldorf, 1989]; idem, "Die Vielfalt der Weisen religiöser Wahrheit und ihres sprachlichen Ausdrucks," in W. Kerber, ed., *Die Wahrheit der Religion* [Munich, 1994], 73–109.)

2. Associated with the uncertainty over the criteria of what can be regarded as theoretically true and practically obliging in a religious context, is the observably dwindling willingness, or motivation, within the faith

communities to accept responsibility for spiritual leadership. In the Catholic Church, the most evident indicator is the growing shortage of priests. (And the delight of the laity at recently being entrusted with responsibilities whereby this dearth has been temporarily counterbalanced seems already to be on the wane.) In the Lutheran Church, the same decline is observable in the compensating inclination of many ministers to shift the center of gravity of their activity from the proclamation of the gospel and the dispensing of the sacraments to other areas of activity, in which not the ability for specifically spiritual leadership but altogether different competence is required. In principle, therefore, other persons, without any ecclesial authority, can function equally well in these fields. What is now generally described as ministers' "role uncertainty," heavily criticized in so many discussions on a new determination of these ministers' "competency" in relation to the "laity," is not only a result of the enduring currency of the old question, become especially acute today, of the relationship between clerical ordination, on the one side, and baptism and the "community priesthood of the faithful," on the other. Rather, we also see that a more general question remains unelucidated, which can only be appositely posed and answered through arguments in terms of the philosophy of religion: What is the specific structure of a religious community (or, expressed theologically, of a "temple of living stones"), and what interplay of activities is necessary if the "upbuilding" of this specific social body is to succeed? In terms of the philosophy of language: What are the specific pragmatics of religious argumentation? Into what sort of relationship do speaker and auditor enter in such argumentation? And what follows for its semantics? How do the elements of such argumentation acquire that relevance and meaning content that bestow on them, within this special manner of argumentation, their convincing character?

In brief: With regard to the difficulties into which theology has come with the attempt to define the conditions determining whether, within a secularized society, the "transmission of the faith" can be secured, the question becomes more urgent how the pragmatics and semantics of argumentation within religious tradition communities are to be determined. Only thus can a criterion, as well, be acquired as to what "counts as argument" within a theological argumentation—that is, what possesses compelling force.

PROBLEMS OF METHOD

Methods of an attempted philosophy of religion today are to be assessed not least of all on the basis of the extent to which they are adequate to do justice to that need for orientation that has recently arisen in the context of an altered situation of religious history and that ought to be summarily discussed in connection with the questions formulated immediately above.

The Method-Combination Suggested in This Book

The survey given in this book of the most important types of philosophy of religion has led to the recommendation that the methods of transcendental philosophy, phenomenology, and speech analysis be used conjointly. Such a combination is *necessary*, because neither transcendental philosophy, when it is made the basis of the philosophy of religion, nor phenomenology, nor the analysis of religious language is immune to self-misunderstandings. Transcendental philosophy, especially when it seeks to ground the consideration of religion by way of the development of a philosophical concept of God, can lead to a manner of thinking as undialectical as it is unhistorical— a manner of thinking that can do justice neither to the specific dialectic of religious experience nor to the historicity of religion. Phenomenology can degenerate into the unstructured collection of religious phenomena that Scheler contemptuously dubbed "picture-book phenomenology"; nor have all phenomenologists of religion been immune to this threat. The analysis of religious language can become a mere description of linguistic oddities, without leading to an understanding of the essential grounds that compel the religious person to precisely this way of speaking; and this destroys the standards for an adequate appraisal and a further critique, on the part of religion itself, of religious speech. Only a critical, and at the same time hermeneutic, reciprocal relationship of these three methods has been seen as suited to solve these possible self-misunderstandings of each of the three methods described (see above, pp. 118ff.)

But the combination of these three methods has been seen to be *possible*, because the said methods refer to one another on their very premises. Phenomenology, as Husserl has understood it from a point of departure in his "ideas," is itself a specific kind of transcendental questioning (see Husserl, *Ideen I*, 216): its responsibility consists in expounding the connection obtaining between the structure of noeses (acts of noesis) and the peculiarity of the objects (noematic correlates) revealed to them in an originating sense. And the analysis of linguistic structure permits a description, in an empirically determinable manner, of the peculiarity of the acts through which objects are revealed to us, as well as the respective manner of this object-relationship in the concrete variety of the manner of their materialization. This places phenomenology, with its investigation of noeses and noemata, out of reach of the debatable methods of "introspection," and lends it surer ground. And linguistic analysis, having at first proclaimed the "linguistic turn" in philosophy, has recently executed a "transcendental turn" for its own part, inasmuch as it has begun to indicate, when it comes to language, the structural conditions of the object relationship (see Peter E. Strawson, *Analysis and Metaphysics* [Oxford, 1992; in German, *Analyse und Metaphysik* (Munich, 1994), esp. chap. 8: "Bedeutung und Verstehen— Strukturelle Semantik"]).

Such a combination of methods is also suggested in more recent publications on the phenomenology of religion and on the analysis of religious language. Particularly worthy of note are the following:

Paul Ricoeur, *Entre herméneutique et sémiotique* (Limoges, 1990); Marco Olivetti, ed., *Religione, Parola, Scrittura* (Padua, 1992); Jean François Courtine, ed., *Phénoménologie et Théologie* (Paris, 1992), especially the following contributions: Paul Ricoeur, "Expérience et langage dans le discours religieux" and Jean-Louis Chrétien, "La parole blessée—Phénoménologie de la prière"); Jean Greisch, ed., *Comprendre et interpréter: Le paradigme herméneutique* (Paris, 1992); and Martin Heidegger's lecture, "Phänomenologie des religiösen Lebens" (Gesamtausgabe, part 2: Vorlesungen, vol. 60, Frankfurt a. M., 1995).

Methodological Objections

Granted, in this connection it must not be left out of account that, in more recent times, fundamental objections have been raised against transcendental philosophy in general and against a transcendental understanding of phenomenology in particular, that bear on the application of these methods within the philosophy of religion as well. Despite the difference of the argumentation's contexts within which these objections are formulated and grounded, still their governing viewpoint is common: transcendental philosophy, inasmuch as it has as its theme the constitution of objects through the acts of regard and thought, is said to proclaim the supremacy of the subject over the world of objects. (As early as 1980, Max Müller published his *Der Kompromiß, oder Vom Unsinn und Sinn menschlichen Lebens* [Freiburg and Munich]), in which he interprets transcendental philosophy as a method of subjectivity's having its way in confrontation with the world.) The same would hold, we hear, even for one's fellow human being, who, if the doctrine of the constitution of the object happened to be correct, could appear to the regarding subject only as the latter's forms of regard and thought permit. In this sense, we are told, phenomenology, as well, if it understands itself transcendentally, is a theory of the universal dominance of intentionality, which allows no space for the other as such (cf. E. Lévinas,

"Die Spur des Anderen," published first in *Tijdschrift voor Filosofie* [Louvain, 1963] and then in *En découvrant l'existence avec Husserl et Heidegger* [Paris, 1967]; in German in idem, *Die Spur des Anderen* [Freiburg and Munich, 1983], 209–35). But since, in the conceptualization of the transcendental philosophers, say their critics, the supreme condition of all object-relationships is the unity of the act "I think," therefore a regard in terms of transcendental philosophy (or transcendental phenomenology) flattens out the diversity of form (the "heteromorphy") of the realms of experience, which diversity finds its expression in the respective autonomy of the linguistic relationship, with its intersubjective regulation or "language play." (See J.-F. Lyotard, *Réponse à la question: Qu'est-ce que le postmoderne?* idem, *La condition postmoderne* [Paris, 1979]; in German: "Was ist postmodern?" and "Das postmoderne Denken," both in W. Welsch, ed., *Wege aus der Moderne* [Weinheim, 1988].) Thus, we are told, even the analysis of language is a corrective, rather than a field of application, of transcendental reflection.

This criticism of transcendental thought acquires an especially sharp edge when turned against the application of that thought to questions of the philosophy of religion. Now the indictment runs: transcendental thinking succumbs to the pressure to knot all phenomena together in systematic unity and to acknowledge as real only what permits insertion into such a systematic oneness. But thereby such thought overlooks precisely that "real" that withdraws from the power of our concepts, and that can be designated adequately only in the invocation of the Name. Vis-à-vis this forcible, systematizing intervention, then, the emphasis maintained by the heteromorphs would seem to function as a vindication of the honor of God. Therefore Jean-François Lyotard can conclude his answer to the question "What is postmodern?" with a programmatic "Total war! Intensify the conflicts, rescue the honor of the Name!" (Lyotard, 203). And on an altogether different premise, E. Lévinas seeks to show that the characteristic primacy of the subject and its intentionality for all transcendental thought must be defeated if it is to be possible that "God occur to the thought" (cf. E. Lévinas, *De Dieu qui vient à l'idée* [Paris, 1982; in German, *Wenn Gott ins Denken einfällt* [Freiburg and Munich, 1985]).

In the following pages, we shall attempt to deal with these objections, not *in abstracto*, by way of general methodological reflections, but by investigating whether the conclusions at which a transcendental and at the same time phenomenological analysis of religious language arrives are necessarily of such a kind as really to be open to this criticism.

ATTEMPTS AT AN APPLICATION

An amalgamation of methods shown to be necessary and possible alike, however called into question, can now be put to a test. We must show what this amalgamation contributes to the explication and solution of those questions of the philosophy of religion that have become especially urgent in more recent times. These questions owe their urgency not only to the state of intra-professional philosophical discussion but also, and far more so, to certain societal developments of which we spoke at the beginning of this "Supplementary Material," as these developments have occasioned an "altered need for orientation." It is to be examined, therefore, whether, by means of the methods here proposed, the philosophy of religion can achieve a contribution to the orientation expected of it. First, then, we may ask whether a philosophy of religion applying methods of this kind can escape the danger of subjecting the content of religious experience to that "supremacy of intentionality," and itself succumb to that "pressure of the system" that critics hold to be the inevitable and corrupting consequences of transcendental thought.

Religion's Rationality and Capacity for Critique

We live in a time when, on the one hand, the conclusions of the criticism of religion are so nearly foregone in the public mind that it seems superfluous to justify them with laborious argumentation, and when, on the other hand, areas of our culture, especially politics and (environmental) ethics, are sacralized in a new way and therefore find themselves exposed to a heightened suspicion of ideology. In these circumstances, the philosophy of religion is expected to deliver a clarification especially of two questions. (1) *Does religion imply its own specific rationality,* overlooked by classic religious criticism and yet forbidding an appeal to that irrationalism that not infrequently arises from weariness with scientific and technological rationality (see above, p. 142)? (2) *Is it possible to see in religions* (if indeed not in all manifestations of the religious) *the possibility of a combination of confidence in the unconditionality of the True and Good with self-criticism of all human cognition and willing?* And can this specifically religious form of criticism be used as an indication of the possibility of a criticism of ideology even in profane contexts—a criticism that does not, on the strength of a logic immanent to itself, compel the universalization of mistrust in ideology and therewith generate a skepticism that renders any responsible theory and practice impossible (see above, pp. 145–46)?

If we ask whether religion implies a specific manner of rationality—and included therein a specific capacity for self-criticism—we shall have to investigate in what manner the religious act (noesis) relates to its object (noema). After all, it depends on the particular nature of religious intentionality whether the religious act sufficiently clearly manifests a difference and relation between the claim of this object and the manner in which we grasp it. In traditional language: Does the particular nature of religious intentionality allow room for the *veritas semper maior*, whose nature as standard of human thought and behavior will indeed be apprehensible, but will be apprehensible in a way in which it is clear at the same time that this apprehension always lags behind the apprehended claim? Then, indeed, the religious act would allow a subject to relate to its content critically and at the same time hermeneutically: critically in distinguishing the *cognoscendum* from the *cognitum*, and hermeneutically in the revelation of the *cognoscendum* in the criticizable form of the *cognitum*, in which form that *cognitum* acquires the manner of its presence for us.

Now, there are examples of religious speech that clearly intimate that this speech exacts of the speaker a language at the boundaries of the enunciable, without thereby diminishing the precision of the expression and thereby the unequivocal character of what is enunciated. Rather, tensions between the grammatical form and the semantics of the expressions applied will be purposely introduced in order to make clear and explicit, in the manner of speech at hand, the boundaries of the enunciable and the ever greater claim of the object of the discourse. Religious language thus becomes the testimonial of a manner of experience in which the subjects of the experience are carried to the frontiers of their experiential capacity (and therefore of their capacity for speech), without falling dumb in the face of what towers before them. Religious speech proves to be the expression, but also the preliminary structural sketch, of a certain kind of experience characteristic of religion (see R. Schaeffler, "Sprache als Bedingung und Folge der Erfahrung," in W. Beinert et al., *Sprache und Erfahrung als Problem der Theologie* [Paderborn, 1978], 11–36). And the semantics of the expressions applied in this speech, especially the particular way in which the names of God applied in religious speech relate to the reality designated therein, becomes understandable only when it is grasped as an expression of that relationship into which the religious speaker enters in order thereby to become capable of religious experience (see R. Schaeffler, "Ein transzendentalphilosophischer Gottesbegriff und seine mögliche Bedeutung für die Theologie," in M. Kessler et al., *Fides quaerens intellectum* [Tübingen, 1992], 97–112).

A like consideration shows that religious subjectivity is never unquestioning self-assurance. Rather it belongs to its peculiarity that religious subjects ascribe their capacity for the execution of the religious act not to themselves but precisely to that reality to which this act relates. In Christian terms: It belongs to faith to grasp oneself as a gift of grace from God, to whom this faith is addressed. But at the same time, a property of the religious act is the consciousness that those who perform it do not subjectively exhaust those possibilities that have become accessible to them objectively through the "opening of the eyes." Thus, even for the special case of religious experience, as it comes to expression in religious speech, Husserl's phenomenological basic law is valid: Between noesis and noema, a "strict correlation" obtains (see *Ideen I*, 232). That means, for the religious act and the reality it intends that only to the religious act is the religiously significant reality (the Holy) "revealed in the first instance"; and only the Holy, understood as the real in terms of a specifically religious peculiarity of essence, represents the specific fulfillment of the religious act. But "correlation" (interrelationship) does not necessarily denote symmetry. And in the special case of the religious act, the relation of noesis and noema is asymmetric in the highest degree: religious noesis is due to its noema, without ever attaining it *adequately*. Indeed, in this case not even the supreme principle of all Cartesian philosophy is valid—the proposition of the essential inerrancy of self-awareness. To the religious act belongs the consciousness that not only does it lack forms of regard and concept adequate to the reality of the Holy, but also that this act fails to grasp itself adequately, since it cannot adequately gather into its own reflection the enlightenment by the Holy by which it has become possible as a religious act. In Christian terms: the act of faith, understood as a gift of the grace of God, is itself a mystery of faith.

This means, for both of the questions posed above that to the peculiarity of the religious act belongs a specifically religious self-criticism, and indeed a radical one. Where it is lacking we are dealing with pseudomorphoses of the religious. These, in turn, are a privileged source of ideologies. And so the exposition and refutation of ideological self-misunderstandings are tasks essentially immanent to religious consciousness, and hence indispensable. But precisely on this account, religious consciousness is actually extraordinarily sensitive to such ideologies, which come forward not within itself, as falsifications of religion, but are produced outside religion. Wherever claims to truth are raised in such a way that, lurking behind them, we discern the impulse to success for its own sake on the part of individual and partial groups in society, there religious consciousness recognizes the danger of a temptation from which it itself has been delivered only through powerful efforts of self-criticism. This holds for the ideological sacralization of politics and morality, as well as for an ideology of science that no longer strives to justify its right through the effort of argument or grasps its provisional character in a spirit of self-criticism, but has made its conclusions unquestioned matters of course, and the standard of judgment of all phenomena of human life—even religion.

For the relationship of religion to criticism of religion and to secularized society, we can conclude that through the extreme asymmetry of noesis and noema, which asymmetry is compelled to a radical self-criticism, religion can sort through even hostile criticism, extracting arguments such as it can assimilate in a spirit of self-criticism; and where this criticism rests on the alleged obvious self-evidence of scientific or technological rationality, it will expose the ideological character of such self-evidences. Thus, vis-à-vis an argumentational criticism of religion, religion is a partner in dialogue; vis-à-vis a self-evidence that eliminates religion, religion is a keen-eyed critic; in both cases, however, religion proves capable of gaining, from its own, specifically religious, sources, a specific manner of capacity for rational argumentation.

Likewise for the evaluation of the phenomena described above as "secularization of politics and environmental ethics" (see above, pp. 142–46), criteria can be extracted from what has been said. After all, to the extreme asymmetry of noesis and noema corresponds in the practical area the just as infinite difference between the task religious persons know to be incumbent upon them, and all of the aims of their behavior that they can set themselves and realize through their activity. Religious praxis, in its self-understanding, is the human being's participation in the divine activity, and this not only in divine worship but also in the activity that shapes the world. Religious praxis misunderstands itself when it misinterprets the divine commission as sacral legitimation of human efforts to succeed, and thus not only when, for example, it legitimates the violent exclusion of one's political opponent as a service to the divine judgment upon the forces of the evil one but also when it abuses the commission of creation, "Subdue the earth," for the justification of an irresponsible exploitation of nature. And so religious criticism opposes the sacralization of the ideology of revolution just as much as to the sacral legitimation of an ideology of scientific and technological progress.

Granted, religious criticism is just as sharp-eyed with respect to attempts to lend a religious legitimation to a hostility toward science, or to an all-too-passionate attitude of anti-mechanization. Participation in the divine "preservation of creation" is not attained by placing obstacles in the way of scientific knowledge of the world or of the technological shaping of the

world—in the hope that the inhabitability of the earth, for coming generations too, will be adequately at hand merely with what the earth "brings
forth of itself." This is just the way to deny specifically human service to that
creator who has not concluded the work of creation once for all, but who
"works until today" (John 5:17). Where a consciousness of the infinite difference between divine commission and human achievement seduces
persons into an attitude of simple noncompliance, there arises the new ideology of those who, with religious and moral pathos, claim for themselves
the privilege of leaving active concern for the future to those whom they
simultaneously defame as contemptuous of creation and hostile to the
divine creator and preserver of the world.

Finally, a position can be taken, on the basis of what has been said, with
regard to the various directions of sacral feminism and feminist theology. If
a criticism of ideology belongs to the constitutive tasks set religious consciousness, then this holds as well for all forms of an ideology of the patri-
archate, to the extent that it can be shown through arguments that an
interest in "male supremacy" has determined the selection and "weighting"
of the content of religious tradition or the interpretation of biblical texts.
But of course this also holds for the no less ideological attempts to select,
from the plenitude of the findings of the history of religion, those that prove
useful for the assertion of "women's interests," or to give preference to
those respective interpretations of biblical texts that seem suited for the
acquisition by women or particular women's groups of a competitive
advantage in their struggle for social influence. In the one case as in the
other, claims to truth in the areas of religious history or theology become
weapons in the interests of particular groups of society, although these
groups each represent the half of humanity. But especially, many arguments
that are brought forward by feminism are examples of that universalization
of mistrust of ideology that renders any rational weighing of evidence and
counterevidence impossible: Those who see nothing else at work in the
whole history of religions and theologies but expressions of the "battle of
the sexes," are open to the suspicion that they admit "truth" only under the
viewpoint of its social effectiveness in the service of their own interests. A
universalized mistrust of ideology, here as always, returns to haunt its representatives, male or female.

But in a methodological respect, the considerations just presented have
shown that it is by the analysis of religious speech that the specifically religious relation of noesis and noema can be seen; and it is from this relationship that the specifically religious manner of capacity for criticism, and of
rationality, flows. It is thus the amalgamation of the methods of linguistic

analysis and phenomenological-transcendental philosophy that makes for the materialization of that special kind of critical self-understanding that is characteristic of the religious act and its object-reference.

Differentiation of the Religious from Its Distortions as Task of Argumentation in Theology and the Philosophy of Religion

In a day when we witness the appearance of the various forms of the "new religions," whose relationship to the religions of tradition is eclectic as well as syncretistic, an old question gains new currency: In what fashion can *criteria for the discernment of the "genuinely religious" from its "pseudomorphoses"* be obtained? In this connection, two questions, especially, arise for the philosophy of religion: To what extent is it essential for religion to develop an *awareness of its own history* (an awareness that can be expressed in allegorization of its own deposit of tradition and in the assimilation of foreign tradition elements)? And within what bounds is the attempt legitimate to surmount, within religious traditions, the "historically contingent" in favor of the "eternally valid" (see above, pp. 152–53)? But here there is a connected question—how an argument must look if it is to protect religious consciousness from ruinous self-misunderstandings. After all, only then can a criterion also be acquired for what "counts as argument" within a theological argumentation—that is, what possesses the power of demonstration (cf. above, pp. 153–55). What we have just said concerning religion's specific rationality and capacity for criticism enables us to answer these questions, as well.

Religious speech, as we have just said, is, in its form, an expression of religious experience; at the same time it renders the speakers capable of the specifically religious experience, since it leads them to give the individual subjective content of an event a place in the specific context of experience. The reference to possible experience, then, becomes the distinguishing characteristic of content-filled religious speech, by contradistinction from that evacuation of content of religious speech that the New Testament calls *kenophōnia,* the "production of empty noise" (1 Timothy 6:20; 2 Timothy 2:16). But since what is supposed to be at stake is the enablement not of simply any experiences but of specifically religious experiences, it must be seen whether the dialectic of this experience comes to expression in the content of what is said: this dialectic always includes what cannot adequately be grasped and expressed, since its ever greater demand finds any human response insufficient. In brief: The extent of specifically religious self-criticism becomes the index by which genuinely religious speech, and therewith genuinely religious experience, can be distinguished from the religious "disguise" of acts and content of an altogether different nature. Especially, it exposes the attempt of competitive self-justification—the core of all ideologies, inasmuch as it settles the speaker in the right and any opponents in the wrong, a priori—as a corruption of religious consciousness. And the criticism of everything that Paul calls "self-justification" becomes a central task of theological argumentation.

To be sure, the reference to the dialectic of religious experience that comes to expression in religious speech implies more than a mere summons to vigilance in terms of criticism of ideology. There are other pseudomorphoses of the religious than its ideological abuse; and therefore there are other tasks and standards of argumentation in theology than the warning against "competitive self-justification." If, structurally, religious speech is an indefatigable testimonial to the necessity of a discourse at the frontiers of the enunciable, and if it thereby both enables and testifies to a kind of experience through which subjects are led to the frontiers of their capacity for experience, then genuine religious phenomena will always have something of contingency (non-necessity and non-coercibility) about them, with which, in passing through a phase of "not understanding," persons have their "eyes opened in a new way." Accordingly, the religious act is always an act of astonished indebtedness, in that the persons who perform this act do not ascribe to themselves the capacity for it. It need not be a question of surprising and extraordinary experiences of enlightenment and conversion. However, the "new light" (that is, the altered shape of all of the subject's cognition) that "dawns" in the religious experience will convict the subjects of the "blindness of their hearts," which heretofore, owing to a struggle of their own for cognition, has prevented them from seeing what has now, after the opening of the eyes, become evident to them.

Among the distinguishing characteristics of the "genuinely religious," therefore, in contradistinction to its distortions or "pseudomorphoses," is the fact that the religious act is owed to an experience beyond any availability to its subject; at the same time, this act makes itself available for future religious experience. A "ground rule" of all theory of experience can be reduced to the formula: No experience is of such a kind that it has rendered future experiences superfluous, or could be made meaningless through future experiences. For the religious experience, whose identifying mark is that the religious act co-grasps the infinite distance between the reality intended by it and its manner of grasping and apprehending, this rule is valid in a special way. No religious experience is of such a kind that it would exclude subsequent novel, astonishing manifestations of the same numinous reality. But neither does any of these novel manifestations of the numinous reality rob of their meaning earlier manners of experience of it.

This rule affords a criterion for the recognition and avoidance of two misunderstandings of religious experience, and two distorted religious attitudes resulting therefrom. First, religious experience can be misunderstood as conveying to its subject an ultimate knowledge of the Holy that has no need of being surpassed in the future. This misunderstanding results in the specific "unteachability of the pious," and the "foolishness of the wise" in matters of religion—those who regard themselves as protected a priori from any possible shock to the orientation of their religious world. But second, religious experience can be misunderstood as revealing, in the novelty of its light, everything heretofore experienced and known as sheer illusion. This misunderstanding results in the specifically religious temptation to an "abandonment of history," whether one's own personal history, or the common history of a tradition community. On the contrary, the rule just formulated indicates that every individual religious act in which the Holy is discovered in a new, surprising manner is seen in retrospect to have been part of a history of encounters with the Holy—a part open to the future, never calculable in advance, and nevertheless consistent—and that these encounters stand with one another in a relationship of mutual interpretation. Or, to put it negatively: Granted that flight from history is repeatedly suggested by the pregnancy of meaning and surprising novelty of the religious experience, nevertheless that flight proves to be a pseudomorphosis of the religious, which corrupts the peculiarity of the religious act and its relationship to the reality of the Holy. Forgetfulness of history, and still worse, repression of history, must therefore be judged as indicators of a false form of the religious (see R. Schaeffler, *Erfahrung als Dialog mit der Wirklichkeit* [Freiburg and Munich, 1995], esp. chap. "Der Aufbau einer Welt religiöser Erfahrung").

To be sure, it would be misguided to erect as a standard for the assessment of religious phenomena a concept of history and historicity acquired outside of religious contexts. Instead, the specifically religious manner of a reference to history must be extracted from the actual religious act and its expressions. This is especially possible in view of the fact that religious speech indicates how it is that community memory, judged as normative, and individual experience are bound together in the religious act. It is always the specifically religious anamnesis, and anticipation of the future in hope, that prepares the context within which—to paraphrase a dictum of Kant—individual experiences are "spelled out" in such a way that they can be read as content of religious experience. But such content of anamnesis and anticipation is transmitted to the individual through religious tradition and its language. When this context is lost, it becomes impossible to distinguish between the mere subjectivity of a religious episode and the objective validity of a religious experience. Many forms of new religiousness, be they "new religions" or attempts at a radical reinterpretation of existing religious traditions, can serve as examples of how the attempted "withdrawal" from history leads to a loss of the criteria that make it possible to distinguish between the subjectivity of religious representations and the objective validity of religious content.

With this we also acquire a standpoint from which to answer the question posed above, namely, what "counts as argument" within a theological argumentation (see above, pp. 153–55). The content of revelation (especially such as bears on religious memory and hope) become instances to which one can apply in assessing religious statements and behavior, since without them the context cannot be furnished in which a subjective episode must find its place if it is to be acknowledged as objectively valid in a religious sense. What is altogether absent from religious revelation thereby becomes the purely subjective play of religious representations. Radical reformers, as well, and even so-called founders of religions, stand in a constitutive relation to those forms of religious tradition that they criticize. True, the normative character of this tradition repeatedly demonstrates its authenticity by the fact that it makes new manners of religious experience possible. What "counts as argument," then, within a religious discourse, and especially within a theological dispute, is not only the citation called to mind by testimonials of revelation but an interpretation that certifies itself by managing to establish a mutual hermeneutic relationship between tradition and present experience—that is, by managing to render present experience understandable in the light of tradition, but also to offer a "new reading" of revelation in the light of new experiences.

For the evaluation of attempts at theological argumentation, this means that a transcendental argumentation is adequate to the self-governance of religious experience—as that autonomy can be discerned in the structure of religious speech—to the extent that it can show religious truth not only to bear on a discrete area of supernatural realities, but to make accessible to the human spirit in a new way all that can in any way be encountered. But transcendental argumentation misses its own argumentational goal if it seeks to transform the contingent element of religious experience subsequently into a priori knowledge that was always available to a person, in however concealed a manner, and that has always directed that person's gaze on the reality of the world.

The case is analogous with a theology that refuses to reduce the capacity for religious experience to a priori concepts, but grasps it as an innate capacity for the production of images that are available in the profound strata of the soul, and that therefore must serve as patterns for the interpretation of every kind of episode or representation. A theology or general theory of religion integrating depth psychology in this manner can elucidate the fact that, in the language of religion, and thus also in the language of the Bible, symbols play an important role, and that these symbols become understandable only when certain basic experiences of human life are interpreted in their light. But such a theology and theory of religion miss their own argumentational goal if, on the basis of their knowledge and interpretation of this kind of image, they regard the content of the most widely varying religious experiences, with all of their contingency and charge of surprise, as equivalent to one another in meaning. No less than do transcendental concepts, images from the depths of the soul manifest their authenticity by making experiences possible that the theoretician cannot anticipate—not by transmitting a pretended a priori knowledge that allows differences in experiential content to seem nonessential. Those who think that they already know this purportedly ever-the-same meaning of religious symbolic discourse can no longer be surprised and instructed by any of these testimonials, and listening to religious testimonials is transformed into a soliloquy by their interpreter.

A theological argument, or even an argument maintained in the philosophy of religion, that means to protect religious consciousness from ruinous self-misunderstandings, then, must first and foremost protect itself against such a self-misunderstanding. It belongs to the task of this kind of argumentation to lay open the ground of possibility of religious experience and to define more precisely the peculiarity of this experience in contradistinction from other kinds of experience. Precisely for this reason, the argument being used in theology or the philosophy of religion misses its object if it generates a purportedly a priori knowledge of such a kind that it has no further need of the always contingent and unforeseeable religious experience, or explains its content as identical in meaning with all others. The hallmark of what counts as argument in the *theological* connection, then, is its suitability for setting forth testimonials of religious acts (experiences) in such a way that the hearers or readers of the testimonial, and addressees of the exposition, become members of a tradition community. Whether these persons have become capacitated, through the hearing of the word, to active participation in a tradition must be demonstrated by their capacitation, through the hearing of the word, for their own experience—that they are trained for an understanding of the word through their own experience. But the test of the *philosophy of religion* consists in its demonstrating, through analysis of religious language and a phenomenological description of the religious act and its specific reference to religious reality, the structure of that context that makes religious experience possible. But this context is always the social context of a tradition community, built up through the reciprocal hermeneutic play of content of revelation and ever new experiences.

Since a contribution to the erection (*oikodomē*) of a religious tradition community of this sort is the goal of all theological argumentation, one can, with Paul, explain the capacity for this "construction" or "erection" as the hallmark of a theological hermeneutics equal to its task. "Strive to excel in [spiritual gifts] for the upbuilding of the church. And so when anyone speaks in tongues, let that one pray that it be interpreted" (1 Corinthians 14:13–14). The *pragmatic function* of hermeneutic discourse—to make the hearer a member of a community in which tradition can be understood in the light of new experience, and in which these new experiences can be understood in the light of tradition—is at the same time the *indicator that such discourse is semantically successful:* that it is to the measure of the object of which it means to speak.

Religion, Culture, and Society

In a time when, through an abundance of intercultural encounters, the necessity of a dialogue among the religions, as well, has been rediscovered, the old question of the *relationship of religion, culture, and society* wins new currency. More specifically, this question bears, on the one hand, on the conditions of the "transculturality" of certain moments of individual religions (that is, their meaning beyond the cultural orbit in which the religion in question has arisen or has borne special fruit), and, on the other, on the conditions of the "inculturation" of religions in societies to which they were not originally native. Or, formulated more generally: In this situation, the philosophy of religion is urgently confronted with the task of redefining the relationship of religion, culture, and society (see above, pp. 146–47). The combination, which we have now repeatedly described, of the methods of linguistic philosophy, phenomenology, and transcendental philosophy permit a preliminary answer to this question, as well.

After all, religious speech is not only a form of expression, and at the same time a condition, of religious experience. It is also, like any speech, the testimonial of a tradition that precedes and renders possible any individual speaking. Speakers find the language in which they speak ready and waiting; and yet there "is" speech only because, and so long as, individuals speak it, and it acquires its particular form through the "usage" of its respective speakers. Experience, precisely to the eye of linguistic philosophy, proves to be not the act of isolated individuals but the testimonial of their relationship to a linguistic community, a relationship charged with "tensions." Speech, then, is always an excellent site at which to study the relation between the conditions of experience, on the one hand, and, on the other, society and its history. This also holds for religious speech: its speakers bring to expression not only their individual experiences but the manner in which, in dealing with a community possessing a religious tradition, they have first had to have been capacitated for their respective individual manners of experience. Religious speech, and its relation to other, profane speech forms in any given linguistic space betray the manner in which religion participates in the respective particular history of a society and its culture—the manifold ways in which religious speech is co-determined through the encounter of its speaker with these or those other religions—providing an exemplary study site for problems of "transculturality" and "inculturation," as well.

Thus, such an investigation of religious speech is always of phenomenological and transcendental significance alike. It is of transcendental significance because the history of any language, and thus of religious language, is always co-conditioned by the fact that each new generation of speakers seeks to bring to expression, in the transmitted language, its new experiences. Precisely thereby, however, the transmitted language is altered, in such wise that its new structure has made possible new manners of synthesizing subjective impressions, and thereby new manners of transforming these into a variety of content of objectively valid experience. Thus, the alterations of the contexts in which all experience content must find its place have a material influence on the history of the language groups and their grammatical form. This kind of diachronic consideration of language is also of phenomenological significance, since the history of each particular genus of language, for example, the religious, brings to expression at once the history of subjectivity and its reference to objects. A consideration in terms of linguistic philosophy, then, permits a conjunction of the transcendental method and the historical: and in this fashion that historicity of subjects and their capacity for the construction of a world of objects becomes visible that Husserl has brought to expression with his "sense sedimentation" or precipitation and "habitus genesis"—each earlier discovered "meaning" enters the manner of later grasping of objects, while any respective earlier performed act founds a "habitus" that defines later manners of act performance.

A consideration of this kind can make it clear that religious speech, within each culture, is a self-governing system of intersubjective speech-relation (an "autonomous language-play"), and thereby shows that the religious act, as well, presents an autonomous manner of intentionality that can validly stand up to other forms of noesis and their reference to their corresponding noemata. Religion is not wholly and entirely a form of expression of the culture in which it lives. And this is the basis not only for its capacity to criticize its own particular culture, but for its possible meaning for foreign cultures (its "transculturality").

On the other hand, without prejudice to its self-governance, religious speech is not an autarchic, self-sufficient system. Within each culture, it stands in reciprocal operational effect with other linguistic forms. It is influenced by the language of poetry, but also by the language of politics, and even by the language of science, and exercises influence of its own on these specialized or "field" languages. This evinces that the act form and object reference of religion stand in a relationship of reciprocal operational effect with other forms of subjectivity and object reference. What we call a "culture" rests not least of all on this reciprocal effect of the various "areas of culture" and their respective specific linguistic forms. In consequence, the religious act cannot be performed in its peculiarity without its standing in reference to differently structured acts. In particular, without reference to aesthetic, ethical, political, and so forth, experience, religion atrophies. In all due critical distance from culture, religion needs to participate in it in all of its variously structured manifestations. A "non-inculturated" religion is an impaired religion.

Granted, the word "inculturation" is generally used in a more specific sense: not to designate the rooting of religion in the overall concrete context of a culture, but to identify the culture-specific assimilation of influences from foreign cultures. For a more exact description of this process, too, a consideration of religious language can be helpful.

The multiple specialized languages spoken in a given culture stand in reciprocal relationship with the corresponding specialized or "field" languages of other cultures. The poetry of each individual culture is influenced by the poetry of other cultures, and exercises, for its part, influence on the language of these others. The same thing holds for the language of politics, economics, and science. Every culture, at least every more highly differentiated culture, develops, in each of these fields, its own, unique language. But no culture, at least no more highly developed one, speaks a language in any of these fields that does not stand in a relationship of reciprocal influence with the corresponding fields of other cultures. The manner in which a culture assimilates other cultures' language forms of scientific discourse, poetry, or political or ethical discourse, into its own language, thereby stamping the latter with the proper, unique peculiarity of each, is the sign of an ongoing culture-specific assimilation of the influences of foreign cultures. Indeed, what we have here is not a specific problem of the relationship and reciprocal influence of religions but a general phenomenon of the reciprocal influence of cultures, which is seen especially clearly in the reciprocal influence of languages. It holds not only for the different "fields" and their languages but also for the various cultures, that they are self-determining (autonomous) in their relationship to one another, but not self-sufficient (not autarchic).

But if "inculturation" occurs continuously in all areas of culture, and belongs to the history of all areas of culture, then neither must a specifically religious "inculturation" represent in principle a threat to the culture that receives the influence of another culture. In each individual case, however, two questions need to be clarified: Can these influences be assimilated in a culture-specific way? And does this assimilation preserve the meaning content of the elements received in the history of the culture in which they have originated?

In connection with the history of religion, these two questions acquire their special urgency when it is a matter of attempts to transfer not only individual elements of religious tradition from one cultural context to another (which constantly occurs in the history of religion), but also that central content of a religious proclamation and practice through which a given religion as a whole distinguishes itself from other religions. This occurs especially clearly in those religions that condemn the gods worshiped in another as false gods (idols), and therefore reject the worship of these gods as false forms of religion (as idolatry or superstition). This is the case with the religion of Zarathustra as well as for Judaism, Christianity, and Islam. Buddhism occupies a special place here, since in its original form it is strictly "without gods." Such religions demand of their audience a decision ("You must choose which [Gods] you wish to serve" [Joshua 24:15]) and a conversion ("You cannot partake of the Lord's table and the table of the demons at the same time" [1 Corinthians 10:21]). To put the question more concretely: Can a monotheistic religion, or, for that matter, a "religion without God," be incorporated into such cultures as—in all areas of cultural life (for example, in art, poetry, and jurisprudence, but also in their specific form of interpretation of the world and view of moral praxis)—are stamped by polytheistic religions? Or does any such attempt at inculturation occasion the alternatives, either of destroying the receiving culture from the inside out or of evacuating of its original content the religious message that seeks its place in this culture?

In order to answer these questions, it is first of all necessary to inquire into the role played by the call to turn from "false gods" in the history of the religious tradition communities within which this demand is made. Here it is to be recalled that the religions that call for a turning from "false gods," or even from all worship of gods, have not always been unquestionably native even to the cultures in which they have developed their effectiveness. In the demand that one turn away from certain gods (in the case of the biblical religion, from the "gods your ancestors served in the region beyond the river," and the "gods of the Amorites in whose land you are living"—Joshua insists that the people choose between these two groups and the "God who brought us and our ancestors up from the land of Egypt, out of the house of slavery"—Joshua 24:15, 17) is reflected rather the experience of a profound crisis of one's own religion and culture. In the consciousness of the members of these religions, this kind of critical experience, to use Husserl's expressions, has "precipitated out," and the resulting manners of religious judgment have been "habitualized." And long before missioners require such a decision on the part of persons belonging to other cultures, it has been in force as an instruction for the management of this crisis and has remained in force as a warning against a return of analogous crises.

To put it more concretely: Monotheistic as well as god-less religions live on the continuing experience that the sacralization of certain areas of life— family (or tribe) and native soil, blood and ground, perhaps we may update by saying society (whose nucleus is the family) and the economy (whose prototype is represented by the cultivation of farmland)—contains a seductive force of its own, which can corrupt the religious act and its reference to religious reality. Linguistic neologisms like "idols" (biblically, "God-nots") and "idolatry," but also ritualized linguistic forms like the liturgical demand for a decision ("Do you reject Satan—and all his works—and all his pomps?") can arise only where, in a tradition community, this sort of experience has been had of the seducibility of religious consciousness and the seductive power of religious representations and forms of relationship.

Behind the missionary demand on the members of other cultures to join in the rejection of "false gods," then, stands not a conviction of the superiority of one's own culture to the foreign one, but the conviction that the threat to religion through its ruinous self-misunderstanding, now called "idolatry" has not only overthrown one's own culture in the remote past, but is a danger threatening everywhere and always, and that therefore the members of other cultures, too, must be called upon to become aware of this danger and to do what is necessary for its overcoming. Monotheists or members of god-less religions, therefore, seen from the point of view of the history of religions, are "once burned, twice cautious," and seek to render their own crisis experience fruitful also for others, as a warning and an instruction.

"Inculturation" in this context means first of all a demand on one's own religious and cultural tradition community: The experience of the grave religious and general cultural crisis arising there, where the worship of the divine itself proves to be the source of a specific temptation, must become a solid component of the religious tradition of the community that has had this experience. In biblical language: "You must choose which gods you wish to serve. . . . As for me and my house, we wish to serve the Lord," must be repeated from generation to generation, in order constantly to maintain watchfulness against the threat of temptation. Only thus can this experience of crisis "precipitate out," and the decision it demands be "habitualized," in the religious tradition community itself. And indeed it is not coincidental that this demand is found primarily in narrative texts whose purpose is to keep alive a normative memory for the tradition community and to interpret successive present experiences in the light of this memory: experiences of how, again and again, many who think to worship the "true God" actually adore "golden calves," and how each generation must rediscover what it means for it to comply with the injunction to "eliminate the idols."

But then a thus "habitualized" watchfulness must find its place in the culture in whose memory the crisis has "inscribed itself"—or to speak with Husserl, has "precipitated" in that culture. In the case of the biblical religion, this means that the warning against the sacralization of tribe and native soil must affect the organization of society and economy, art and science, if the "monotheism" that has emerged from this crisis is to take root in the culture of the tradition community. The new consciousness even of religious subjects who have become critical of their own piety must, in a "second look," survive the test of the reality of experience—not in the sense of an anti-religious skepticism that universalizes a wariness of idolatry and suspects all piety of superstition, but in the sense of a critical differentiation between the God who means to be worshiped and the earthly ways in which this God's operation is manifested.

Only when the warning against idolatry has thus been "inculturated" into one's own culture, can it thereupon be offered, in a missionary situation, to other tradition communities, in order to capacitate them to two sorts of experience: experiences of the potential for seduction that can issue even from their way of worshiping God, and experiences of how a sharpened self-critical understanding of religion can alter and further develop their own culture. Thus understood, the call to "do away with the false gods" becomes not a directive to esteem one's own history as nonessential but an invitation to understand it in a new—and now, granted, critical—way. Even in the missionary context, the rule holds: The religious proclamation is anything but a monologue on the part of pious souls. After all, it indicts not only godlessness but also piety. It does not, however, reduce its audience to silence: rather it qualifies them for experiences of their own that, in the light of the word that has been heard, they can now have and can even testify to before their teachers. The religious word renders the experience of the hearer not superfluous but finally possible in an altered fashion—and, in the light of the experiences of which the word of proclamation makes its audience capable, the message, too, that has been brought to it, becomes understandable in a new way. If transcendental philosophy leads to the insight that all experience has a dialogic character, and if linguistic philosophy endorses this finding, inasmuch as it shows that hearing proves itself in responding, and responding further develops the speech spoken in common, then it follows that missionary inculturation too is a dialogic event, in which an audience is told what they could not say on grounds of their own tradition, but in which this audience makes a response to the message it has listened to, which also gives the missionaries to hear something that they themselves would not have been able to say.

On the Question of Method: Primacy of Intentionality?

We have just attempted to indicate, at least in outline, the manner in which a philosophy of religion utilizing the method suggested here of conjoining methods of linguistic analysis, transcendental philosophy, and phenomenology can do justice even to the tasks assigned it by more recent societal developments: In its way, and within its bounds, it satisfies the "need for orientation" that we considered at the beginning of this "Supplementary Material" (see above, pp. 139–55).

We do not intend to argue the results of this attempt any further here; rather, let them be left for discussion on the part of readers. However, let us conclude with an attempt to answer the objection raised in more recent times, with manifold modifications, against the transcendental method in general and its application to problems of the philosophy of religion in particular. The transcendental method is suspected of reflecting the modern pretension to a primacy of the subject over its objects, of intentionality over the reality intended, and above all, of the concept over the inconceivable God—and then of making this pretension a general guide to epistemology and thereby of legitimating it.

Now, all transcendental reflection indeed arises out of a criticism of the seemingly so modest, but in reality most pretentious, "self-evidence" of those who maintain that their thought and speech describe only "what is shown on its own basis," and transmit only "what is and as it is." Now, inasmuch as this self-evidence on the part of the knower belies the active participation that we have, in our regard, thought, and speech, in the manner of the "self-manifestation of objects," it simultaneously withdraws this activity of ours from possible criticism. To the contrary, transcendental philosophy emphasizes that there is no cognitional receipt that is not at the same time a shaping, an organization. Of course, this organization has a responsorial character: we seek to respond to a claim on the part of the real—to think this claim for ourselves, and at the same time to make it comprehensible to others by speaking. But we must always have already regarded, thought, and spoken if this claim is to come to hearing for ourselves and others. Transcendental reflection serves to render this responsorial shaping, or organization, of ours conscious, and self-critically to take responsibility for it (see R. Schaeffler, *Erfahrung als Dialog mit der Wirklichkeit* [Freiburg and Munich, 1995]).

This holds for religion, as well, and all the more for philosophical reflection on religion. There is no self-notification on the part of the Holy, no revelation of God, without the active participation if its hearing, seeing, thinking, and speaking addressees. We "have," to put it in Christian fashion, the word of God only in the echo of the response the prophets and apostles have given to this word. And we hear their answering word only inasmuch as we answer to it for our own part. It is this response of ours that seeks our critical responsibility. A "primacy" of the subject, of its intentionality, of its concepts, materializes only inasmuch as this answer or response of the seer and hearer is constitutive of the self-notification of the Holy and divine. Human beings are "hearers of the word" only to the extent, and only in the manner, that they submit to the claim of this word that they make answer—to be sure, only to the extent, and only in the manner, that they "see through" their answer to the extent of perceiving, self-critically, its inadequacy.

Therefore, there is no religion without religious speech or language. And on the same grounds, religious speaking is always at the frontier of the enunciable—not, however, in order to reduce human discourse to silence, rather in order, through this discourse, to make the call to ever new responses audible. The relationship between the "external word" that hearers cannot themselves say, and their own response, of which they cannot be deprived, since they are called to this response precisely through the word, is repeated in the relationship between the religious tradition already at hand as a standard for the religious individual and the personal experience of which this word makes its hearer capable, and in the relationship between the call to change and conversion and the new light that falls upon hearers' own experiences. To put it theologically: The Spirit who is God's way of self-communication is at the same time the Spirit "who makes tongues speak."

A philosophy of religion utilizing the methods both of linguistic analysis and transcendental phenomenology furthers not the subordination of the Holy and divine to the human subject—any more than transcendental philosophy furthers any such primacy of the subject—but precisely the subjects' self-critique, as, in the inadequacy of their response to the assertion of the divine (and of all reality), they seek to "keep on track." Our attempt in the considerations set forth here has been to offer specimens of a transcendental philosophy of religion in this sense, a philosophy that seeks to do justice to the questions arising out of more recent societal developments.

Works Cited

Anselm of Canterbury	*Prosl.*	*Proslogion.* In *S. Anselmi Opera Omnia,* edited by F. S. Schmitt, Tomus 1, vol. 1. Stuttgart-Bad Cannstatt, 1968.
	CDH	*Cur Deus Homo.* In *S. Anselmi Opera Omnia,* edited by F. S. Schmitt, Tomus 1, vol. 2. Stuttgart-Bad Cannstatt, 1968.
Aristophanes	*Clouds*	*Die Wolken.* In *Aristophanis Comoediae,* edited by Hall/Geldart, vol. 1, 11th ed. Oxford, 1967.
Aristotle	*Eth. Nik.*	*Nikomachische Ethik.* In *Arisotelis Opera,* edited by J. Bekker, 1094–1181. Berlin, 1831.
	Metaphys.	*Metaphysica.* In *Aristotelis Opera,* edited by J. Bekker, 980–1093. Berlin, 1831. Reprint, 1960.
Augustine	*Conf.*	*Confessions.* In *Corpus Scriptorum Ecclesiasticorum Latinorum* 33.1, edited by P. Knöll. Prague/Vienna/Leipzig, 1896. Reprint, New York/London, 1962.
	GLA	*De gratia et libero arbitrio.* In *Patrologia Latina,* edited by J. P. Migne, 44:881–912. Turnholt.
	Lib. arb.	*De libero arbitrio.* In *Corpus Scriptorum Ecclesiasticorum Latinorum* 74, edited by G. M. Green. Vienna, 1956.
	VR	*De vera religione.* In *Corpus Scriptorum Ecclesiasticorum Latinorum* 77, edited by G. M. Green. Vienna, 1961.
Austin, J. L.	1962	*How to Do Things with Words.* Oxford, 1962. Cited according to *Zur Theorie der Sprechakte,* revised by E. v. Savigny. Stuttgart, 1972.
Barth, K.	1931	*Fides quaerens intellectum: Anselms Beweis der Existenz Gottes im Zusammanhang seines theo-*

		logischen Programms. Munich/Zollikon, 1931. Reprinted in *Gesamtausgabe Karl Barth,* edited by E. Jüngel and J. U. Dalferth, vol. 14. Zurich, 1981.
	1934	*Nein! Antwort an Emil Brunner.* Munich, 1934.
	KD	*Die Kirchliche Dogmatik,* vol. 1/2, 5th ed. Zurich, 1960.
Bertholet, A.	1942	"Der Sinn des kultischen Opfers." In *Forschungen und Fortschritte XVIII.* Akademie der Wissenschaften, phil.-hist. Klasse 2, 167f., 1942.
Bloch, E.	AiChr	*Atheismus im Christentum.* In E. Bloch, *Gesamtausgabe,* vol. 14. Frankfurt a.M., 1968.
	GdU	*Geist der Utopie.* Munich/Leipzig, 1918. Cited according to E. Bloch, *Gesamtausgabe,* vol. 16. Frankfurt a.M., 1971.
	PH	*Das Prinzip Hoffnung.* In E. Bloch, *Gesamtausgabe,* vol. 5. Frankfurt a.M., 1959.
Bonaventure	ImD	*Itinerarium mentis in Deum.* In *S. Bonaventurae Opera Theologica Selecta,* vol. 5, edited by A. Sepinski, 177–214. Quaracchi/Florence, 1964.
Braithwaite, R. B.	1955	*An Empiricist's View of the Nature of Religious Belief.* Cambridge, 1955. Cited according to Dalferth 1974, 167–89.
Brugger, W.		*Summe einer philosophischen Gotteslehre.* Munich, 1979.
Brunner, A.		*Die Religion: Eine philosophische Untersuchung auf geschichtlicher Grundlage.* Freiburg i.Br., 1956.
Brunner, E.	1925	*Philosophie und Offenbarung.* Tübingen, 1925.
	1928	*Religionsphilosophie evangelischer Theologie.* Munich, 1928. 2nd ed., 1948.
	1934	*Natur und Gnade: Zum Gespräch mit Karl Barth.* Tübingen, 1934.
Buber, M.	IuD	*Ich und Du.* Leipzig, 1923. Reprinted in M. Buber, *Werke I,* 77–170. Munich/Heidelberg, 1962.
Bultmann, R.	GuV	*Glauben und Verstehen: Gesammelte Aufsätze.* Tübingen, 1933–65.
Carnap, R.	1928	*Scheinprobleme in der Philosophie: Das Fremdpsychische und der Realismusstreit.* Berlin, 1928. Reprinted with an Epilogue by G. Patzig. Frankfurt a.M., 1966.
Casper, B., ed.	1981	*Gott nennen: Phänomenologische Zugänge.* Freiburg/Munich, 1981.

Cassirer, E.	PsF	*Philosophie der symbolischen Formen*, vols. 1–3. Berlin, 1923–29. Reprint, Darmstadt, 1964.
Chantépie de la Saussaye, P. D.		*Lehrbuch der Religionsgeschichte*. Freiburg i.Br., 1887.
Chrétien, Jean Louis	1992	"La parole blessée—Phénoménologie de la prière." In Courtine 1992.
Cohen, H.	BR	*Der Begriff der Religion im System der Philosophie*. Gießen, 1915.
	RV	*Religion der Vernunft aus den Quellen des Judentums*. 1928. Reprint, Wiesbaden, 1966.
Collins, A.	1713	*A Discourse of Free-Thinking*. London, 1713. Edited by G. Gawlick. Stuttgart-Bad Cannstatt, 1965.
Colpe, C., ed.		*Die Diskussion um das "Heilige."* Wege der Forschung 305. Darmstadt, 1977.
Courtine, J. F., ed.	1992	*Phénoménologie et Théologie*. Paris, 1992.
Crombie, J. M.	1957	"The Possibility of Theological Statements." In *Faith and Logic*, edited by B. Mitchell, 31–83. London, 1957. Here cited according to Dalferth 1974, 96–145.
Dalferth, I. U., ed.	1974	*Sprachlogik des Glaubens: Texte analytischer Religionsphilosophie und Theologie zur religiösen Sprache*. Munich, 1974.
	1981	*Religiöse Rede von Gott*. Munich, 1981.
Descartes, R.	Medit.	*Meditationes de Prima Philosophia*. In *Oeuvres de Descartes*, edited by Ch. Adam and P. Tannery, vol. 7. 2nd ed. Paris, 1964.
Ebeling, G.	1959	*Das Wesen des christlichen Glaubens*. Tübingen, 1959.
	1966	*Gott und das Wort*. Tübingen, 1966.
	1971	*Einführung in theologische Sprachlehre*. Tübingen, 1971.
Eliade, M.	HC	*Histoire des croyances et de idées religieuses*. Paris, 1976ff.
	HR	*The History of Religions: Essays in Methodology*. Chicago, 1959.
	MeR	*Le mythe de l'éternel retour: Archétypes et répétition*. Paris, 1949.
	RuH	*Traité d'Histoire des Religions*. Paris, 1949. Cited according to *Die Religion und das Heilige: Elemente der Religionsgeschichte*. Salzburg, 1954.
Evans, D. D.	1969	*The Logic of Self-Involvement*. New York, 1969.
Feuerbach, L.	WdChr	*Das Wesen des Christentums*. Leipzig, 1841. Cited according to L. Feuerbach, *Sämtliche*

| | | *Werke*, edited by W. Bolin and F. Jodl, vol. 6. 2nd ed. Stuttgart-Bad Cannstatt, 1960. |

Flew, A.   1955   "Theology and Falsification." In *Essays in Philosophical Theology*, edited by A. Flew and A. MacIntyre, 96–108. London, 1955. Cited according to Dalferth 1974, 84–95.

Freud, S.   1948   *Die Zukunft einer Illusion*. Cited here according to S. Freud, *Gesammelte Werke 14*, edited by A. Freud et al., 323–80. London, 1948.

Gogarten, F.   1926   *Illusionen: Eine Auseinandersetzung mit dem Kulturidealismus*. Jena, 1926.

                            1953   *Verhängnis und Hoffnung der Neuzeit: Die Säkularisierung als theologisches Problem*, 2nd ed. Stuttgart, 1958.

Gollwitzer, H., and   *Denken und Glauben*, 2nd ed. Stuttgart, 1965.
W. Weischedel

Gregory Nazianzen   *Hymn.*   *Hymnus an Gott*. In *Patrologia Graeca*, edited by J. P. Migne, 37:507f.

Greisch, J., ed.   1992   *Comprendre et interpréter: La paradigme herméneutique*. Paris, 1992.

Hamann, J. G.   *MPV*   *Metakritik über den Purismum der Vernunft.* 1784. In *Mancherley zur Geschichte der metakritischen Invasion*, edited by F. T. Rink. Königsberg, 1800. Reprinted in J. G. Hamann, *Sämtliche Werke*, edited by J. Nadler, 3:275–80. Vienna, 1951.

                            UdS   "Des Ritters von Rosenkreuz letzte Willensmeinung über den göttlichen und menschlichen Ursprung der Sprache. Königsberg, 1772. Reprinted in *Sämtliche Werke*, 3:25–33. Vienna, 1951.

Hegel, G. W. F.   *Ästh.*   *Vorlesungen über die Ästhetik*. In G. W. F. Hegel, *Sämtliche Werke*, edited by H. Glockner, vol. 12, 4th ed. Stuttgart-Bad Cannstatt, 1964.

                            Gesch.   *Vorlesungen über die Geschichte der Philosophie.* In *Sämtliche Werke*, vol. 17, 4th ed. Stuttgart-
                            Phil.   Bad Cannstatt, 1964.

                            Phän.   *Phänomenologie des Geistes*. In *Sämtliche Werke*, vol. 2, 4th ed. Stuttgart-Bad Cannstatt, 1964.

                            Phil.   *Vorlesungen über die Philosophie der Geschichte.*
                            Gesch.   In *Sämtliche Werke*, vol. 11, 4th ed. Stuttgart-Bad Cannstatt, 1961.

                            Phil. Rel. *Vorlesungen über die Philosophie der Religion.*
                            I, II   In *Sämtliche Werke*, vols. 15 and 16, 4th ed. Stuttgart-Bad Cannstatt, 1965.

	Syst. Phil. III	System der Philosophie, III. Teil. In Sämtliche Werke, vol. 10, 4th ed. Stuttgart-Bad Cannstatt, 1965.
Heidegger, M.		Phänomenologie des religiösen Lebens. (Gesamtausgabe II. Abt.: Vorlesungen, vol. 60). Frankfurt a.m., 1995.
Heiler, F.	EWR	Erscheinungsformen und Wesen der Religion. Stuttgart, 1961.
	Gebet	Das Gebet: Eine religionsgeschichtliche und religionspsychologische Untersuchung. 1918. 4th ed., Munich, 1921.
Henry, Michel	1992	"Parole et religion—La parole de Dieu." In Courtine 1992.
Heraclitus		Fragmente. In Die Fragmente der Vorsokratiker, edited by H. Diels and W. Kranz, 1:150–82, 1st ed., 1903. 12th ed., Dublin/Zurich, 1966.
Herder, J. G.		Abhandlung über den Ursprung der Sprache. Preischrift Berlin, 1770. Reprinted in J. G. Herder, Sämtliche Werke, edited by B. Suphan, vol. 5. Berlin, 1891; Hildesheim, 1967.
	Metakr.	Eine Metakritik zur Kritik der reinen Vernunft: 1 Teil, Verstand und Erfahrung; 2 Teil, Vernunft und Sprache. Leipzig, 1799. Reprinted in J. G. Herder, Sämtliche Werke, edited by B. Suphan, vol. 21. Berlin, 1881; Hildesheim, 1967.
Hirsch, E.		Hauptfragen christlicher Religionsphilosophie. Berlin, 1963.
Hogrebe, W.	1974	Kant und das Problem einer transzendentalen Semantik. Freiburg/Munich.
Holm, S.		Religionsphilosophie. Stuttgart, 1960.
Horace	Epist.	Epistulae. In Horace, Sämtliche Werke, edited by H. Faerber and W. Schoen, 2:134–229. Munich, 1970.
Hudson, W. D.	1969	"Some Remarks on Wittgenstein's Account of Religious Belief." In Talk of God, edited by G. N. A. Verey. London, 1969.
Hübner, K.	1978	Kritik der wissenschaftlichen Vernunft. Freiburg/Munich, 1978.
	1985	Die Wahrheit des Mythos. Munich, 1985.
Humboldt, W. von	VmS	Über die Verschiedenheiten des menschlichen Sprachbaues (1827–1829). In W. v. Hunboldts Werke, edited by A. Flitner and K. Giel, 3:144–367. Darmstadt, 1963.
		Über die Verschiedenheit des menschlichen Sprachbaues und ihren Einfluß auf die geistige Entwick-

		lung des Menschengeschlechts (1830–1835). In *Werke*, 3:368–756. Darmstadt, 1963.
Husserl, E.	*Ideen I*	*Ideen zu einer reinen Phänomenologie und phänomenologischen Philosophie, 1.* Halle, 1913. Cited according to *Husserliana: E. Husserl Gesammelte Werke*, vol. 3, edited by W. Biemel. The Hague, 1950.
Kant, I.	*Diss.*	*De mundi sensibilis atque intelligibilis forma ac principiis.* Königsberg, 1770. In I. Kant, *Werke*, edited by W. Weischedel, vol. 3. Darmstadt, 1966.
	KpV	*Kritik der praktischen Vernunft.* Riga, 1788. In I. Kant, *Werke*, vol. 4. Darmstadt, 1966.
	KrV	*Kritik der reinen Vernunft.* Riga, 1781. In I. Kant, *Werke*, vol. 2. Darmstadt, 1966.
	Logik	*Vorlesungen über Logik*, edited by G. J. Jäsche. Königsberg, 1800. In I. Kant, *Werke*, vol. 3. Darmstadt, 1966.
	Prol.	*Prolegomena zu einer jeden künftigen Metaphysik, die als Wissenschaft wirt auftreten können.* Riga, 1783. In I. Kant, *Werke*, vol. 3. Darmstadt, 1966.
	Religion	*Die Religion innerhalb der Grenzen der bloßen Vernunft.* Königsberg, 1793. 2nd ed., 1794. In I. Kant, *Werke*, vol. 4. Darmstadt, 1966.
	SF	*Der Streit der Fakultäten.* Königsberg, 1798. In I. Kant, *Werke*, vol. 6. Darmstadt, 1966.
Kerstiens, F.	1968	*Die Hoffnungsstruktur des Glaubens.* Mainz, 1968.
Lanczkowski, G.		*Begegnung und Wandel der Religionen.* Düsseldorf/Cologne, 1971.
Lévinas, E.	1963	"Die Spur des Anderen." *Tijdschrift voor Filosofie.* Reprinted in *En découvrant l'existence avec Husserl et Heidegger.* Paris, 1967. German trans., "Die Spur des Anderen." Freiburg/Munich, 1983.
		De Dieu qui vient à l'idée. Paris, 1982. German, *Wenn Gott ins Denken einfällt.* Freiburg/Munich, 1985.
Loisy, A.		*L'évangile et l'église.* Paris, 1902.
Lotz, J. B.		*Transzendentale Erfahrung.* Freiburg/Basel/Vienna, 1978.
Lübbe, H.		*Religion nach der Aufklärung.* Graz, 1986.
Luhmann, N.		*Die Funktion der Religion.* Frankfurt a.M., 1977.

Lucretius (Titus
    Lucretius Carus)
De rerum natura: Welt aus Atomen, edited by K. Büchner. Zurich, 1956. Cited according to edition of Stuttgart, 1973.

Luther, M.   SA   *De servo arbitrio.* 1525. In *D. Martin Luthers Werke,* Kritische Gesamtausgabe Weimar-WA, vol. 18, edited by A. Freitag. Weimar, 1908. Reprint, 1964.

Lyotard, J. F.   "Réponse à la question: Qu'est-ce que le postmoderne?" "La condition postmoderne." Paris, 1979. German, "Was ist postmodern?" and "Das postmoderne Denken," in *Wege aus der Moderne,* edited by W. Welsch. Weinheim, 1988.

Maréchal, J.   AdM   *Le point de départ de la métaphysique (Der Ausgangspunkt der Metaphysik),* Cahiers 1–5, 1922–47. Cited according to Cahier 5, Löwen, 1926. 2nd ed., Brussels/Paris, 1949.

                    Mél.   "Le point de départ de la métaphysique, Première rédaction." Louvain, 1917. In *Mélange Joseph Maréchal,* edited by J. B. Lotz, 1:288–98. Brussels/Paris, 1950.

Marx, K.   KHegRPh   "Zur Kritik der Hegelschen Rechtsphilosophie—Einleitung." In K. Marx and F. Engels, *Werke I,* 378–91. East Berlin, 1964.

Metz, J. B.   Apol.   "Apologetik." In *Sacramentum Mundi: Theologisches Lexikon für die Praxis,* 1:266–76. Freiburg/Basel/Vienna, 1967.

                    1973   "Erlösung und Emanzipation." In *Erlösung und Emanzipation,* edited by L. Scheffczyk, 120–40. Freiburg/Basel/Vienna, 1973.

Mitchell, B., ed.   *Faith and Logic: Oxford Essays in Philosophical Theology.* London, 1957. 3rd ed., 1968.

Moltmann, J.   Bze   "Die Kategorie 'Novum' in der christlichen Theologie." In *E. Bloch zu ehren,* edited by S. Unseld, 243–63. Frankfurt a.M., 1965.

                    1972   *Der gekreuzigte Gott: Das Kreuz Christi als Grund und Kritik christlicher Theologie.* Munich, 1972. 4th ed., 1981.

Moltmann, J., ed.   1967   *Ernst Bloch: Religion im Erbe.* Munich, 1967.

Müller, M.   *Der Kompromiß, oder: Vom Unsinn und Sinn menschlichen Lebens.* Freiburg/Munich, 1980.

Nietzsche, F.   Antichrist   *Der Antichrist (1888–1889).* In *Nietzsche Werke,* edited by G. Colli and M. Montinari, vol. 6.3. Berlin, 1969.

	GdM	*Zur Genealogie in der Moral (1886–1887).* In
		Nietzsche Werke, edited by G. Colli and M.
		Montinari, vol. 6.2. Berlin, 1968.

Nygren, A. *Meaning and Method: Prolegomena to a Scientific Philosophy of Religion and a Scientific Theology.* Philadelphia, 1972.

Oelmüller, W., ed. *Wahrheitsansprüche der Religionen.* Colloquium Religion und Philosophie 2. Paderborn/ Munich, 1986.

Olivetti, M., ed. *Religione, Parola, Scrittura.* Padova, 1992.

Otto, R. GdÜ *Das Gefühl des Überweltlichen (Sensus Numinis).* "Aufsätze, das Numinose betreffend, Part 1." Stuttgart-Gotha, 1923. Reprint, Munich, 1932.

Hl. *Das Heilige: Über das Irrationale in der Idee des Göttlichen und sein Verhältnis zum Rationalen.* Breslau, 1917. Cited according to the edition of Munich, 1947.

Palmer, H. "Understanding First." *Theology* 71 (1968): 107–14. Cited according to Dalferth 1974, 237–47.

Phillips, D. Z. 1965 *The Concept of Prayer.* London, 1965. 2nd ed., 1968.

1968 "Religious Belief and Philosophical Enquiry." *Theology* 71 (1968): 114–22. Cited according to Dalferth 1974, 247–57.

1970 "Religious Beliefs and Language-Games." *Ratio* 12 (1970): 26–46. Also published in Phillips, *Faith and Philosophical Enquiry,* 77–110. London, 1970. German in Dalferth 1974, 258–88.

Pindar *Pindari Carmina cum Fragmentis,* edited by C. M. Bowra. Oxford, 1935. 2nd ed., 1947.

Pius X Pasc. Encyclical *Pascendi.* Acta Sanctae Sedis 40 (1907): 593–650.

Plato Apol. *Apologie des Sokrates.* In *Platonis Opera,* edited by J. Burnet, vol. 1. Oxford, 1900. Reprint, 1967.

Charm. *Charmides.* In *Platonis Opera,* vol. 3. Oxford, 1903. Reprint, 1967.

Gorg. *Gorgias.* In *Platonis Opera,* vol. 3. Oxford, 1903. Reprint, 1967.

Hipp. M. *Hippias Maior.* In *Platonis Opera,* vol. 3. Oxford, 1903. Reprint, 1967.

Phaedo *Phaidon.* In *Platonis Opera,* vol. 1. Oxford, 1900. Reprint, 1967.

	Phaedr.	*Phaidros.* In *Platonis Opera,* vol. 2. Oxford, 1901. Reprint, 1967.
	Pol.	*Politeia.* In *Platonis Opera,* vol. 4. Oxford, 1902. Reprint, 1967.
	Symp.	*Symposion.* In *Platonis Opera,* vol. 2. Oxford, 1901. Reprint, 1967.
	Tim.	*Timaios.* In *Platonis Opera,* vol. 4. Oxford, 1902. Reprint, 1967.
Plotinus	*Enn.*	*Plotini Opera: Enneades I–VI,* edited by P. Henry and H. R. Schwyzer. Paris/Brussels, 1951–73.
	Enn. III,1	Vom Schicksal.
	Enn. III,2-3	Von der Vorsehung, books 1–2.
	Enn. III,7	Über Ewigkeit und Zeit.
	Enn. IV,1-2	Vom Wesen der Seele, books 1–2.
	Enn. IV,7	Von der Unsterblichkeit der Seele.
	Enn. V,4	Wie aus dem Ersten das hervorgeht, was auf das Erste folgt.
Porphyry		*Über die Philosophie aus den Orakelsprüchen— De Philosophia ex Oraculis haurienda,* edited by G. Wolff. Berlin, 1866. Reprint, Hildesheim, 1962.
		Über Götterbilder. In J. Bidez, *Vie de Porphyre.* Gent, 1913. Reprint, Hildesheim, 1964. Appendix. See also reports here on the lost works *On Divine Names* and *On Homer's Philosophy.*
Proclus		*Theologie im Sinne Platons.* In *Platonis Theologiam Libri Sex.* Frankfurt/Hamburg, 1618. Reprint, Frankfurt a.M., 1960.
Rahner, K.	An. Chr.	"Die anonymen Christen." In Rahner, *Schriften zur Theologie,* 6:545–54. Einsiedeln/ Zurich/Cologne, 1965.
	Glaubens-zugang	"Glaubenszugang." In *Sacramentum Mundi: Theologisches Lexikon für die Praxis,* 2:414–20. Freiburg/Basel/Vienna, 1968.
		Hörer des Wortes: Zur Grundlegung einer Religionsphilosophie. Munich, 1941. 2nd ed., 1963.
	N. Rel.	"Das Christentum und die nichtchristlichen Religionen." In Rahner, *Schriften zur Theologie,* 5:136–58. Einsiedeln/Zurich/Cologne, 1962.
	Transz.	"Transzendentaltheologie." In *Sacramentum*

		Mundi, 4:986–92. Freiburg/Basel/Vienna, 1969.
	1976	*Grundkurs des Glaubens: Einführung in den Begriff des Christentums.* Freiburg/Basel/ Vienna, 1976. 11th ed., 1980.
Ramsey, I. T.	1957	*Religious Language: An Empirical Placing of Theological Phrases.* London, 1957. 3rd ed., 1973.
Ricken, F.		"Sind Sätze über Gott sinnlos?" *Stimmen der Zeit* 193 (1975): 435–52.
Ricoeur, Paul	1977	"Nommer Dieu." In *Études théologiques et religieuses* 52:489–508. German in Casper 1981, 45–79.
	1990	*Entre herméneutique et sémiotique.* Limoges, 1990.
	1992	"Expérience et language dans le discours religieux." In Courtine 1992.
Robespierre, M.	*Werke*	*Über die Beziehungen der religiösen und moralischen Vorstellungen zu den republikanischen Prinzipien und über die nationalen Feste: Rede in der Nationalversammlung 1794.* French in *Robespierres Werke,* edited by Bouloiseau and Soberui, 10:442–65. Paris, 1967. German in *M. Robespierre: Ausgewählte Texte,* translated by M. Unruh, 653–96. Hamburg, 1971.
Robinson, J. A. T.	1963	*Honest to God.* London, 1963. German, *Gott ist anders.* 11th ed., Munich, 1966.
Rosenzweig, F.	Coh	"Hermann Cohens jüdische Schriften." Reprinted in *F. Rosenzweig: Kleinere Schriften,* edited by E. Rosenzweig, 299–350. Berlin, 1937.
	SE	*Der Stern der Erlösung.* Frankfurt a.M., 1921. Cited according to 3rd ed. of Heidelberg, 1954.
	Urz. SE	"'Ruzelle' des Stern der Erlösung: Brief an Rudolf Ehrenberg vom 18.ll.1917." In *F. Rosenzweig: Kleinere Schriften,* 357–72. Berlin, 1937.
Ryle, G.	1931	"Systematically Misleading Expressions." In *Proceedings of the Aristotelian Society* (1931). German in *Sprache und Analysis,* edited by R. Bubner, 31–62. Göttingen, 1968.
Sartre, J. P.	1946	*L'Existentialisme est un humanisme.* Paris, 1946. German in J. P. Sartre, *Drei Essays,* 7–51. Frankfurt/Berlin/Vienna/Zurich, 1975.

Saussure, F. de   1916   *Cours de Linguistique Générale.* Lausanne/
                            Paris, 1916. German, *Grundfragen der allge-
                            meinen Sprachwissenschaft,* edited by Ch. Bally
                            and A. Sechehaye, translated by H. Lommel.
                            2nd ed., Berlin, 1967.

Schaeffler, R.   1973   *Religion und kritisches Bewußtsein.* Freiburg/
                            Munich, 1973.

                   1974   "Der Kultus als Weltauslegung." In B. Fischer
                            et al., *Kult in der säkularisierten Welt,* 9–62.
                            Regensburg, 1974.

                   1976   "Zum Verhältnis von transzendentaler und
                            historischer Reflexion." In *Von der Notwendig-
                            keit der Philosophie in der Gegenwart: Festschrift
                            für K. Ulmer zum 60. Geburtstag,* edited by H.
                            Kohlenberger and W. Lütterfelds, 42–75.
                            Vienna/Munich, 1976.

                   1978   "Sprache als Bedingung und Folge der
                            Erfahrung: Das religiöse Wort als Beispiel für
                            die Geschichtlichkeit des Verhältnisses von
                            'Sprache' und 'Rede.'" In W. Beinert et al.,
                            *Sprache und Erfahrung als Problem der Theolo-
                            gie,* 11–36. Paderborn, 1978.

                   1979   *Was dürfen wir hoffen? Die katholische Theologie
                            der Hoffnung zwischen Blochs utopischem
                            Denken und der reformatorischen Rechtferti-
                            gungslehre.* Darmstadt, 1979.

                   1980   *Die Wechselbeziehungen zwischen Philosophie
                            und katholischer Theologie.* Darmstadt, 1980.

                   1981a   "Die Vernunft und das Wort: Zum Religions-
                            verständnis bei Hermann Cohen und Franz
                            Rosenzweig." *Zeitschrift für Theologie und
                            Kirche* 78 (1981): 57–89.

                   1981b   "Kant als Philosoph der Hoffnung: Zu G. B.
                            Salas Kritik an meiner Interpretation der kan-
                            tischen Religionsphilosophie." *Theologie und
                            Philosophie* 56 (1981): 244–58.

                   1982   *Fähigkeit zur Erfahrung: Zur transzendentalen
                            Hermeneutik des Sprechens von Gott.* Freiburg/
                            Basel/Vienna, 1982.

                   1989   *Das Gebet und das Argument: Zwei Weisen des
                            Sprechens von Gott.* Düsseldorf, 1989.

                   1992   "Ein transzendentalphilosophischer Gottes-
                            begriff und seine mögliche Bedeutung für die
                            Theologie." In M. Kessler et al., *Fides quaerens*

intellectum: Festschrift für Max Seckler, 97–112. Tübingen, 1992.

1994 "Die Vielfalt der Weisen religiöser Wahrheit und ihres sprachlichen Ausdrucks." In *Die Wahrheit der Religion*, edited by W. Kerber. Munich, 1994.

1995 *Erfahrung als Dialog mit der Wirklichkeit*. Freiburg/ Munich, 1995.

Scheler, M. *EiM* *Vom Ewigen im Menschen*. Leipzig, 1920. Cited according to Max Scheler, *Gesammelte Werke*, vol. 5, edited by Maria Scheler. Bern, 1954.

Schelling, F. W. J. v. *Einl. Mythol.* *Historisch-kritische Einleitung in die Philosophie der Mythologie*, aus dem Nachlaß hrsg. von K. F. A. Schelling, 1856. Cited according to *Schellings Werke*, edited by M. Schröter, vol. 6. Munich, 1965.

WmF *Philosophische Untersuchungen über das Wesen der menschlichen Freiheit und die damit zusammenhängenden Gegenstände*, Landshut 1809. Cited according *Schellings Werke*, edited by M. Schröter, 4:223–308. Munich, 1965.

Schleiermacher, F. *Über die Religion: Reden an die Gebildeten unter ihren Verächtern*. Berlin, 1799.

Schroedter, H. *Analytische Religionsphilosophie: Hauptstandpunkte und Grundprobleme*. Freiburg/Munich, 1979.

Schulz, W. 1957 *Der Gott der neuzeitlichen Metaphysik*. Pfullingen.

Searle, J. R. 1969 *Speech Acts*. Cambridge, 1969. German, *Sprechakte*. Frankfurt a.M., 1971.

Sherry, P. 1972a "Truth and the Religious Language-Game." *Philosophy* 47 (1972): 18–37.

1972b "Is Religion a 'Form of Life'?" *American Philosophical Quarterly* 9 (1972): 159–67.

1977 *Religion, Truth and Language-Games*. London, 1977.

Smart, N. *Reasons and Faiths: An Investigation of Religious Discourse, Christian and Non-Christian*. London, 1958. Reprint, 1971.

Soe, N. H. *Religionsfilosofi*. German, *Religionsphilosophie: Ein Studienbuch*. Munich, 1967.

Spinoza, B. de *E* *Ethica, Ordine Geometrico demonstrata*. In *Spinoza Opera*. Heidelberger Akademie der

		Wissenschaften, edited by C. Beghardt, vol. 2. Heidelberg, 1925.
Splett, J.		*Die Rede vom Heiligen: Über ein religions-philosophisches Grundwort.* Freiburg/ Munich, 1971.
Spranger, E.	PPR	"Philosophie und Psychologie der Religion." In E. Spranger, *Gesammelte Schriften,* edited by H. W. Bähr, vol. 9. Tübingen, 1974.
Statius of Thebes		"Thebais." In *P. Paini Stati Thebais et Achilleis,* edited by H. W. Garrod. Oxford, 1906. Reprint, 1962.
Staudenmaier, F. A.		*Geist der göttlichen Offenbarung oder Wissenschaft der Geschichtsprinzipien des Christentums.* Gießen, 1837. Reprint, Frankfurt a.M., 1967.
Strawson, P. E.		*Analysis and Metaphysics.* Oxford, 1992. German, *Analyse und Metaphysik.* Munich, 1994.
Thomas Aquinas	*Comm. de an.*	*In Aristotelis Librum De Anima Commentarium,* edited by A. M. Pirotta. Rome, 1959.
	De an.	*Quaestiones Disputatae de Anima,* edited by M. Calcaterra and T. S. Centi. In *S. Thomae Aquinatis Quaestiones Disputatae,* edited by P. Bazzi et al., 2:277–362. 2nd ed., Turin/Rome, 1948.
	De verit.	*Quaestiones Disputatae de Veritate.* In *S. Thomae Aquinatis Quaestiones Disputatae,* 8th ed., Turin/ Rome, 1949.
	S. Th.	*Summa Theologiae,* edited by von P. Caramello. Turin/Rome, 1952–63.
Tillich, P.		*Religionsphilosophie.* Stuttgart, 1962.
Trillhaas, W.		*Religionsphilosophie.* Berlin/New York, 1972.
Unsere Hoffnung	UH	"Unsere Hoffnung: Ein Bekenntnis zum Glauben in dieser Zeit." In *Gemeinsame Synode der Bistümer in der Bundesrepublik Deutschland,* vol. 1, *Beschlüsse der Vollversammlung,* edited by L. Bertsch et al., 84–111. Freiburg i.Br., 1976.
Vahanian, G.	1961	*The Death of God: The Culture of Our Post-Christian Era.* New York, 1961. German, *Kultur ohne Gott?* Göttingen, 1973.
van Buren, P.	1963	*The Secular Meaning of the Gospel, Based on an Analysis of Its Language.* New York, 1963.
	1972	*The Edges of Language: An Essay in the Logic of a Religion.* New York, 1972.
van der Leeuw, G.	1920/1921	"Die 'Do-ut-des'-Formel in der Opfertheorie." *Archiv für Religionswissenschaft* 20:241–53.

	EPR	*Inleiding tot de Phaenomenologie van den Gods-dienst.* Groningen. German trans., *Einführung in die Phänomenologie der Religion.* 2nd ed., Gütersloh/Darmstadt, 1961.
	PdR	*Phänomenologie der Religion.* Tübingen, 1933. 2nd ed., 1956.
Vatican II	GS	*Gaudium et Spes.* In *Acta Apostolicae Sedis* 58 (1966): 1024–1120. German in K. Rahner and H. Vorgrimler, *Kleines Konzilskompendium.* Freiburg/Basel/Vienna, 1966.
Virgil	Aeneid	*Äneis.* In *P. Vergilii Maronis Opera,* vols. 2 and 3, edited by G. P. E. Wagner. Leipzig/London, 1832.
Verweyen, Hj.		*Ontologische Voraussetzungen des Glaubensaktes: Zur transzendentalen Frage nach der Möglichkeit von Offenbarung.* Düsseldorf, 1969.
Wainwright, G.	EE	*Eucharist and Eschatology.* London, 1971. 2nd ed., 1978.
	1980	*Doxology: The Praise of God in Worship, Doctrine and Life—A Systematic Theology.* London/New York, 1980. 2nd ed., 1982.
Welte, B.		*Religionsphilosophie.* Freiburg/Basel/Vienna, 1978.
		Vom Wesen und Unwesen der Religion. Frankfurt a.M., 1952.
Widengren, G.		*Religionens värld.* German, *Religionsphänomenologie.* Berlin, 1969.
Wisdom, J.	1944/1945	"Gods." In *Proceedings of the Aristotelian Society* 45 (1944/1945): 185–206. German in Dalferth 1974, 63–83.
	1965	"The Logic of God." In *Paradox and Discovery.* Oxford.
Wittgenstein, L.	PU	*Philosophische Untersuchungen.* 1953. In L. Wittgenstein, *Schriften,* 1:279–544. Frankfurt a.M., 1960.
	Tract.	*Tractatus logico-philosophicus: Logisch-philosophische Abhandlung.* 1921. In L. Wittgenstein, *Schriften,* 1:7–83. Frankfurt a.M., 1960. 2nd ed., 1963.
	VuG	*Vorlesungen und Gespräche über Ästhetik, Psychologie und Religion,* edited by C. Barret. Oxford, 1966. German, 2nd ed., Göttingen, 1971.
Wobbermin, G.		*Religionsphilosophie.* Berlin, 1924.
		Das Wesen der Religion. Systematische Theologie nach religionspsychologischer Methode 2. Leipzig, 1921.

Index

act, religious, 61, 65–67, 116–17, 165, 166, 171
acts of evaluation, 116–17
acts of prayer, 117. *See also* prayer
anonymous Christians, 42–43, 48
Anselm of Canterbury, 17
  and faith and knowledge, 24–25
  and Ontological Proof for God, 24–25
Aquinas. *See* Thomas Aquinas
Aristophanes, 1
Aristotle, 21, 40
  and capacity for speech, 99
  and first cause, 22–23
atheism, 16
  in Christianity, 15
  and the decision for religion *simpliciter*, 9
  onto-theology and, 23, 38, 42
  versus religion, 45
Augustine, 8, 9–10, 17, 22, 31
  biblical religion and, 17
  and decision for religion *simpliciter*, 9
  human freedom and, 11
  and Neoplatonic philosophy, 9
Austin, J. L., 78, 92, 94–95

Barth, Karl, 25, 39, 82
beatific vision, 25
being
  God and, 22–24, 109
  transcendental meaning of, 41

Bertholet, Alfred, 116
Bloch, Ernst, 17, 39, 43–45, 46, 48, 49, 125, 143
  and religion without God, 14–16
Bonaventure, 29
Braithwaite, R. B., 79, 80
Brunner, E., 82
Buber, Martin, 91–94
Bultmann, Rudolf, 82

Carnap, R., 74
Casper, Bernhard, 105
Cassirer, Ernst, 86–89, 111
Chantépie de la Saussaye, P D., 51
Chrétien, Jean-Louis, 157
Christianity
  philosophy and, 13
  at end of history of religion, 39
  as true religion, 42
cognition, 35, 40
cognitive ascent, 8
Cohen, Hermann, 91–96, 105, 111, 122, 128
Collins, A., 2
Copernican revolution
  onto-theology and, 25–30
Courtine, Jean François, 157
creation, 22–23
Crombie, Jan M., 75, 83

Dalferth, Ingolf U., 82, 83, 100–102
demiourgos (divine "artisan"), 22

Descartes, 25
    and proof for God, 30–32, 34
dialectic
    reason and, 35, 36
    of religious experience, 164–65
discourse
    Christian, 100–102
    hermeneutic, 169
    language and, 71, 99
    mythological, 20
    religious (*see* religious discourse)
    upon God, 100
        linguistic analysis and, 75–78
        philosophical, 37
        philosophical theology and, 46
        in transcendental philosophy,
            30–45, 111
doxa (manifestation), 7, 54, 128, 131,
    133

Ebeling, Gerhard, 97–100
eidos (essential form), 52, 110, 129
    See also Wesengestalt
Eliade, Mircea, 51, 56, 60–61, 62,
    64, 72
    and dialectic of the hierophanies,
        64, 69, 72
empiricism
    and object of cognition, 40
encounter, intercultural, 139, 146–49,
    169
error, 78
    Descartes and, 31
    Kant and, 34–35
    reason and, 34–35
    understood as sin, 31
ethics, law of, 36
experience, religious, 164–68
    misunderstanding of, 166
    religious speech and, 169–70

faith
    act of, 24
    as form of religion, 24
    as opposed to knowledge, 24–25
    and will, 25

fear, 2–3
    rationality and, 1
feminism, 144, 163
Feuerbach, L., 14, 16, 17, 39, 95, 112,
    149
Flew, Antony, 77
freedom
    divine, and hierophany, 64
free will
    Descartes and, 31
French Revolution, 32–34
Freud, Sigmund, 3, 4

German Idealism
    See Idealism, German
God
    being of, 17, 22–24, 109
    as "the Being," 24
    of the Bible. 22–23
    death of, 13, 39, 102, 107
    doctrine of, in transcendental
        philosophy, 39–40
    essence of, 17–18, 24
    existence of, 17–18, 24
    as metaphor, 14
    names of, 18, 26, 48, 62
    oneness of, 21
    proofs for the existence of, 17, 30,
        31, 34
    revealed as Spirit, 13
    service to, 17
    transcendental doctrine of, 120–23
    as unmoved mover, 22–23
    "word," 14, 19–21, 37, 100–102
Gogarten, Friedrich, 39
grace
    of forgiveness, 11
Gregory of Nazianzus, 68, 136
Greisch, Jean, 157

Hamann, J. G., 85
Hegel, G. W. F., 10, 12–13, 15, 16,
    39, 53, 54, 62
    and historicity of religion, 63–65
Heidegger, Martin, 157
Heiler, Friedrich, 68–71, 117

Heraclitus, xv, 21, 24
Herder, J. G., 85
hermeneutics
  of religion, 21–25
hierophany, 58–59, 72
  apparition and, 63
  dialectic of, 59, 63–65
  divine freedom and, 64
  typology of, 60–61
  withdrawal and, 63
history
  phenomenology of, 71
  religious consciousness and, 61
history of religions
  Christianity and, 13, 15, 39
  phenomenology of religion and,
    61–62
  philosophy and, 16
Hogrebe, Wolfram, 72
Holy, the, 128, 133, 134, 161
  apparition of, 63
  concept of, 116
  knowledge of, 63
  phenomenology of religion and,
    57–61, 62
  service to, 144
  unnameability of, 63
hope, 2–3
  as center and norm of religion,
    43–45
  content of, 37
  eschatological, 62
  religious, 45
  theology of, 38–45
Horace
  Epist., 2
Hübner, Kurt, 192
human being
  as image of God, 103
  needs of, and religion, 14
  relationship of, to infinite God,
    11–12
  self-consciousness of, 31
  as sinner, 11, 31
  will of, 11
human ego
  Descartes and, 30

Husserl, Edmund, 51, 53–57, 62,
    71–72, 110, 156, 161, 170,
    174
  historicity of religion and, 63–65

Idea, divine, 8
Idealism, German, 10, 12
Idealists, 16, 38
Ideas, Platonic, 52
idolatry, 9, 173
inculturation, 169–70, 172–75
intellect, 25

Jesus
  death of, 13
Judaism, 90–91
Jung, Carl Gustav, 140

Kant, Immanuel, 23, 92, 94, 112,
    123, 124, 131, 132, 136, 166
  and critique of ontology, 26–27, 40,
    41
  Critique of Practical Reason, 36–37
  and "Copernican revolution,"
    25–30
  and doctrine of the postulates, 30,
    36–37
  and Jewish religion, 90
  error and sin and, 34–35
  and rejection of onto-theology, 27
  religion and, 37, 90–91
  and Ontological Proof for God, 26
  reason and, 33–34, 45
  and secularization of philosophy,
    38–40

Kerstiens, Ferdinand, 45
Kessler, M., 160
knowledge
  act of, 24
  foundation of, 34
  and necessity, 25
  as opposed to faith, 24–25

Lanczkowski, Günter, 51
language
  discourse and, 71, 99

of faith, 102–5
about God, 50
grammar and, 70
of prayer, 69
philosophy of, 96–105
religious, 19, 71–72, 121, 129, 160
analysis of, 73–105, 126–29, 136
autonomy of the play of, 78–84
nonpropositional character of,
78–84
positivism and, 74–81
philosophical, 19
semantics and, 70
leadership, spiritual, 154–55
Leibniz
and argument for existence of
God, 34
Lévinas, E., 157–58
linguistic analysis
philosophy of religion and, 74, 110,
156–57
transcendental, 72, 111, 114, 119,
130
"linguistic turn," 73–105
philosophy of religion and, 108–10,
111, 157
transcendental philosophy and,
84–96
linguistic philosophy
in Germany, 84–86
logos, 20, 58, 133
Plotinus and, 8
Loisy, Alfred, 153
Lübbe, Heinrich, 142
Lucretius
De rerum natura, 2
Luhmann, Niklos, 142
Luther, Martin, 81
Lyotard, J.-F., 158

Maréchal, Joseph, 29–30, 40, 41
Marx, Karl, 2, 4, 14, 16, 17
Marxism, 141
Marxists
psychotherapy and, 3
metaphysics, 74
method, phenomenological, 61–71

Metz, Johannes Baptist, 45
modernism, 32
Moltmann, Jürgen, 39, 44, 48
Müller, Max, 157
multiplicity, from divine Oneness, 9–10
mystery
in the New Testament, 24
myth, 19–20
allegorization of, 5
history of, 62

necessarily existing being, 24
necessity
and knowledge, 25
Neoplatonism, 8–9
idealism and, 10–12
Neoplatonists, 16
Nietzsche, Friedrich, 2, 38
noema (any object intended), 54, 55,
119, 120, 135, 160–62
religious, 62, 68–69, 71, 72, 125,
134, 136, 163
retreat of, 59
noemata, 54, 133
religious, 58, 171
noesis (knowing), 54, 55, 110, 120,
133, 135, 156, 160–62
collapse of, 59
religious, 57–59, 62, 68–69, 71, 72,
125, 134, 136, 163, 171
Nous
divine, 8
as divine Spirit, 10
as foreseeing, 10
and Psyche, 8

Oelmüller, Willy, 142
Olivetti, Marco, 157
Ontological Proof for God, 24–25
Immanuel Kant and, 26
ontology
philosophy as, 22, 26
reconciliation of, with transcendental philosophy, 40
theology and, 23
onto-theology, 21–25, 37
crisis of, 25–30

and faith and knowledge, 24–25
and philosophy of religion, 26
transcendental variants of, 42-43
other
and divine Spirit, 10, 12
Otto, Rudolf, 51, 53, 57–58, 68–69, 137

pacifism, prophetic, 143
Palmer, Humphrey, 82–83
perception, act of, 66
phenomenology, 156
    concept of essence in, 53
    regional, 56–58, 72
    of the spirit, 63
phenomenology of religion, 50–72, 118
    and history of religions, 61–62
    and the Holy, 57–61, 63–64
    Max Scheler and, 65–67
    and philosophical phenomenology, 51–53
    and philosophy of religion, 110
    and transcendental method, 111, 114, 119
    the term, 51
Phillips, D. Z., 80, 82
philosophical theology
    and content of religion, 110
    Descartes and, 30
    philosophy of religion and, 17–49, 108–10, 120
    questions of, 18–19
    theme and argumentation of, 18–21
    and transcendental methods, 129
philosophy
    as analytics of pure understanding, 26
    Christianity and, 13
    as ontology, 22, 26
    Platonic, 6–8
    secularization of, 38–40
    as service to the world, 8
    Socratic, 5
    of symbolic forms, 86–87
    in terms of religion, 8
    transcendental, 29, 30–38, 156
        doctrine of God and, 39

reconciliation of, with ontology, 40
philosophy and science, 3, 107
    origin of, from religion, 4
philosophy of religion
    in antiquity, 1
    application of method in, 159–77
    basic question of, 37–38
    and Christian theology, 96–105
    on the basis of transcendental theology, 40–42
    central task of, 39
    as conversion of religion into philosophy, 5–16
    as criticism of ideology, 39
    as critique of a prerational consciousness, 1–4
    elements of, 46
    of German Idealism, 10
    as grammar of commandment and prayer, 91–94
    and human will, 11
    as interpreter of religious tradition, 7
    linguistic analysis and, 74
    and "linguistic turn," 108–10, 111
    methodological approaches to, 106–38, 155–58
    methodological objections, 157–58
    and onto-theology, 26
    and phenomenology of religion, 110
    and philosophical theology, 17–49, 108–10, 120
    point of departure of, 7, 106
    questions for, 153–55
    types of, 106–10
Pindar, 24
Pius X (pope), 27, 32
Plato, 5, 7, 16, 19, 29, 30, 31, 52, 100
    and critique of religion, 21
    and highest principle, 22
    Socrates in, 6, 7, 20
Platonism
    Christian, 29, 30
    doctrine of ideas, 52
    and object of cognition, 40

Plotinus, 8–11
polytheism, 49
Porphyry, 9
postulates, doctrine of, 30, 36–37
prayer, 67
    acts of, 117
    dialectic of, 68
    language of, 69
    mystical, 68
    phenomenology of, 67–69
    prophetic, 68
pre-Socratics, 22
Proclus, 9
Pronoia, 10

Rahner, Karl, 30, 41–43
    non-Christian religions and, 49
Ramsey, I. T., 79, 80
rationalism, age of, 34
rationality, 141–42
reason
    autonomy of, 35
    deification of,
        defeat of, 34–37
        and religious rationalism, 32–34
    dialectic of, 35, 36
    error and, 34–35
    French Revolution and, 33
redemption
    concept of, 45
religion
    abolition of, 13–14, 16
    biblical, 23
    core of, 15
    critique of, 20, 120, 139, 159–64
    and culture and society, 169–75
    definition of, 37
    demise of, 3, 15
    dissolution of, 14
    distortions of, 164–69
    emergence of, from fear, 3
    essence of, 24
    form of, 24
    historicity of, 58–59, 61–62, 69
    Idealist understanding of, 13
    as illusion, 3, 4
    justification for the existence of, 3

    matter of, 24
    of mysticism, 68
    natural and revealed, 10
    needs of human beings and, 14
    as origin of philosophy and
        science, 4
    rationality of, 159–64
    as "other," 48
    phenomenology of (see phenome-
        nology of religion)
    of revelation, 68
    as service to God, 17
    science of, 63
    in terms of philosophy, 8
    pseudomorphoses of, 149–53, 164,
        165, 166
    question of, 75
    transculturality of, 169–71
    transformation of, into philosophy,
        10, 16, 38–39, 107
    true, 22–24, 32, 42, 48
    truth of, 78
religions
    comparison among, 42–43
    dialogue of the, 146–49
    inculturation of, 169
    new, rise of, 139, 149–53, 164
religious, the
    genuine, 149–53, 164
religious consciousness, 14, 61–62,
        120–23
    corruption of, 165
religious discourse, 20, 21
    historicity of, 67
religious phenomena
    criteria for, 115–17, 129–33, 164
religious rationalism
    and deification of reason, 32–34
Ricoeur, Paul, 105, 157
Robespierre, 32
Robinson, J. A. T., 102
Rosenzweig, Franz, 91–96, 105, 128
Ryle, Gilbert, 76

sacralization, 139, 143–46, 159, 173
Sartre, Jean-Paul, 38–39
Saussure, Ferdinand de, 99

Schaeffler, R., 16, 23, 27, 44, 49, 69,
    87, 91, 99, 125, 131, 141, 146,
    154, 160, 166, 176
Scheler, Max, 51, 56, 64, 65–67, 68,
    69–71, 116, 117, 134, 156
  religious conservatism and, 70
Schelling, F. W. J., 12
  myth and, 6
Schulz, W., 34
science
  and technology, 141–42
Searle, J. R., 92, 94–95
secularization, 139–46, 153–54
  Christian faith and, 39
  of environmental ethics, 142–46,
    162
  as opposed to secularism, 39
  of politics, 142–46, 162
  of thought, 38–40
self-thinking thought, 22, 24
sensus numinis, 57–58
  See also Holy, the
Sherry, P., 82
sin
  consequence of, 31
socialism, prophetic, 143
speech
  capacity for, 99
  concerning God, 102–5
  phenomenology of, 71
  prayer as, 71
  religious, 164, 169–70
speech acts, 70, 72, 92, 93
  religious, 94–96, 102
speech logic of faith, 100–102
Spinoza, B., 12, 34
spirit
  dialectic of, 10
  Plotinus and, 10
Spirit, divine, 10, 12
  and community, 39
  and doctrine of Trinity, 10
  indwelling of, 11
  as metaphor, 14
Spirit, predetermining (Pronoia), 10
Spranger, E., 116
Statius of Thebes, 1

Strawson, Peter E., 157
subjectivity
  theory of, 30–32
  Kant and, 34

theology
  ontology and, 23
  systematic, 102–5
  transcendental, 29, 30
    and philosophy of religion, 40–42
  of the word, 96–105
Thomas Aquinas, 17, 22, 23, 25, 40,
    41, 46, 116
  function of the intellect and, 40
transcendental method, 111, 114, 119,
    129–30
transculturality, 169–71
Trinity, dogma of, 12, 104
truth, 154
  contained in religious concepts, 3
  existence of God and, 34
truths, religious, 154
  available to philosophical argumen-
    tation, 9–10
  known only through divine
    revelation, 9–10

unmoved mover, 22–23, 29
Unnameable, the, 58

Vahanian, G., 39
van Buren, Paul M., 100, 102
van der Leeuw, Gerardus, 51, 53, 116
von Humboldt, Wilhelm, 85–86, 94

Wainwright, Geoffrey, 102–5, 128
Welsch, W., 158
Wesengestalt (essential structural form),
    50, 52
will
  freedom of, 25
Wisdom, J., 79, 80
Wittgenstein, 77, 78, 80, 87, 88, 89,
    101
worship, history of, 62

Zinzendorf, Count, 58